Praise for *Unknown Pleasures*

"Honest, punchy, and rough-hewn . . . a portal into a vivid moment in rock history . . . the life and times of a working band transformative power of m

"As a founding member of Joy Division t influential bands, Hook has a wealth of i is eye-opening account . . . outspoken and h Joy Division fans the closure they've been waiting decades for." —***Nylon* magazine**

"Vivid, funny, and unexpectedly touching, Peter Hook's memoir strips away the shroud of myth surrounding Joy Division to offer a refreshingly gritty perspective on the story of four ordinary young men who together made extraordinary music."
—Simon Reynolds, author of *Rip It Up and Start Again: Postpunk 1978–1984*

"There is perhaps no better demonstration of the complexities of life and art than the fact that a history of Joy Division is often laugh-out-loud funny. *Unknown Pleasures* gives back this mythologized band its humanity [and] shows hindsight truly can be great. It is also heartrending, ruthless, and redemptive." **—Michael Azerrad, *Wall Street Journal***

"A surprisingly funny—and gleefully profane—portrait." ***—Entertainment Weekly* (The Must List)**

"An immense account of Joy Division's rise, cataloguing the group's struggle for recognition, their rapidly gained superiority on the Manchester scene and the epic numbness following Ian Curtis' shock suicide. Having read Hook's book, you'll feel like you were the fifth member of the band." ***—GQ***

"Intimate." ***—San Francisco Chronicle***

"Brutally honest." ***—Salon***

"Hook has hit upon something not normally associated with the almost mythical Ian Curtis and crew: rampant piss-taking humor. . . . This was a group that wrote, gigged, and recorded hard, beyond all costs." ***—Rolling Stone,* 3 ½ stars**

"We couldn't have guessed Joy Division's legacy was founded upon this much mischief and laughter, and not half the heartbreak we're lead to believe . . . it's one of those rare rock tomes that hits upon a magical balance because its writer relays historical facts without allowing time and distance to sugarcoat his delivery . . . a candid, revelatory, and unexpectedly witty survey of post-punk's greatest (if shortest-lived) band." ***—Cleveland Music Examiner***

"A tiny gem written by a monster musician. It's the best document yet to be produced on Joy Division." ***—Rock Cellar Magazine***

"Rich in detail." ***—LA Weekly***

"From a musical-history perspective, there's plenty to gnaw on in *Unknown Pleasures*. . . . The passages where Hook details the recording of the *Unknown Pleasures* album are fantastic and insightful, with minute-by-minute details on the genius of Ian Curtis and producer Martin Hannett." **—*The Onion A.V. Club***

"Revealing and vivid. . . . Hook has restored a flesh-and-blood rawness to what was becoming a standard tale. Few pop music books manage that." **—Andy Beckett, *The Guardian***

"Reading *Unknown Pleasures* . . . is like talking to a bawdy uncle after his fourth beer. But better, unless your uncle has stories about trying cocaine for the first time at the *Pretty in Pink* premiere. Apparently being in the saddest post-punk art-goth band in history can occasionally be pretty fucking funny." **—MTV Hive**

"The most colorful and intimate account of Joy Division ever written . . . a marvelous raconteur, Hook evokes the spirit of the age with a bluff authenticity that no outsider could hope to emulate . . . explaining the creation of his band's remarkable music with all the passion and insight it deserves." **—Keith Cameron, MOJO**

"A comprehensive, illuminating portrait of the band that often takes the piss out of its doom-ridden legacy." **—*Cincinnati City Beat***

"A colorful and surprisingly upbeat read." **—Yahoo! Music**

"Fans can finally hear the band's story from someone who was there from the very beginning." **—*SF Weekly***

"Hook provides [Ian Curtis] with a fitting tribute. . . . Simply but vividly told, it wrestles movingly and boldly with contradictions." **—PopMatters**

"An enthralling read." **—*Dayton Daily News***

"One of the warmest, most honest musical memoirs in recent memory." **—*Publishers Weekly***

"A bittersweet, profanity-filled recollection of their brief existence . . . recalled with Hook's winning Manc gallows humor. . . . If you like Joy Division you really have to read it." **—Ian Harrison, Q Magazine**

"Unflinchingly honest. . . . Hook peels away the romantic sheen colored by [Joy Division's] dark history and gives unfettered insight into the band's origins and inspirations . . . this is required reading for anyone who ever felt moved by Joy Division's cold, dark music." **—*Kirkus*, starred review**

"A window like no other into the reality of life in this most aloof of bands." **—*Metro* (London)**

ALSO BY PETER HOOK

The Hacienda: How Not to Run a Club

JOY
DIVISION

UNKNOWN PLEASURES

· INSIDE JOY DIVISION ·

PETER HOOK

Image credits: Photo insert page 7, top: Paul Welsch © Getty Images; Photo insert page 9, top: Kevin Cummins © Getty Images; Photo insert page 9, bottom: Attempts have been made to track down the copyright holder to no avail; Photo insert page 14, bottom: © Christopher Hewitt; page 15, top: Pierre Rene Worms.

This book was originally published in the UK in 2012 in slightly different form by Simon & Schuster UK.

A hardcover edition of this book was published in 2013 by It Books, an imprint of HarperCollins Publishers.

First It Books paperback published 2013.

Interior designed by Jennifer Daddio / Bookmark Design & Media Inc.

Library of Congress Cataloging-in-Publication Data is available upon request.

ISBN 978-0-06-222257-2

HB 02.06.2023

DEDICATED, WITH LOVE

to my mother

IRENE

and her sister

JEAN.

This book is the truth, the whole truth,

and nothing but the truth . . .

as I remember it!

PETER HOOK, 2012

· CONTENTS ·

PART THREE: "TRANSMISSION"

PART FOUR: "LOVE WILL TEAR US APART"

PART FIVE: "CEREMONY"

· INTRODUCTION ·

It's a strange life. Normally I don't include any other people in my writing. Everyone remembers the same things completely differently. The contradictions really confuse you and spoil everything, making you question yourself and what happened. I proved it to myself by letting a very close friend see what I had written. He replied with a great comment: "What's the point of all this?"

So, answers on a postcard, please.

Hooky

X

PROLOGUE

JANUARY 1978

Our first gig as Joy Division and it ended in a fight. Typical.

Not our first gig. Before that we'd been called Warsaw but, for reasons I'll explain later, we couldn't carry on being called Warsaw, so we'd had to think of a new name. Boys in Bondage was one of the many suggestions and we very nearly went with another, the Slaves of Venus, which just goes to show how desperate we were getting.

It was Ian who suggested Joy Division. He found it in a book he was reading, *House of Dolls*, by Ka-Tzetnik 135633. He then passed it round for all of us to read. In the book, "Joy Divisions" was the name given to groups of Jewish women kept in the concentration camps for the sexual pleasure of the Nazi soldiers. The oppressed, not the oppressors. Which in a punky, "No Future" sort of way was exactly what we were trying to say with the name. It was a bit like Slaves of Venus, except not crap.

So that was decided: we were Joy Division. Little did we know what we were letting ourselves in for, that for years people would be asking us, "Are you Nazis?"

"No. We're not fucking Nazis. We're from Salford."

So anyway, we had this gig at Pips Discotheque (formerly Nice 'N' Easy) on Fennel Street in Manchester. It was our first official gig as Joy Division, though it had been advertised as Warsaw (the name change came over Christmas), and we were pretty excited come the night—me especially, because that day I'd been out and bought a brand-new guitar.

I'd been paranoid about my old one since recording our EP *An Ideal for Living.* Barney had told me it was out of tune between the F and the G. I didn't know what that meant, but it sounded serious. So I'd saved up for a new one, a Hondo II, Rickenbacker Stereo Copy (I beat the guy down from £99 to £95) and tonight was its debut. Not only that but I had a lot of mates coming to see us—the Salford lot, we'll call them: Alex Parker and his brother, Ian, Twinny, and all the lads from the Flemish Weaver on Salford Precinct, my local pub.

Before the show started, Ian Curtis had been listening to *Trans-Europe Express* by Kraftwerk over the PA. He loved that record. He must have given it to the DJ to play as our intro music, and I'm not sure if he was planning to get up onstage from the dance floor, or what he was intending to do really, but he was on the dance floor and he was sort of kicking broken glass around as "Trans-Europe Express" was playing. Kind of kicking it and moving round to the music at the same time.

We already knew Ian was driven, and recently we'd been seeing how volatile he could sometimes be. He was going through a phase of acting up a bit, shall we say. A front-man thing, of course, and partly his Iggy Pop fascination, but also frustration—frustration that we weren't getting anywhere, that other Manchester bands were doing better than us, getting more gigs than us. The Drones had an album out. The Fall, the Panik, and Slaughter & the Dogs all had singles out, and their records weren't all muffled and shit-sounding like ours. To cap it all, here we were, our first gig as Joy Division, and only about thirty people had turned up—twenty of them my mates.

All of this got to me, Steve, and Bernard, too, of course, but Ian had it worse than we did. Probably because we all lived with our parents but he was married, so maybe the group felt more like real life for him somehow, more like something he *had* to make work.

Or perhaps I'm talking out my arse. Maybe Ian was just kicking glass because he was pissed and felt like it. Not that it mattered anyway: the bouncer didn't care whether Ian was developing his stage persona or acting out his career frustration or what. He just saw a twat kicking glass. He stormed over, grabbed him by the scruff of the neck, marched him to the door, and threw him out.

Great. Someone came and told us; so, instead of going on, the three of us had to go to the door and beg the bouncer to let him back in.

He was going, "Fuck off, he's a wanker kicking broken glass round . . ." And we were going, "Yeah, but that wanker's our singer, mate—he's the singer of our band—you've got to let him in. Come on, mate . . ."

Eventually, and after much begging, the bouncer relented and let Ian back in, and at last we got onstage, about twenty minutes late, looked out into the crowd—if you can call it that—and there were all my mates right at the front going, like, "Hiya, Hooky. Are you all right, Hooky?" grinning at me and giving me the thumbs-up. I was thinking that it was nice of them to turn up, but the grinning and thumbs-upping I could have done without. In Joy Division we were very serious. We were more into scowling.

Meanwhile Barney was giving me daggers, like, "Your mates better behave themselves." Ian as well, the cheeky bastards.

Then Ian went, "Right, we're here now. We're Joy Division

and this is . . . 'Exercise One,'" and I struck a pose with my brand-new Hondo II and hit the first note of the first song, an open E.

Except that instead of the first note of "Exercise One" there was a massive *boing* sound, and everyone looked at me.

Oh, fuck. The string had flipped off the guitar. I pushed it back over the nut so it clicked into the hole and hit it again.

Boing.

It jumped out again.

Fuck, fuck, fuck-a-duck.

It was a fault on the guitar, honest. I had to hold the string in with my thumb and my finger as I was playing. I was just getting to the point of mastering that when I looked down and saw Alex Parker, who was a very good friend of mine, and his brother, Ian, all of a sudden start fighting.

No worries, I thought. *The rest of them'll sort that out.* Sure enough, a load more of the Flemish Weaver mob waded in to split them up. But then more punches were thrown, one of them went crashing to the floor and instead of the fight stopping it got worse, gradually escalating until *all* of my mates were involved, a huge mass punch-up. Like a giant ball of them rolling up and down in front of us as we were playing. Oh my God! The rest of the band were looking at them and then at me and giving me daggers as this big ball of fighting blokes rolled across the front of us and then back again. Of course the bouncer who'd thrown Ian out was nowhere to be seen, and they were just left to roll about, so we just kept on playing. Flat as fuck but the band played on.

But then it escalated. These other kids kept running forward from the back, starting on my mates, lashing out at them as they rolled past. Which of course wound me up. So I started kicking these kids from the stage.

"Don't fucking kick my mate, y'bastard!"

"Hey, la, pack it in!"

"Bleedin' Scousers!"

So there I was, kicking them in the head, trying to play "Exercise One" while trying to hold my string in, the rest of the band really pissed off with me for bringing along my daft scally mates. *Shit!*

At last the bouncer reappeared. He had a bunch of mates with him and they started knocking heads together, kicked out the Flemish Weaver lot and then the Scousers, which left us finishing the gig to an empty room, me holding my string, Ian, Barney, and Steve all looking at me like they wanted to throttle me. It was terrible, absolutely fucking awful. Our first gig as Joy Division and we didn't play another one for almost two months, which back then seemed like a long, long time. I felt like the worst thing in the world.

Little did we know, eh?

PART ONE

"INSIGHT"

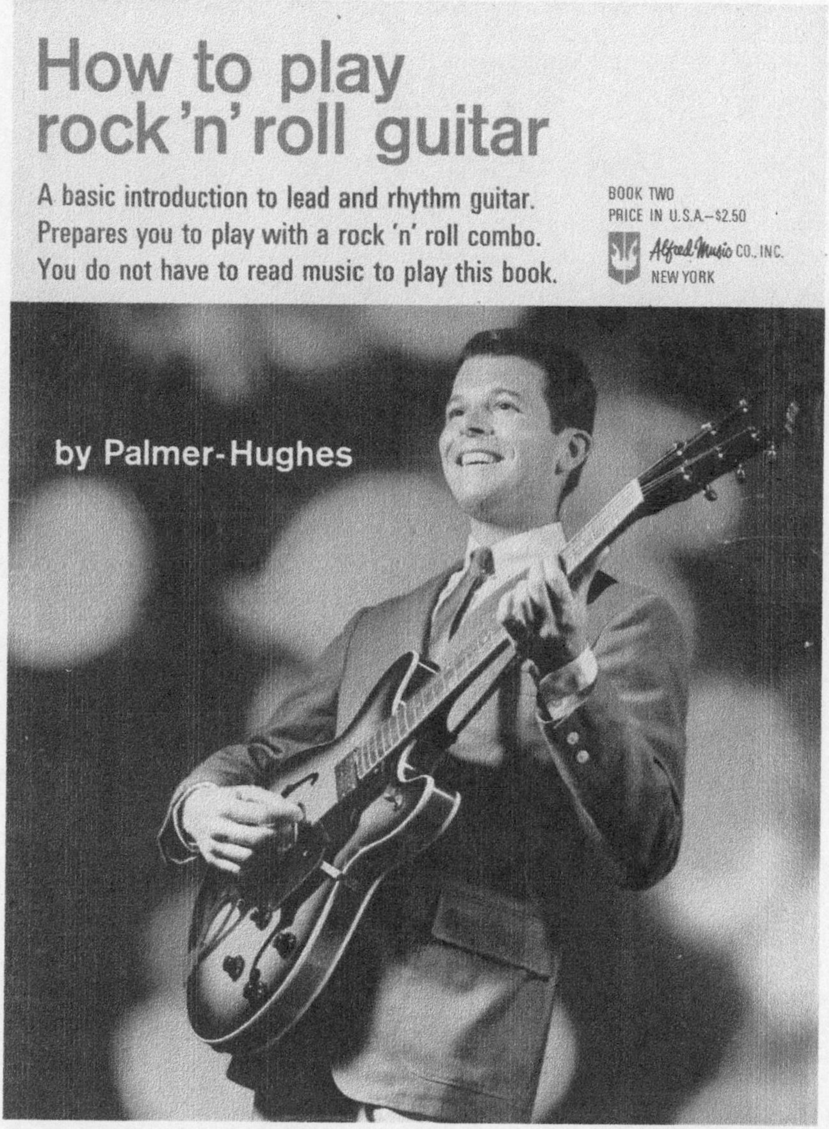

How to play
rock 'n' roll guitar
A basic introduction to lead and rhythm guitar.
Prepares you to play with a rock 'n' roll combo.
You do not have to read music to play this book.
BOOK TWO
PRICE IN U.S.A.—$2.50
Alfred Music CO., INC.
NEW YORK
by Palmer-Hughes

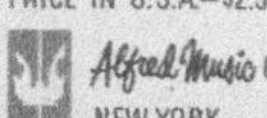

• Chapter 1 •

"Oh, fuck, it's Steve Harley"

I'd started getting interested in pop music around twelve or thirteen, when, like every other kid back in those days, I was glued to *Top of the Pops* every week. Then somebody gave me a reel-to-reel tape recorder that already had a load of music on it, and I used to listen to that over and over again—stuff like "Chirpy Chirpy Cheep Cheep." Still, though, nothing could eclipse *Top of the Pops*, which I lived for. You forget now, what with MTV, YouTube, and the fact that music's shoveled into your ears in every shop, restaurant, and supermarket, but back then *Top of the Pops* was the only way you could get to see pop music being performed. For a kid from Salford it was mind-blowing to see Deep Purple doing "Black Night," Sabbath ripping through "Paranoid," Family doing "The Weavers Answer," Marc Bolan, Bowie . . . It was like having a window on a wonderful other world, even if they were lip syncing. Plus it annoyed your parents.

As I got older I became a skinhead. This was way before skinheads were associated with the National Front. Back then it meant being into ska and reggae, ironically enough, and from that

I discovered the Upsetters, the Pioneers, Desmond Dekker, Dave & Ansel Collins. It wasn't until the fourth year that I got my first record player, though, when I bought one from Martin Gresty, who needed some quick cash. I don't think his mum even knew he was selling her Dansette, to be honest, but I gave him eleven quid for it, which was all the money I had and a fortune in those days. Of course that meant I couldn't afford to buy any records, which my mother thought was hilarious. So I nicked some. There was a shop on Langworthy Road that used to have old ex-jukebox singles for sale in a box outside and I swiped a couple sight-unseen, just to have something to play on my Dansette. When I got round the corner to take a look at my haul I wasn't exactly overjoyed: "Ruby, Don't Take Your Love to Town" by Kenny Rogers and "The Green Manalishi" by Fleetwood Mac. I'd never heard of either. Still, at least I finally had something to listen to. Or so I thought. Turned out I couldn't play them—since they were for a jukebox they needed an adaptor—and it took me another week to steal one! Years later I appeared on that BBC program *The One Show*, talking about the first record I ever bought: I told them it was "Ruby, Don't Take Your Love to Town"; I didn't tell them that I'd nicked it, though.

But when I *really* got into music—when the bug didn't so much bite as take a huge fuck-off chunk out of my leg—was on holiday in Rhyl. This was just before I left the Town Hall for Butlin's (a popular British holiday camp): 1973, it would have been. There was me and my mates: Deano, Stuart Houghton, Danny Lee, and Greg Wood, five of us in a four-berth caravan. Christ it was freezing, and there was no electricity—there were gas mantles for lights—but it was the first proper holiday I'd ever had, and we spent it roaming the streets of Rhyl and listening to Radio Luxembourg in the caravan. They kept playing a song called

"Sebastian" by Cockney Rebel. That was it for me. For the first time, I listened to a record and really thought, *Wow.* Why, I don't know. Because it was different, I suppose; it seemed so different. It had a slow, orchestral start and built to a climax—it was very long, too, which was something unheard of for a pop record back then. It just grabbed me—grabbed my attention and held it. Strange how we'd be doing another very long song with "Blue Monday" years later.

When I got back from holiday I bought the single. It was nine minutes long and you had to turn the record over halfway through, which just added to the experience: it was part of the ritual of playing it, gave the song a dramatic pause and made me like the record even more. After that I became a fan of Cockney Rebel and bought their first LP, *The Human Menagerie*—a great record. They became my gateway to music. Before this when I'd watched *Top of the Pops* I'd just goggled at it, but now it was like I was part of it; I understood it. Bowie, Roxy, Ian Dury—I started to get them now.

Years later I was at an awards ceremony with New Order getting an award for "Blue Monday." I'd given up drinking by then, so I was straight as an arrow when Steve Harley strolled up to me, and I thought, *Oh, fuck, it's Steve Harley from Cockney Rebel.*

He went, "Hello, Peter, how are you?"

And I thought, *Not only is it Steve Harley, but he knows who I am and he's* dead *fucking nice.*

He went, "Oh, it's so lovely to meet you. I believe that our first record was one of your inspirations?"

I was like, "Yeah, yeah, it was," and ran away. Just couldn't deal with it. Left him standing there looking around and no doubt thinking, *That was fucking bizarre.* But it wasn't as bizarre for him as it was for me. "Sebastian" had got me into the whole thing. If it hadn't been for Steve Harley, I wouldn't have been standing at that awards ceremony talking to Steve Harley. Very, very weird, that was.

After that—Rhyl, I mean, not the awards—I started reading *NME* and *Sounds*. Then we began going to gigs with Barney, who I'd met in my first year at Salford Grammar. He still gets really annoyed when I call him Barney.

"You're the only fucking person who calls me Barney. Everyone else calls me Bernard," he bleats. But at school they used to call him Barney Rubble—this even cropped up in an early Joy Division review—and his surname was Dickin, so they took the piss out of him about that, too, as you can imagine. He changed it to Sumner after he finished school.

Barney wasn't in my class, though. He wasn't even in the same house. I was in Lancaster and he was in Gloucester, the other two being Warwick and York. There were a few lessons we shared, but not many. My first memory of him is standing outside the gym and him coming up, and I just went, "All right?" and he went, "All right?" and that was it; that was the first time we had any kind of contact. No indication that we'd be spending the rest of our lives together, in one way or another, and change the world of music not once but twice. Even then we didn't really become friends at first, not really until the third year, when we both became skinheads. Both of us had scooters but Barney got his first; they'd changed the driving age from sixteen to seventeen and he lied about his age to get his. My birthday being in February meant I had to wait a year. We were both gradually getting into music: starting with soul and reggae, moving into pop. Barney's scooter was adorned with stick-on letters spelling "Santana," his favorite group, and I had "Abraxas" on mine, the name of their second album, and we used to ride around

Langworthy Road on our Santana-themed scooters, looking for girls to chat up.

A right pair of right bastards we were, too. Always in trouble. Always stealing things, which we continued to do when we were in bands. We were *terrible* for nicking things in Joy Division and New Order. We used to go to these wonderful gigs with all this beautiful stuff backstage and nick it all. Now you've got bands like the Happy Mondays or Oasis (in the early days) who had big scally reputations, but they had the same background as us: just working-class thieves. You never had anything so you took it. Same attitude to music: you've got to start somewhere. The difference was that nobody expected that sort of behavior from us in Joy Division or New Order because we had an arty, intellectual image.

So anyway, we'd started going to gigs and we saw Led Zeppelin; Cockney Rebel, of course; and half of a Deep Purple set before Barney made us leave because he had a toothache. It wasn't just him who had to leave: it was all of us. He's always got away with fucking murder, that one.

I first read about the Sex Pistols in April 1976, on another holiday. Me, Stuart Houghton, Danny Lee, and Danny McQueeney decided to go to Torquay and Newquay in my new car, a Mark Ten Jag 420G, registration KFR 666F (funny how I can remember all the numbers)—the same model the Krays had—that I'd bought for £325. We weren't staying anywhere, just sleeping in the car. Needless to say it was tough but enjoyable; we got on well—it was one of those holidays I'll never forget. The tires were knackered and we couldn't go more than fifty miles an hour—took us hours and hours to get there. But one thing I do remember was sitting in a car park in Newquay at about seven in the morning, still pissed from the night before, reading *Melody*

Maker. It had the Sex Pistols in it, and there was a picture of them taken at their gig at the Nashville Rooms where a huge fight had broken out. Sitting there in the car park in Cornwall, with the sun coming up and all my mates snoring in the Jag, I had an *epiphany.*

First off, I was intrigued by the idea of a group who seemed, I don't know, *human* compared to bands like Led Zeppelin and Deep Purple, who seemed, to a working-class tosser from Salford, so out of my league they might as well have lived on another planet. I mean, I'd never have looked at Led Zep and thought, *I'm going to be the next John Paul Jones.* He was like some kind of god up there. I loved the music. I loved watching it. But the idea of emulating them was ludicrous.

The Sex Pistols, though: they looked like working-class tossers *too,* which automatically made them completely different from anything I'd seen in music before. I was a great fan of James Dean; I'd seen *Giant* and *Rebel Without a Cause.* And now I felt a connection between him, these *punks,* and me. That real snotty, rebellious, arrogant-kid type of thing, only not in glossy-looking 1950s America but in gray old 1970s Britain. The Pistols were the link somehow. And the fact that they had a reputation for fighting at every gig and were part of this movement—this *punk* movement . . .

I was like, *I have* got *to see this lot.*

TIMELINE ONE

MAY 1948–APRIL 1976

MAY 31, 1948

Martin Hannett born, Miles Platting, Manchester.

From an early age Hannett showed an aptitude for mathematics and science, interests he would carry through to his musical theory. Gaining a chemistry degree from Manchester's UMIST, he played bass for Greasy Bear before forming the Invisible Girls, the backing band for John Cooper Clarke and, in later years, Pauline Murray and Nico. Together with Tosh Ryan he helped set up the musicians' collective Music Force, then Rabid Records, the home of Slaughter & the Dogs. Styling himself Martin Zero, he went on to produce the Buzzcocks' Spiral Scratch EP, the first release on the independent New Hormones label run by the Buzzcocks' manager, Richard Boon. He produced Slaughter & the Dogs' debut single, "Cranked Up Really High," then worked with Chris Sievey (later known as Frank Sidebottom) and his band the Freshies, before scoring a top 3 hit producing Graham Fellows's "Jilted John" in July 1978. (Indeed, Hannett can be seen playing bass on a Top of the Pops *performance of that song.) Shortly afterward, he produced Joy Division for the first time.*

APRIL 26 (HE ASKED ME NOT TO PUT THE YEAR IN)

Alan Erasmus born, Didsbury.

Erasmus and Tony Wilson became friendly when they met at a Christmas party and bonded over a spliff. For a while Erasmus managed Fast Breeder but parted company with them and instead sought out Wilson, the two joining forces to put together a new band, the Durutti Column. The flat Erasmus shared with best friend Charles Sturridge (a Granada director who went on to make Brideshead Revisited*) was at 86a Palatine Road, and doubled up as the Factory HQ.*

FEBRUARY 20, 1950

Tony Wilson born, Salford.

Wilson attended the De La Salle Grammar School in Salford, developing a love of drama and literature thanks to a performance of Hamlet *at Stratford-upon-Avon. At seventeen he worked as an English and drama teacher at the Blue Coat School in Oldham; he then attended Cambridge, graduating with an English degree in 1971. After working for ITN as a trainee reporter he returned to Manchester in 1973, joining Granada and presenting* Granada Reports *as well as the music program* So It Goes. *However, the end of* So It Goes *left Wilson pondering ways in which he could continue and extend his involvement in the music business. . . .*

JANUARY 15, 1953

Rob Gretton born; raised in Newall Green, Wythenshawe.

A fierce Manchester City fan, Gretton worked as an insurance clerk before leaving the job to work on a kibbutz with girlfriend Lesley Gilbert. He returned to the UK in 1976 and became involved in the emerging Manchester punk scene, working with Slaughter & the Dogs, then the Panik.

OCTOBER 9, 1955

Peter Saville born; raised Hale, Manchester.

Saville attended St. Ambrose College before studying graphic design at Manchester Polytechnic. Envious of contemporaries Linder Sterling and Malcolm Garrett, who had already made their names designing for the Buzzcocks and Magazine, and learning of the soon-to-open Factory club, Saville approached Tony Wilson at a Patti Smith concert. Not long afterward, the pair met in the canteen at Granada, where Saville showed Wilson a book of Jan Tschichold typography . . .

JANUARY 4, 1956

Bernard Sumner born; raised Lower Broughton, Salford.

Sumner attended the Salford Grammar School, where he met Peter Hook.

Years later, me and Barney went back to school. We were doing an article for *NME* and the photographer was going on about how it would be great to get some pictures of us at our old school. So we were like, "Right, mate," and went and picked this guy up and drove over to Salford Grammar. But for some reason he hadn't organized it properly. I think he may have phoned up the cleaner or something, who would have been like, "Who's the group? No Order? Are they famous? 'Blue Monday'? Never heard of it. Oh, bring 'em along anyway."

So we turned up, me and Barney, in our leather jackets, biker boots on—1982 or 1983, this was, so we were still pretty punky. But however weird we looked was nothing compared to how weird we felt trooping up to the gates of our old school. It had become a comprehensive by then but otherwise hadn't changed at all: there were still the same grand old 1960s buildings, and they still had all the old prize cups in the cases, the wood paneling and pictures of all the head boys on the walls. What blew our minds was how it all looked the same except so much smaller. We were like, "Fucking hell, this is wild being back here." It even smelled the same.

We reached the headmaster's office and the guy from *NME* said to the secretary, "Oh hello, I've got Peter Hook and Bernard Sumner here from the successful group New Order, and they're old boys from the school. We just wondered if it was possible to take their pictures in the hall for the *New Musical Express*, the biggest music paper in England."

She was nice enough, quite excited really, and said, "If you wait one second I'll just ask the headmaster." And she disappeared off into his office. Then all of a sudden we heard, "*What?* That pair of dickheads!" Then the office door flew open and out burst our old geography teacher, Dave Cain, now the headmaster, roaring at us: "You pair of bastards!"

Oh dear—we used to make his life a misery.

"Get out!" he screamed at us. "Get out, you pair of twats!"

And you know what? Straightaway we were schoolkids again. It was like going back in a time machine. In a flash we were out of there, the head on our tails, clattering along the old wooden corridors in our jackboots. Not a word of a lie: we had to run off the premises, laughing hysterically, kicked out by our old geography teacher.

Not to be outdone, we skulked back when the coast was clear; the *NME* guy going slowly nuts because he needed to get his picture. Outside the school was a board with the name of the school on it. The photographer thought this board would make a nice image, so he positioned us near it, one on either side, and got ready to take his picture. But the head must have been keeping watch, because all of a sudden we heard, "*Oi, you!* I thought I told you pair of bastards to fuck off!"

Again he came charging out. Again we legged it. The *NME*

guy was still pointing his camera at the sign but we were off, so he still couldn't get the picture he wanted—all he managed to get was a Polaroid, which I have. We ended up doing the proper photo shoot near Barney's old flat in Greengate, Broughton.

FEBRUARY 13, 1956

Peter Hook born.

JULY 15, 1956

Ian Curtis born, Stretford, Manchester.

Early academic prowess saw Curtis admitted to the King's School, Macclesfield; while there he met Deborah (Debbie) Woodruff. He was also friendly with Helen Atkinson Wood, who later found fame playing Mrs. Miggins in Blackadder, *and gave her his copy of* The Man Who Sold the World. *He passed seven O Levels but dropped out of school midway through studying for his A Levels to begin a job at Rare Records in Manchester. He became engaged to Debbie on April 17, 1974. After a spell running a record stall, he took jobs in the civil service, eventually settling in Oldham after his marriage in 1975. Still dreaming of a career in the music business, Ian placed an advert in the music press, signing himself "Rusty," which attracted the services of guitarist Iain Gray.*

DECEMBER 13, 1956

Deborah Woodruff born, Liverpool.

Having left Liverpool when she was three, Deborah's parents set up home in Macclesfield, where she attended Macclesfield High School for Girls, a sister school to the King's School. She became acquainted with Ian in 1972 when she was seeing his friend Tony Nuttall. When she and Tony split, she agreed to go on a date with Ian, to see David Bowie at the Hardrock Concert Theatre in Manchester. Soon they were a couple. Deborah was Ian's second serious girlfriend.

OCTOBER 12, 1957

Annik Honoré born, southern Belgium.

To satisfy a voracious musical appetite, Annik traveled to gigs throughout Europe, seeing Siouxsie & the Banshees more than a hundred times, as well as Patti Smith, the Clash, Generation X, Iggy Pop, and David Bowie. Like Ian Curtis, her favorite album was Bowie's Low. *Annik became involved with the fanzine* En Attendant, *and then made plans to move to London. In the meantime she saw Joy Division for the first time at the Nashville Rooms on August 13, 1979, having traveled from Belgium especially to see them, and two weeks later interviewed the entire band at the Walthamstow flat that a friend of the band, Dave Pils, shared with his girlfriend, Jasmine. By September that year Annik was living in London, in Parsons Green, and working at the Belgian embassy.*

OCTOBER 28, 1957

Stephen Morris born, Macclesfield.

Morris attended the King's School, Macclesfield but was expelled for drinking cough syrup. Morris had drummed with the Sunshine Valley Dance Band, a group of school friends, and worked for his father's firm, G Clifford Morris, a local plumbers' merchants. He spotted two adverts in the window of Jones's Music Store in Macclesfield: "Drummer wanted for punk band the Fall" and "Drummer wanted for local punk band Warsaw." Luckily for him he responded to the advert with the local phone number.

AUGUST 23, 1975

Ian Curtis and Debbie Woodruff marry, Henbury.

APRIL 23, 1976

The Sex Pistols play the Nashville Rooms, London.

It was by all accounts an unremarkable concert until Vivienne West-

wood decided to "liven things up" by slapping a female audience member. The girl's boyfriend rushed to help her, at which point Malcolm McLaren came to the aid of Vivienne, then the band to the aid of them both. All of which was captured in what were to become iconic images of the Pistols and reported in Melody Maker *and* NME *(in a piece written by a pre–Pet Shop Boys Neil Tennant), marking the beginning of the Pistols' notoriety and the aura of violence that was to accompany them from then on.*

· PART TWO ·

"DISORDER"

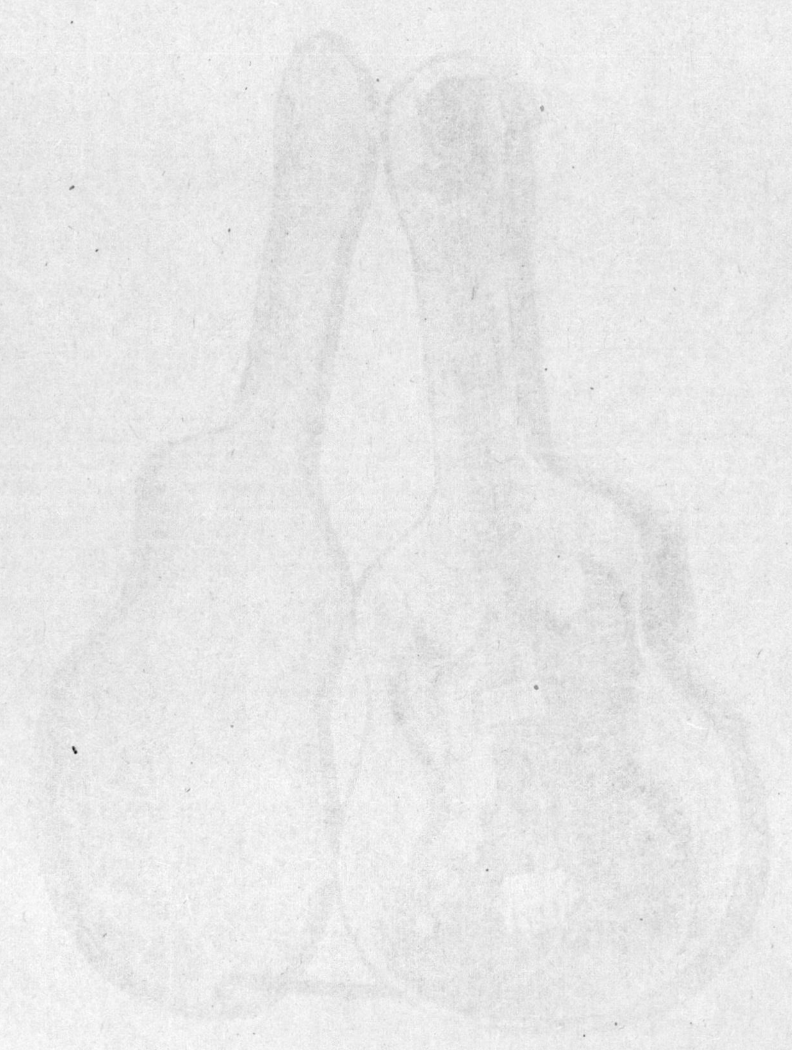

· *Chapter 2* ·

"Normal band, normal night, few people watching, clap-clap, very good"

Inspired by the Velvet Underground, friends Howard Devoto and Pete Shelley had formed a band, taking their name from a headline in Time Out *that read:* FEELING A BUZZ, COCKS? *Having made a pilgrimage to see the Sex Pistols in High Wycombe, they resolved to stage the Pistols in Manchester—with themselves supporting. A gig was scheduled for June 4, 1976, at Manchester's Lesser Free Trade Hall—although, as it turned out, the Buzzcocks were not ready to play, and support was instead provided by rock band Solstice.*

*Very few attended. Fifty at most. Yet the concert has been immortalized in two films (*24 Hour Party People *and* Control*), is the subject of a book (*I Swear I Was There: The Gig That Changed the World, *by David Nolan) and is popularly believed to have been the wellspring for years of musical innovation that was to follow, not just in Manchester but globally: in punk, post-punk, and ultimately dance-music culture.*

Among those who were definitely at the gig were Peter Hook and

Bernard Dickin, who went on to form Warsaw/Joy Division/New Order; Steven Morrissey, later of the Smiths; Mark E. Smith, later of the Fall; Mick Hucknall, later of Frantic Elevators, then Simply Red; John the Postman; photographer Kevin Cummins; and writer Paul Morley. They and others went away inspired: bands were formed, fanzines published, wardrobes overhauled—and the word about the Pistols was spread, so that the next concert, on July 20, also at the Lesser Free Trade Hall, was far better attended. Most of those at the first gig returned, along with Ian Curtis and producer Martin Hannett.

I've always read the *Manchester Evening News* cover to cover, ever since I was a kid. Don't ask me why, it's just something I've always done. Home is Becky and the kids and the *MEN.*

Reading the small ads in the *MEN* was how I found out that the Pistols were playing at the Lesser Free Trade Hall, 50p a ticket.

Now, my mates—and I mean this in the nicest possible way—have always been dead normal, so they weren't interested. But I'd been going to gigs with Terry and Bernard and (apart from the infamous toothache incident) having a laugh, so I phoned Bernard up.

"The Sex Pistols are on—do you want to go and see them?"

He went, "Who?"

I said, "Oh, it's this group. They have fights at every gig and it's really funny. Come on, it's only 50p."

"Yeah, all right, then."

Terry was up for it too, so it ended up being me, him, Barney, and Sue Barlow, who was Barney's fiancée. I think they'd met at Gresty's house when he was sixteen or so. They'd been going out for a few years and used to fight like cat and dog. With the possible exception of Debbie and Ian, they had the most tempestuous, argumentative relationship I've ever known in my life. *And* they ended up getting married. . . .

So that was it anyway, the group of us who went and saw the Sex Pistols at Lesser Free Trade Hall. A night that turned out to be the most important of my life—or one of them, at least—but that started out just like any other: me and Terry making the trip in Terry's car; Barney and Sue arriving on his motorbike; the four of us meeting up then ambling along to the ticket office.

There to greet us was Malcolm McLaren, dressed head to toe in black leather—leather jacket, leather trousers and leather boots—with a shock of bright-orange hair, a manic grin, and the air of a circus ringmaster, though there was hardly anyone else around. We were like, *Wow*. He looked so wild, from another planet, even. The four of us were in our normal gear: flared jeans, penny collars and velvet jackets with big lapels, all of that. Look at the photographs of the gig and you can see that everybody in the audience was dressed the same way, like a *Top of the Pops* audience. There were no punks yet. So Malcolm—he looked like an alien to us. Thinking about it, he must have been the first punk I ever saw in the flesh.

Wide-eyed we paid him, went in and down the stairs into the Lesser Free Trade Hall (the same stairs I'd laid down on many years before). At the back of the hall was the stage and set out in front of it were chairs, on either side of a central walkway, just like it was in *24 Hour Party People*—although I don't remember many people sitting down like they are in the film. I don't think there was a bar that night, so we just sat around, waiting.

The support band was called Solstice, and their best number was a twenty-minute cover version of "Nantucket Sleighride." The original, by Mountain, was one of my favorite records at the time so we knew it really well, and we were like, "This is great. Just like the record."

Still, though, nothing out of the ordinary. Normal band, normal night, few people watching, clap-clap, very good, off they went.

The Sex Pistols' gear was set up and then, without further ceremony, they came on: Johnny Rotten, Glen Matlock, Steve Jones, and Paul Cook. Steve Jones was wearing a boiler suit and the rest of them looked like they'd just robbed a thrift store. Rotten had on this torn-open yellow sweater and he glared out into the audience like he wanted to kill each and every one of us, one at a time, before the band struck up into something that might have been "Did You No Wrong" but you couldn't tell because it was so loud and dirty and distorted.

I remember feeling as though I'd been sitting in a darkened room all of my life—comfortable and warm and safe and quiet—then all of a sudden someone had kicked the door in, and it had burst open to let in an intense bright light and this even more intense *noise*, showing me another world, another life, a way out. I was immediately no longer comfortable and safe, but that didn't matter because it felt great. I felt alive. It was the weirdest sensation. It wasn't just me feeling it either—we were all like that. We just stood there, stock still, watching the Pistols. Absolutely, utterly stunned.

I was thinking two things. Two things that I suppose you'd have to say came together to create my future—my whole life from then on.

The first was: *I could do that.*

Because, fucking hell, what a racket. I mean, they were just dreadful; well, the *sound* was dreadful. Now, the other band didn't sound that bad. They sounded *normal*. But it was almost as though the Pistols' sound guy had deliberately made them sound awful, or they had terrible equipment on purpose, because it was all feeding back, fuzzed-up, just a complete din. A wall of noise. I didn't recognize a tune, not a note, and considering they were playing so many covers– the Monkees, the Who—I surely would have recognized something had it not sounded so shit.

So, in fact, sound-wise it was as much the sound guy who inspired us all as it was the Sex Pistols, who were, as much as I hate to say it, a pretty standard rock band musically. I'm not saying it's a bad thing that they played straightforward down-the-line rock 'n' roll, but it didn't make them special.

No. What made them special, without a shadow of a doubt, was Johnny Rotten. The tunes were only a part of the package—and probably the least important part of it, if I'm honest. Close your eyes and, like I say, you had a conventional pub-rock band with a soundman who either didn't have a clue or was being very clever indeed. But who was going to close their eyes when he, Johnny Rotten, was standing there? Sneering and snarling at you, looking at you like he hated you, hated being there, hated everyone. What he embodied was the *attitude* of the Pistols, the attitude of punk. Through him they expressed what we wanted to express, which was complete nihilism. You know the way you feel when you're a teenager, all that confusion about the future that turns to arrogance and then rebellion, like, "Fuck off, we don't fucking care, we're shit, we don't care"? He had all of that and more.

And, God bless him, whatever he had, he gave a bit of it to us, because that was the second thing I felt, after *I can do that.* It was: *I* want *to do that.* No. *I fucking* need *to do that.*

Tony Wilson said he was there, of course, but I didn't see him, which is weird because he was very famous in Manchester then; he was Tony Wilson off the telly. Mick Hucknall was there, and Mark E. Smith and everyone, but of course we didn't know anybody—all that would come later. The only people we knew there were one another: me and Terry, Barney and Sue. I don't know what Sue made of it all, mind you; I'd love to know now. But me, Barney, and Terry were being converted.

The Pistols were on for only about half an hour and when they finished we filed out quietly with our minds blown, absolutely and utterly speechless, and it just sort of dawned on me then—that was it. That was what I wanted to do: tell everyone to Fuck Off.

· *Chapter 3* ·

"Is that a bass guitar?"

On the way home that night we decided to form a band. If they can do it, we said, meaning the Pistols, then so can we.

We decided to follow the rules of punk . . .

Rule one: act like the Sex Pistols.
Rule two: look like the Sex Pistols. One guitar, one bass.

Terry volunteered to be the singer. Barney had been given a guitar and a little red practice amp for Christmas, which made him the guitarist, so I thought, "Right, I'll get a bass."

Of course, I'm pleased it worked out like that because I ended up learning the bass guitar, really making it my own and developing a very distinctive style, whereas (who knows?) if I'd tried learning the guitar I might just have been a run of the mill rhythm guitarist. It's one of the strange things about writing a book like this, actually. You start seeing your life as series of chance happenings that somehow come together to make you what you are. You start thinking, *What if I hadn't bought that week's* Melody Maker *or seen the advert for the Sex Pistols in the* Manchester Evening News*?*

What if Barney's parents had bought him a Johnny Seven for his birthday instead of a guitar?

But they didn't. They bought him a guitar, so I became a bassist. The very next day I borrowed £40 off my mam, and got the bus to Mazel's on London Road, Piccadilly, in Manchester. I had no idea how much guitars cost. But I think Barney's was about £40. Mazel Radio was one of those shops that always felt dark, it was that filled with weird indecipherable stock. (I used to go there with Terry for fun most weekends.) It was an Aladdin's cave stuffed with transistors, valves, accumulators, TVs, radios—all kinds of electrical doo-dahs.

And cheap guitars.

"Can I have one of those, please?" I said, pointing at them.

"Well, what kind do you want, son?" said the bloke behind the counter.

"A bass one."

And he went, "Well, how about this one?"

"Is that a bass guitar?

"Yeah."

"That'll do."

So I bought my first guitar, which I've still got: a Gibson EB-0 copy. No make on it. They tried to sell me a case, but after bus fare I didn't have enough money so I took it home in a black garbage bag they fished out from behind the counter. Very punk.

Barney had been playing a bit so he showed me a couple of notes. He'd go, "Hold your finger there, then move your finger to there. Move your finger back. . . ."

We were off. Not long later, we got books on how to play: the Palmer-Hughes *Book of Rock 'n' Roll Guitar* and *Rock 'n' Roll Bass Guitar.* Mine came with stickers for the neck of the bass so you knew where to put your fingers. When the stickers wore off with sweat, I painted them on with Tippex. We'd be sitting round practicing, with Barney shouting out the chords, like, "Play A, A, A, A, and then we'll change to G, G, G, G." I'd practice by myself, too, but it was far more interesting learning together than it was playing on your own at home.

Teaching myself meant I ended up learning it wrong, though, because I picked up the bad habit of playing with three fingers. A teacher would have made me play with four, but the Palmer-Hughes *Book of Rock 'n' Roll Bass Guitar* didn't talk back, so I started off—and have ended up—a three-fingered bass player; and having to hold down my little finger as I play makes me slower. Saying that, I suppose it also gave me my style, which is slower and more melodic compared to most bassists. It's a different way of playing, and it came through learning badly.

We began by practicing in Barney's gran's front room. I told you she was a lovely lady. She had an old stereogram record player, and Barney, who was always good with electronics, wired up our guitar leads to the two input wires on the needle cartridge so we could play through it. It worked as well. I mean, it sounded fucking diabolical, and if we both played at the same time you couldn't hear anything but a wall of noise, but it worked. So we'd made it, we'd arrived—right up until his gran discovered that we'd wrecked her stereo and went berserk and threw us out. Then we ran down Alfred Street laughing.

But we didn't care. We were punks. We raided a used-clothing store and cut up the clothes we stole; I spiked up my hair and took the dog collar off the dog to wear. My mam went mad yet again. At first we were just copying the look from *Melody Maker* and *NME*, and wearing what the London punks were wearing, but pretty soon we were developing our own style. Barney discovered the Scout Shop on New Mount Street and started wearing a more military look (typical of him, he wanted to be a neat-and-tidy punk) while I used masking tape on my blue blazer to put stripes on it, and we both sprayed prison arrows on our clothes.

You used to get shouted at in the street for dressing like that; you were treated like a leper. I mean, these days nobody would bat an eyelid, but back then it was really shocking to see these kids walking round with hair in spikes and their clothes cut up. Which was, of course, why we did it—we wanted to be shocking; we wanted people staring at us. We loved that our mums hated it and that we had to get changed on the bus. It was all part of being a punk.

This was it for us: we'd get the guitars out, play around for a bit, go out so that people in the street could treat us like lepers, then come back and play around on the guitars some more. It was great.

The next punk happening in Manchester was the Pistols' second gig, on July 20, also at the Lesser Free Trade Hall. Apart from the venue it was completely different: for a start, we were punks now and knew what to expect from the band; plus there were a lot more people there, not only because the word had spread in Manchester but also because the Pistols, unless I'm very much mistaken, had brought a busload of supporters with them, which was exciting straightaway. At that time if you put a group of Londoners—Cockneys, in other words—and a group of Mancunians into a municipal building at the same time, the, shall we say, "regional differences" meant a fight was bound to break out—which it did.

We were in the bar talking to these kids who'd come over to us, one of them going, "Hey, are you fucking Cockneys or what?" all up in our faces.

And we went, "No, fuck off, mate, we're from Salford."

Turned out they were from Manchester too: Wythenshawe. "We're a group," they said.

"Oh, right. We're a group, too. Sort of."

"Well, we're Slaughter & the Dogs. We're supporting tonight."

Wow—it was Slaughter & the Dogs; and this bloke's name was Mick Rossi, the guitarist. Slaughter & the Dogs was one of the earliest punk bands in Manchester—and they were on the bill that night along with the Buzzcocks.

"What's your group called?" said Mick Rossi.

We looked at one another. "Dunno. We haven't got a name yet."

Didn't have a name. Didn't have songs. Didn't have a lead singer unless you counted Terry, which—after a couple of disastrous practice sessions—we didn't. But still, we were a band.

"Right, the Cockneys are here," said Rossi, clenching his fists. "We're having the Cockneys, we're fucking having them."

And this was the support band. So there was a hell of an atmosphere right from the beginning and, true to form, there was as much fighting as there was pogoing and moshing, everyone rolling around the room. It was more good-natured than you might have expected, but, even so, pretty chaotic and, because of all the scraps breaking out, a lot more exciting than the first gig. At the first gig it all went off onstage. At the second gig it all went off in the audience *and* onstage.

Looking back, I don't know which of the gigs was the most important in terms of the influence it had. A lot of people say the second because there were more people there, the Pistols were better known, and punks had started to get going in the city, but for me and Barney it was the first because that's when we decided to form the group. Overall I think you'd have to say they were each as important as the other. I mean, after those two gigs, bands had formed and venues were putting them on and there was a group of us who soaked up whatever punk we could. That autumn we saw the Stranglers at the Squat on Devas Street; in September, Eater played the first-ever gig, at Houldsworth Hall on Deansgate. Eater was supported by the Buzzcocks, who played at just about every gig in Manchester and were also doing a lot to help other punk bands find their feet. They'd encouraged us; their manager, Richard Boon, had come up with our first name, the Stiff Kittens, and later we found out that Ian had been in touch with them too. Together with the Drones and Slaughter & the Dogs they were the backbone of the punk scene and helped make Manchester the major punk city after London. They all played regularly at the Squat and at a gay bar on Dale Street called the Ranch, owned by Foo Foo Lammar, as well as at the Electric Circus on Collyhurst Street, which quickly became the city's main punk venue.

Debbie Curtis remembers Ian talking to me and Barney at that second Pistols gig. (He wasn't there for the first one, which annoyed him to no end, but he brought Debbie along to the second.) Maybe we did share a few words that night but he certainly didn't really register with me then. The first time I remember Ian making an impact was at the Electric Circus, for the third Pistols gig. He had "Hate" written on his jacket in orange fluorescent paint. I liked him immediately.

· *Chapter 4* ·

"He was just a kid with 'Hate' on his coat"

The Electric Circus was an older, normal rock venue, in that it was a redbrick building, with a pointed roof like a church. The front door opened into one big, dark room with a high ceiling. The bar was on the right-hand side and there was a balcony, which I never saw open. In fact, the only reason I knew it had a balcony was that I was hanging around one night—this was later, when we were Warsaw—and somehow we got on to it, and there sat the Drones' PA.

By that time the Drones were like Slaughter & the Dogs—real fucking loudmouth, football-hooligan types, and we hated them. I mean, with the exception of the Buzzcocks, who were like the father figures of Manchester punk, all the bands hated one another and were forever trying to get one over on each other, and Slaughter & the Dogs and the Drones were the worst of the lot. The second time the Pistols played the Lesser Free Trade Hall, Slaughter & the Dogs had their own posters made up that had their name above the Pistols and missed out the Buzzcocks altogether. That's the kind of thing I'm talking about. Horrible twats.

They made us look like angels. The Drones were just as bad. So . . . Well, let's just say something happened to their equipment. Something nasty.

All of which is a roundabout way of saying that, once we'd put our knobs away, I knew there was a balcony in the Electric Circus.

Even before the Pistols played there the Circus was a big punk venue; and because there was only that and the Ranch, which was a punk club on Thursday nights, you got to start recognizing all the punks because they were going to the same two places on the same nights. The people who stuck out tended to be the well-known ones, like the Buzzcocks and Slaughter & the Dogs, or the guys with big personalities—people like John the Postman, the noisy bastard. Me and Barney were pretty quiet. We'd just stand on the sidelines and not get noticed, but you'd see the faces and you'd let on. "All right, mate, how are you?" something like that. People got to know you.

The night of that third Pistols gig there was a really lively atmosphere, to say the least. You've got to bear in mind that this was December 9, 1976, a week or so after the Pistols had done their *Today*-program interview, when they'd gone on TV and told Bill Grundy he was a "fucking rotter." Next day it was all over the papers—THE FILTH AND THE FURY!—and suddenly the Pistols were public enemy number one. They were about to go on their Anarchy tour with the Damned (who ended up getting thrown off it, for some reason), the Clash, and Johnny Thunders & the Heartbreakers, and because of the outcry most of the gigs were canceled. Seventeen of the twenty-four dates were stopped by local councils. Among those that went ahead were two at the Electric Circus, and consequently a lot more people came along. The place was fucking rammed.

Even so, we recognized Ian. He stood out. Me and Barney were at the top of some stairs looking down and he came up the stairs with his donkey jacket on and we got talking to him because we'd seen him around. What were our first words to him? Fucked if I can remember. "Didn't I see you at the Squat?" something like that. I'm not sure we even found out his name that night, to be honest. He was just a kid with "Hate" on his coat, just a normal kid. Of course, we were all punks, so we must have looked pretty wild compared to everybody else, but he looked normal compared to us. He was nice. Softly spoken. Sharp sense of humor. Of the two portrayals of him on film, I prefer the one in *24 Hour Party People.* The guy in *Control,* Sam Riley, played him as being much more arty and conventionally pretty than he was in real life, whereas Sean Harris in *24 Hour Party People* had a bit more of the real-life Ian's edginess and intensity. Neither was perfect and neither was totally off the mark, but for my money Harris was the more accurate.

It was at that same Pistols gig that we spoke to a guy from *Sounds,* who quoted us in his report of the gig—our very first national write-up.

> *The sentiments [that the Pistols were great] were echoed by most every kid I spoke to—they were certainly all in the process of forming bands. Stiff Kittens (Hooky, Terry, Wroey and Bernard, who has the final word) being the most grotesque offering.*
>
> PETE SILVERTON, *SOUNDS,* DECEMBER 18, 1976

"Grotesque," eh? Cheers, mate. Wroey was someone Barney had met in Broughton, a friend of his cousin Grimmie. We were trying him out as singer at the time, which is why he got a mention in *Sounds.* Like most of our singers, he didn't last and we added him to a growing pile of rejects. The problem wasn't that they were terrible as such, just that they were the wrong sort of terrible. I mean, we just needed someone to sound horrible and shit—we were a punk band after all—but they weren't right for it. For some reason they couldn't do proper singing or horrible and shit singing, just awful singing, but not in a good way. I suppose it's one of those star-quality things. You recognize it when you see it.

Our search was taking too long. So we decided to advertise for a singer with a notice on the board in Virgin Records in Piccadilly, and in response got the biggest bunch of weirdoes you've ever met in your life. Barney went to meet a couple of them on his own, and we saw a few together, but none of them really stuck out. Getting a bit frustrated, we decided to ask Martin Gresty from school because he was the craziest person we'd ever met in our lives. He was an absolute psycho, but in a nice way—the terror of the school. We thought he'd be ideal as a punk singer. We went round to his house, just near Langworthy Road, and knocked on his door.

"Is Martin there?" we asked when his mother answered the door.

"Sorry, love, he's gone out plane-spotting."

Turned out the scourge of Salford Grammar had calmed down. He was a plane-spotter now. Not trains but planes: he joined coach trips to different airports to spot planes. Very weird. (I mean, how hard can it be to spot a plane at an airport?) Anyway, we gave our numbers to his mum but Nidder (as we called him) never got in touch. Too busy spotting planes, probably. Which was a shame because I'm sure his lunatic tendencies would have been reawakened by being in the group. Plus he and Barney would have had mad fights. At school they used to wind each other up like crazy, and every Friday night they'd have a fight. We'd all go and watch them in the park but we'd be bored because they were so evenly matched—we'd be like, "Oh come on, lads, it's five o'clock, we want to go home. . . ." Anyway, it wasn't to be.

Then Danny Lee, my mate from Sorbus Close, tried out for the singer, but he wasn't much cop.

In the meantime we were becoming more and more friendly with Ian. We started seeing him out more often and we'd recognize him because he'd either be wearing his jacket with "Hate" on it or his mackintosh, which he wore when he came straight from work. We'd found out his name, that he was from Oldham and married, which came as a bit of a shock—not that he was from Oldham, but that he was married. I mean, *married*. We'd only just graduated high school. At least, it felt like we had.

He'd got a band together as well. That was the thing about that period. We'd all been inspired. We were all desperate to just go ahead and do it. Ian had returned from a punk festival in France, having seen Iggy and the Damned, all fired up about doing his own stuff. So far he'd managed to recruit a drummer and a guitarist and, like us, had been getting help (advice mainly) from Richard Boon and Pete Shelley.

We wanted a singer and a drummer but Ian had a drummer and a guitarist, so—remembering the rules of punk—we couldn't join up, even though we desperately needed a singer and he desperately needed a bassist. We had to follow the rules.

We'd meet in the pub. "Hiya, mate. How are you? How's it going? How's the band?"

"Oh, me drummer's left."

Ian's drummer was Martin Jackson, a very good drummer. We ended up trying to get him for Warsaw but he said no and went to play for Magazine initially then ended up with Swing Out Sister, among others. I bet he still kicks himself now.

So anyway, he'd left Ian.

"Still got me guitarist, though," said Ian. That was Iain Gray, a close friend of Ian's and another familiar face on the punk scene. He'd been at the first Pistols gig.

There are two schools of thought on how Ian ended up joining us. The first is that Ian answered another ad we put in Virgin Records, but that's not what I remember. (Saying that, there are a lot of things I don't remember. . . .) The way I thought it happened was that the next time we saw Ian, at the last Sex Pistols gig at the Electric Circus, we said to him, "All right, mate. How's it going? How's the group? You still got Iain as your guitarist?"

"Nah, he's fucked off."

And we had a Eureka moment. "Well, come in with us, then. You can sing for us."

Either way, the result was the same: we had our lead singer. We met the Saturday after the gig and took him with us for a scramble round Ashworth Valley in Rochdale, getting him well and truly wet and covered in mud. A great way to audition singers; I highly recommend it.

But back to that fourth and last Pistols gig. It was a virtual riot, the kind of night you look back on and wonder how the fuck you escaped with your life. Like I said, the Damned were off the tour, so the Buzzcocks opened instead, followed by the Clash, Johnny Thunders & the Heartbreakers, and then the Pistols, who'd been kicked out of not one but two Manchester hotels earlier that day. It was absolutely packed, inside and out, a riot outside and a riot inside. Loads of football fans had come looking for a fight and the Pistols played under a hail of spit and bottles, with constant fights taking place in front of the stage. Even in the queue outside you risked life and limb, with the kids on the flats raining bottles and bricks down from the roofs on to the punks below. They'd even gone to the trouble of taking the spikes out of the railings round the Electric Circus, to use as ammunition. After the gig it was bedlam outside, with the punks getting hammered left, right, and center. We flagged down a passing cop car and asked for help getting past these lunatics and the copper said, "Run behind the van and we'll escort you to your cars." We all trooped behind, but as he set off he put his foot right down and sped off—leaving us at the mercy of the mob. The bastard. Luckily Terry's car was nearby so we dived in and escaped.

Looking back I wonder if that last Pistols gig at the Electric Circus was the night that the allure of punk started to fade for some of us. Once you get football fans coming—the twats who just want to spit and throw bottles—it's time to move on, and people like the Buzzcocks and then us, Magazine, the Fall, and Cabaret Voltaire were eventually able to find a way forward. We'd already decided that the name the Stiff Kittens was too "cartoon punk" and were looking for something else. Also, we'd started writing some songs. We still needed a drummer, though. Terry tried for that, too, but alas it wasn't going to be him.

· *Chapter 5* ·

"He was one of us"

Even though Terry was a bit shy and awkward in company, and all our schoolmates picked on him, we liked him all the same. Whereas my other mates preferred to stay in the pubs in Salford, Terry was into Bowie and Roxy and he introduced us both to the discos in town, Pips or Time & Place. Plus he was there right at the beginning. He was there for the Pistols, and he was in on the conversations about starting the group. He was one of us.

Like I say, I thought we'd given him a go as the singer and it didn't work. He disputes that, but agrees that he then tried his hand at guitarist and that didn't work. Then he became the drummer. By that time we'd recruited Steve, but Terry kept up with the lessons for himself. So he became the manager and he wasn't very good at that, either. No killer instinct—he was too nice. Then he became the sound guy, and he was shit at being a sound guy too, because Harry DeMac had taught him—as a joke, presumably—to turn things up with the "gain pots" on the desk instead of the faders (ask your roadie), which resulted in some pretty wild mixes. (Saying that, if you listen to the tapes now they sound great. Quite a few have been released to much acclaim.)

After we found OZ PA, a local Manchester sound company, Terry became our roadie, eventually becoming New Order's tour manager, and we had a great time. He was my oldest friend and my sounding post for the start of my moaning about Barney. We were always very close; Barney hated this and he took it out on Terry sometimes. I remember at the sound check for one New Order gig, in the Midwest somewhere, some kid gave Terry four E's, saying, '"Give them to the band, buddy!"

Terry took one, but Barney, who didn't do sound checks at that time so wasn't even there, somehow found out and demanded Terry be sacked for it. I wouldn't mind, but American E is shit anyway; it wasn't worth moaning about, especially with the amount we were earning then—something like a million dollars per gig with merchandising—and we were carrying ounces of coke! Me and Rob told Barney to fuck off and he stormed out after the gig.

So anyway, by 1989 Barney had had enough of him. They hated each other. The Barney-and-Terry hate was even more intense than the me-and-Barney hate—and Barney threatened to leave New Order many times if Terry didn't go. Eventually Terry moved to Los Angeles. With the advent of technology he reckoned he could work from anywhere so why not somewhere sunny? Thirteen years he'd worked with us by this point: through thick and thin, a loyal colleague and friend—still is, hopefully.

I mean, the trouble was that he started off as our lead singer and went right down the ladder, or up the ladder, all the way to the bottom or the top depending on how you think. It was actually Terry who discovered distortion for us. Ian had a small WEM amp and two columns of ten-inch speakers he used for his vocals.

Terry didn't have an amp that day so plugged into the WEM while Ian wasn't singing . . . Oh my God, it sounded like choirs of angels, distorted choirs of angels: heavenly. Barney elbowed him out of the way immediately, saying, "You and Ian use mine!"

Barney discovered distortion.

Still, things certainly improved and we started practicing more regularly at night, often going straight from work. I was working at the Ship Canal; Ian was working at the Employment Exchange in Macclesfield and Barney was at Cosgrove Hall Films helping to make cartoons for ITV: *Count Duckula*, *Danger Mouse*, and all that. His job was to color in *Danger Mouse*—although he used to tell the girls he was a graphic artist. It was a cool place to work, actually, much more relaxed than the Town Hall. They let us practice there in the early days; it was one of the many places we used when we pinged around from place to place. It used to be very difficult to find rehearsal rooms. Every pub you'd go in you'd say, "We're a band and we're just looking for a rehearsal room."

And they'd say, "Oh right. Why don't you rehearse in the main room and you can play your songs and the punters will love it."

Which sounded horrific to us. "Oh no, you wouldn't like us. . . ."

So we got a lot of offers but not many that were suitable, and we ended up shuttling around: the Albert pub in Macclesfield; Bernard's gran's front room; the Swan in Salford, which the landlady let us use for free if we bought a pie and a pint; disused mills and warehouses all over the place, where we used to go and drag gear up and down stairs then set up and play in the freezing cold. None of them was a fully fledged rehearsal room apart from the Big Alex, where twelve bands practiced at once and you couldn't concentrate because it was like being in an engine room. You'd have a reggae band going on, a heavy metal band sawing away. To try to compete, Ian had to go and buy himself the WEM PA system.

Up till then he'd just been hollering, which didn't bother us because it sounded like the Sex Pistols, which is what we aspired to: that volume and attitude. Our first songs were like that, all just punk-copy songs. We had one called "BL"—bleedin' 'ell—which was about Danny Lee's sister Belinda, who I went out with and who broke my heart. I wrote it and Ian used to sing it, God bless him. I wrote "At a Later Date" and "Novelty," too—I was writing a lot of lyrics at work because I was bored. I could get rid of the whole month's work in a week, so all I had to do for the other three weeks was go up and down the canal collecting the rent, piss about, fall asleep in the file room, and write lyrics. Most of them were terrible but Ian was so nice and gracious like that he used to sing them anyway. Then we'd do one of his songs and it sounded so much better—and that was before we even knew what he was saying. What was obvious about Ian was that he was pouring everything into it; he wasn't playing at being in a band. My lyrics were just words on a page whereas his were coming from somewhere else, his soul.

We were getting to know him a bit better, too. When we first met him, he and Debbie lived in Oldham, but they sold up—either because she wanted to move back to Macclesfield or they just weren't getting on in Oldham, whatever. But while they sorted out the house in Macc he lived at his gran's in Stretford. Me and Barney would go round there to practice and usually go out to gigs and, as he was spending so much time with us . . . Well, I suppose you'd have to say we corrupted him a bit. Like, when we first met him he was a married man and behaved like one. If an attractive girl walked by on the street, me and Barney would look but Ian wouldn't give her a second glance. He was just that bit more of a gentleman than we were, I suppose you'd have to say. Well, a *lot* more of a gentleman.

But he didn't stay that way for long. Soon enough he was behaving the same way: if a girl walked down the street, he'd be looking too. But that was his personality, though I'm not sure I realized this at the time. (Probably didn't, if I'm honest.) But looking back that's exactly what he was: a people pleaser; he could be whatever you wanted him to be. A poetic, sensitive, tortured soul, the Ian Curtis of the myth—he was definitely that. But he could also be one of the lads—he *was* one of the lads, as far as we were concerned. That was the people pleaser in him, the mirror. He adapted the way he behaved depending on who he was with. We all do a bit, of course, but with Ian the shift was quite dramatic. Nobody was better at moving between different groups of people than he was. But I also think this was an aspect of his personality that ended up being very damaging to him. He had three personas he was trying to juggle: he had his married-man persona, at home with the wife; the laddish side; and the cerebral, literary side. By the end he was juggling home life and band life, and had two women on the go. There were just too many Ians to cope with.

I've realized all this in the years since, of course. At the time I just thought he was a great guy. And he was a great front man. You could tell.

Now, if only we could find a drummer.

· *Chapter 6* ·

"I can't actually think of anything less 'us' than a wet-towel fight"

So we asked around for a drummer and when that drew a blank, we tried advertising. Our first reply was from a student whose name I can't remember. We took him on but he really got on our tits, so even though he was an okay drummer we decided to get rid of him. Being a right pair of shits, me and Barney decided that the only way to ditch him was by telling him he was "too good" for us.

We drove to Middleton College to give him the good news to his face—it's where Steve Coogan went, funnily enough, a famous college in the area—and made our way up to his dorm, only to find him and his mates flicking one another's bare arses with their towels. If we'd had any doubts about sacking him, they were laid to rest at the sight of that because offhand I can't actually think of anything less "us" than a wet-towel fight.

Out of breath from his jolly larks he came bounding up to us: "All right, lads! How's it going?"

"We think you're too good for us," we said as rehearsed, heads down. "You know, the sound we're going for, you know, it's . . . And . . . You're too . . . Good."

"Right," he beamed, and ran back to whipping his mates' arses with his towel while we sloped off to wrestle with the thorny issue of finding another drummer—an issue that was about to get even thornier: we had our first gig coming up.

When we'd started the group, me and Bernard had got in touch with Pete Shelley from the Buzzcocks. (I can't remember how—he must have given us his phone number.) We met him in a pub in Broughton, where we picked his brains. We were a bit star-struck, a bit in awe of him because he was in a band and they were like Manchester punk royalty, but mainly we were just pleased that he'd agreed to see us, because in those days there were no books on starting a band. You couldn't take a course or look it up on the Internet. Being in a group gave you instant social-leper status. It meant you were ostracized by your family and shunned by passing strangers in the street, and your workmates made no bones about what they thought of it all.

"Why do you want to be in a group? Fuck off, do some work why don't you?"

So to actually talk to someone with firsthand experience was very valuable. And, though the Manchester punk scene would go on to resemble a snake pit of petty jealousy, backbiting, and rivalry, the Buzzcocks and especially Pete seemed above all that. Right from the word go they were about being inclusive—the proper punk ethos. It was just the rest of us who squabbled like kids over a bag of sweets.

Because we'd met up with Pete, and because Pete was a nice, gracious guy, he'd ask me and Bernard how it was going. We told him that Ian was really working out as a lead singer, which was good because Pete knew Ian, too, and Pete asked us if we'd like a support slot with the Buzzcocks, and even though we still didn't have a name that we all liked, and we were "between drummers," we virtually bit his hand off. This was it. This was what we were getting ready for.

The first thing we did was work on the look. I went shopping with Terry at the Army & Navy Store on Tib Street, where a black plastic cap set me back 50p.

"You have to have a gimmick, our Peter," as my mother always said. These were probably her only words of advice about the band other than "You should give it all up and settle down." (I remember once arriving late for my Sunday lunch at home because I'd been doing an interview for *NME* in town. When I told her, I thought she'd go mad: dinner was ruined. Instead she burst out crying, hugged me, and said, "At last. You're getting a proper job!" That was in 1986.) But it wasn't bad advice as it goes, and that was my gimmick at first: the cap and a mustache. Terry, who by this point was trying his hand at being our manager/roadie, got his tank commander's goggles; Barney no doubt invested in a fresh supply of Scout clothes from the Scout shop, and of course Ian had his own Ian thing going on. One thing they got dead right in *Control*, actually, was how Ian looked. He didn't go in for the jackboots (ex–German Army, £3.50 a pair from Tib Street; wore them for years) or the tank hats or Scout stuff. He was just Ian, and he was always much cooler than us without really trying to be. Just was.

Next we needed a new name, Stiff Kittens being too "London punk." We chose Warsaw. Just like that. For any group the name's your most important thing, definitely as important as the music, and I've always found it tough to choose one. But Warsaw was a piece of piss, far easier than any of the name changes that came later. We picked it because it was cold and austere. It was either that or Berlin, and because we all liked "Warszawa," the track on

Bowie's *Low*, we chose that. Too late for Richard Boon, though: the Buzzcocks' manager had been screaming at us for a name but by the time we eventually we came up with Warsaw it was too late, or so he said, and he'd gone with Stiff Kittens on the poster. This annoyed us and kind of led to us falling out with the Buzzcocks a bit—because we would have been very, well, *vocal* about our annoyance.

But we still didn't have a drummer. For a while it looked like we might have to cancel the gig or maybe even go back to the wet-towel kid, but in the end we got a guy called Tony Tabac, who we recruited a night or two before the gig. Nothing like cutting it fine; it was straight in at the deep end for him. Quite a nice guy he was, too, and a good drummer. I remember his audition: a bit meat-and-potatoes, but good—and he'd decorated his bass drum with all kinds of shit, like cigarette ends and cigarette packets, which we liked because it looked punky.

On May 29, 1977, at the Electric Circus, the band played their first-ever gig, supporting Penetration and the Buzzcocks. Tony Wilson was in the audience, as well as Paul Morley, who by this time was writing for NME *and was impressed by Warsaw's "twinkling evil charm." "The bass player had a moustache," he later wrote. "I like them and will like them more in six months' time." Photographer Kevin Cummins was also there, as well as Steve Shy of local fanzine* Shy Talk; *John the Postman, who led the crowd in a rendition of "Louie Louie" at the end of the night; and punk poet John Cooper Clarke, who performed after Warsaw.*

I remember driving there in the afternoon, and I remember getting there and loading the gear in. I don't remember the sound check. We had one, I think, but we had no idea what to do because we'd never done one before. No one had the foggiest.

Not knowing what to do made it exciting, though. Like, now, everybody's got a stage manager and a sound guy, lights, and so on. The bands know all about sound checks and levels, equipment and all that. Now they even have music schools to teach you that kind of stuff. Back then you knew fuck-all. You didn't have anyone professional, just your mates, who, like you, were clueless; you had a disco PA and a sleepy barmaid. It's something I find quite sad about groups today, funnily enough, the careerism of it all. I saw this program once, a "battle of the bands" sort of thing. It had Alex James from Blur on it and Lauren Laverne and some twat from a record company, and they'd sit there saying what they thought of the band: "Your bass player's shit and your image needs work; lose the harmonica player."

All the bands just stood there and took it, going, "Cheers, man, we'll go off and do that."

I couldn't believe it. I joined a band to tell everyone to fuck off, and if somebody said to me, "Your image is shit," I'd have gone, "Fuck off, knob head!" And if someone had said, "Your music's shit," I would have nutted them. That to me is what's lacking in groups. They've missed out that growing-up stage of being bloody-minded and fucking clueless. You have to have ultimate self-belief. You have to believe right from the word go that you're great and that the rest of the world has to catch up with you. Of us lot, Ian was the best at that. He believed in Joy Division completely. If any of us got downhearted it was always him who would cheer us up and get us going again. He'd put you back on track.

Anyway back to our first gig. Clueless or not, we got set up. The changing rooms were in the old projection rooms. (Not that we ever changed clothes as such—in fact, we used to look down on bands who did. I bet those bands on the Alex James program "change" . . .) I remember walking down the steps to the stage, and Ian saying, "We're not Stiff Kittens. We're Warsaw," and that was it—we were off—and I can't remember a thing more about it because I was so frightened. When we came off we felt we'd done okay and there was a lot of relief that we'd got through it, that first step of playing in front of people. Because it's the weirdest sensation: I mean, I find it pretty weird even when I do it now, to be honest. . . .

Warsaw's next gig was on May 31 at Rafters on Oxford Street, supporting the Heartbreakers, who were fronted by Johnny Thunders, an ex-member of proto-punks the New York Dolls. The Heartbreakers had arrived in the UK in time to ride the punk wave and found themselves much admired by the English groups. Their heroin use, however, was legendary.

Getting that gig was a massive thrill. You've got to remember that in those days we played just to play. It didn't matter that we weren't getting paid: we did it anyway, and fucking loved it. I'd get so worked up before a gig that I had to run off the excitement. There was that much adrenaline in me I just had to get rid of it somehow and I'd set off running like Forrest fuckin' Gump. And supporting Johnny Thunders was mega because, well, he was Johnny Thunders of the New York Dolls; I was a huge fan. He was American. The Heartbreakers were the first group we'd met who we didn't already know, which made them otherworldly, as far as we were concerned.

So when we got into Rafters in the afternoon, loaded our gear in raring to go, dead excited to be meeting the Heartbreakers, we were very surprised to find them all laid out on the seats. Sparkled, comatose, passed-out.

We stood there looking at them, mouths hanging open, thinking, "Oh my God! How can you be in a group and be *asleep*?" There's me, so excited to be doing a gig I was charging about. There's the Heartbreakers, so hungover or smacked-up or whatever, just laying there. We couldn't believe it.

What's more, it became our problem, because we had to wait until they'd sound checked before we could do anything, and it took something like four hours for them to get their shit together. They had a road crew, but the road crew was just as wasted, and it was like the lot of them were running on half speed, like watching punk skeletons staggering in slow motion, and as a result we never got to sound check. When they eventually played they were almost as much of a shambles onstage as they'd been during the afternoon. During their set they played "Chinese Rocks," which was their big hit, three times. I was looking at the crowd, thinking, *You're pissed off? We've had to put up with this all day.*

So it was a bit disillusioning, really, because we'd thought it would be like before, with the Buzzcocks, where everybody was dead excited and enthusiastic and planning on changing the world. But it wasn't. These guys could barely stay awake, let alone change the world. It was a relief to get back to "our world" for our next gig.

This was where Barney's infamous sleeping bag made its first appearance. We had been invited by Penetration to support them, the Adverts, and Harry Hack & the Big G at Newcastle Town Hall. It was the first time we'd used borrowed equipment, meaning we had to walk on, plug in, and play, so we sounded dreadful, and I think also the first time we got paid. Twenty quid. I'd asked Danny McQueeney to drive us up there in his three-and-a-half-ton van, which just had three seats in the front. Obviously there was me, Barney, Ian, Tony, Terry, and Danny, which makes six; so this meant that three of us had to go in the back. One of them being me. Now, if you've never been in the back of a three-and-a-half-ton van all the way from Manchester to Newcastle, let me tell you, it's like being locked in a box. A freezing box. Newcastle's a long way. It was hell. So, when the gig ended and Danny announced that he was too pissed to drive back (and none of us were insured to drive), we weren't too fussed about postponing the hellish journey back and staying the night.

Until it got cold, that is. Really. Fucking. Cold. One minute we were milling around outside the van where we'd parked—under the big Tyne Bridge, just by the docks—still a bit pissed and having a laugh. Next thing you know, about four a.m., the temperature had dropped and we were diving into the van for any shred of warmth. Then we watched in amazement as Bernard first got a deck chair out, and next wrapped a scarf around his neck and put a hat on. Then pulled out a sleeping bag, wriggled into it, and settled himself into his chair for the night. Slack-jawed, we were, green with envy and turning blue with the cold, wishing that we'd thought of bringing warm clothes and wondering why Barney had thought of it.

We couldn't put the heater on. There was only just enough fuel to get us back as it was. So for the rest of the night we took turns trying to kip in the cab, where it was warmest, and Barney sat there, snug as a bug and twice as smug, while we froze. Whoever it was who said that "no man is an island" never met Bernard.

Around this time we played at the Squat on Devas Street. The Squat was in an almost derelict building in the middle of wasteland off Oxford Road. It had been part of the Royal Manchester College of Music but it became a punk venue, only a really rough one—really dingy—where you could just turn up and play, and there would always be more people from bands than there were audience members in there. We played with the Drones, the Negatives, the Fall, and the Worst—a real gathering of Manchester punks that was—for the Stuff the Jubilee festival. Suddenly it felt like we were part of something. Us, the Fall, the Worst: after the Buzzcocks and Slaughter & the Dogs we were the next wave of punk bands and we'd be following one another around for years.

Word was beginning to spread about Warsaw, with the second Squat gig, on June 25, reviewed for Sounds *by Tony Moon, who wrote, "[Warsaw] have slightly better gear than the Worst and since they have done a couple more gigs are a bit tighter. Tony Tabac is on drums [. . .] he only joined a few weeks ago. Pete Hook is on bass/plastic cap, Barney Rubble is on guitar and Ian Curtis is the voice. Lotsa action and jumping in the air [. . .] to [. . .] 'Tension', 'The Kill'."*

Bernard never referred to himself as Barney Rubble, and it's unclear where that name originated outside of Salford Grammar. The gig would also be Tony Tabac's last, as he was arrested shortly afterward.

Tony, it turned out, was a bit of an entrepreneur. As far as I can remember he came up with a foolproof plan to sell some dope. He would drop the price; undercut all the other dealers. Brilliant: why had no one thought of it before? Why? Because as soon as the other dealers heard, they shopped him and he got busted by the cops. He got bailed, but his head went and his parents clamped down on him too. I remember going to his house to practice once, and the family was obviously very well-to-do, very posh: they had games machines, pinball machines in the living area, all shit like that, and we were like, *Wow.* It was the nicest house I'd ever seen. Huge. He had his own room and everything, which was unusual back then. His sister was dead fit as well, and he'd written "Warsaw" on the bass-drum skin next to the cigarette ends and cigarette packets, which we all thought was *dead* fucking cool: "Whoa, look, we've made it. We've got our name on a bass drum." All in all, what with the cool house and the fit sister and the fact that he was obviously into the band, we were pretty sad to lose him.

So we got another drummer. A small, thin guy by the name of Steve Brotherdale. Again a meat-and-potatoes drummer, but not bad apart from he'd always be banging on the ride cymbal. It's a fucking hateful sound, the ride cymbal; used to drive us mad. Me and Barney used to run over and swipe it off him. Plus he had his girlfriend with him all the time. Even while we were rehearsing this poor cow was sat there. And he was horrible to her, which rubbed us up the wrong way into the bargain. We were always falling out with him about it. I chucked him out of the car once in the middle of Piccadilly, on the way home one night, closely followed by his drums. Told him to fuck right off.

He was with us when we next played at Rafters (on June 30), though, where we first came across Martin Hannett and Alan Erasmus, and saw a new side to Ian. A bit of a worrying side.

· *Chapter 7* ·

"The twats were flicking the V's up at us"

The gig had been organized by Martin Hannett, who by then had formed a promotions company called Music Force. We were supposed to be headlining, but when we got there the other band were sound checking first. This was Fast Breeder. They were from South Manchester and they were shit, absolute fucking rubbish. They went, "No, no, no: we're headlining; we're headlining!" and we were going, "No, no: we're headlining; fuck off. We arranged it with Martin Hannett!" and before you know it we were all having a massive row, us lot saying we should be sound checking first because we were on last, them lot saying the same, all squaring up to each other. Well, me and Ian were, while the rest of the group stayed out of it, which was pretty much how it went for the rest of our career, come to think of it. Only Ian ever got involved in arguing and then only if he'd had a few.

Anyway, me and Ian were squaring up to them, secretly shitting it because they were much bigger than us, when their manager got involved. A black guy wearing a flat cap, he looked quite tasty and we were thinking, "We'd better be careful here . . ." and it turned out to be Alan Erasmus, who later became a partner in Factory and who was indeed very tasty. I think he threatened to throw Peter Saville out of a window once. Can't blame him for that, though: Peter can be very annoying sometimes.

To our immense credit we didn't back down and, with neither side budging, we decided to phone the promoter, Martin. I went to the back, where the pay phone was, called, and found him very laid back about it all, like he'd been smoking, just going, "You know what, it doesn't make much difference really," which was easy for him to say. There was pride at stake here.

I went back and said, "Right, Martin's just confirmed. We're headlining."

Then some twat from Fast Breeder went, "I'm not having that. I'm not having that!" And he stormed off to the phone, came back and said, "Martin says that *we're* headlining."

So Ian went back to the pay phone to try Martin again, but by this time he'd stopped answering; so we carried on arguing until they eventually backed down—or seemed to—and agreed that we were headlining so we should sound check. So we did. Then they set up their gear. But what they did—and this is a trick I've seen repeated many times since, a really sneaky one—they did their sound check then fucked off, leaving their gear onstage.

They were supposed to be on at half-nine. Support band: half past nine. That's the way it goes. But at half nine they weren't there. Their roadies were assuring us that the band was on their way but it was all a ruse. In the end they came back really late—about the time of the headline slot, funnily enough, so it looked like they were headlining—did their set and by the time they came off most of the audience had gone home. The twats were flicking the V's up at us as they packed up.

By now the place was nearly empty. One of the few left was a punk girl called Iris with her friend Pauline. I'd seen them around, and I'd been talking to them while we were waiting for Fast Breeder to turn up. We got together that night, started going out, ended up having two lovely kids and stayed together for ten years. Saying that, I was away for eight-and-a-half of them.

Anyway, while I was chatting up the future mother of my kids, Ian had been knocking the beers back. All of us were fucked off at being kept waiting, but he was the only one who showed it by getting pissed. Really pissed, he was. So pissed that a couple of songs into the set he suddenly jumped off the stage and up-ended a table. Glass went everywhere. We played on. Maybe he'd come back . . . Then he tipped up another table. He'd stopped singing, of course: too busy going berserk. He picked up a third table, smashed it on the dance floor and the top sliced off, sending shards of it everywhere that nearly hit Iris.

Still we played on. We were looking at one another, like, "What the fuck? He seemed so nice . . ." as Ian threw himself to the floor and began writhing around in the broken glass, cutting himself in the process. Any remaining audience members were either scared half to death or laughing at him, while we were just freaked out. This was our mate going mental here. In the end he returned to the stage and we finished the gig, watching as what was left of the crowd scarpered rather than risk another outburst. Nobody fancied being pelted with more broken glass or bits of broken table. It was one of our worst gigs ever.

Looking back, I think there was a bit of showmanship involved. Ian was really into Iggy and always pushing us in that direction musically. But I think this was a time that he took on the physicality of Iggy too, prompted partly by him being pissed and partly by this huge fallout with Fast Breeder. Even so—even knowing where it was all coming from—it was a massive shock to see him like that. We'd witness other examples of it, of course, when he'd lose his temper—usually when he was pissed—and start screaming and shouting. But that was the first time.

That was Steve Brotherdale's first gig—what an initiation. His second was at Tiffany's in Leicester, when he blotted his copybook with us all by coming to the front of the stage, bringing his high-hat with him, and then playing said high-hat. Ian just looked at him with his gob hanging open then told him to get the fuck back, which he did. But the writing was on the wall from that moment on.

He was still with us for our very first recording session: the Warsaw demo, which we did at Pennine Sound Studios, a converted church on Ripponden Road in Oldham. We'd pooled what money we had to buy some recording time and in we went, green as you like. Paul the engineer walked us through the process: he'd mike it all up, sound check, and we'd record it all in one take, no overdubs. He listened back. "Great. There's your master, lads." Five tracks—"Inside the Line," "Gutz for Garters," "At a Later Date," "The Kill," and "You're No Good for Me"—all done in three or four hours, which was all we could afford.

"Inside the Line" and "The Kill" were Ian's; "Gutz for Garters," "At a Later Date," and "You're No Good for Me" were mine. Listening back now you can hear what a punk band we were then. "You're No Good for Me" in particular was proper sub-Buzzcocks rubbish. Just about the only indication to our future sound was "The Kill," which we later rerecorded during the *Unknown Pleasures* sessions, when it sounded very different indeed. Overall, the demos were the sound of a band still finding its feet, but "The Kill" still showed that we were getting somewhere. More important, for the time being at least, we now had demo tapes we could use to try to get lots more gigs outside of Manchester.

Terry, still our manager, had the job of copying the demos and sending them out to venues. The idea was that he'd ring the venue a bit later, find out what they thought of the tape, and see if they'd give us a spot. "All right, it's Terry Mason, manager of Warsaw—just wondered what you thought of the demo I sent you?" That sort of thing.

But every time he rang someone he was getting the same reaction.

"Terrible."

"Absolutely shit, mate."

"Fuckin' awful."

So Terry was saying to us, "No one wants you, lads. They all say you're shit," which we couldn't understand because other groups who were much shitter than us (like the Drones, for example) were getting gigs out of town. Us? Nothing.

So I said to Terry, "Terry, give us one of them tapes and let me have a listen to it, and make sure it's all right."

He went, "All right, Hooky, here y'go," and fished one of out his jacket, one of those tapes you get—or used to get—in a pack of three; TDK, something like that. I put it on in the car and it started off okay. Bit muffled, a little distant, but you could hear my bass, Barney sawing away, Steve Brotherdale doing the business, Ian doing his punky singing—yet to fully develop his baritone, of course; still doing the punky shouting back then but sounding great. We're sounding like a band, a good band. The kind of band you'd want playing at your venue, surely. . . .

Then suddenly I heard the theme tune to *Coronation Street* drown it all out. And next I hear this voice, Terry's mum, Eileen, saying, "Come on now, Terry, your tea's ready. . . ."

Now, back then the only way we could afford to record tape-to-tape was by using two little flat cassette players, put speaker-to-speaker, which was what Terry had been doing. But the dozy bugger had been recording them while he was watching telly and waiting for his mum to do his tea. No wonder no one wanted to book us.

So Terry stopped being our manager and became our road manager, or head roadie or whatever, and we started doing the managing ourselves. We sent out new demo tapes, made some calls and sure enough we got some bookings—the first being for Eric's in Liverpool. Result. Except our drummer up and left.

Rob Gretton was a high-profile member of the Manchester music scene. He'd missed the two Pistols concerts, having been on a kibbutz in Israel with long-term partner Lesley Gilbert, but on his return became involved with Slaughter & the Dogs and helped to finance their first single, "Cranked Up Really High" (produced by Martin Hannett, then working as Martin Zero). Next he produced a fanzine, Manchester Rains, *before setting up Rainy City Records, which released the one and only EP by the Panik,* It Won't Sell. *He had also promoted Siouxsie & the Banshees at the Oaks in Chorlton.*

We didn't yet know Rob, but he was already doing us a favor in a weird kind of way—because for some insane reason the Panik asked Steve Brotherdale to join them and off he went. They were a lot punkier than us, and he was a hard, fast drummer, so he suited them, plus he thought they had more potential than we did. He probably regrets leaving us—well, he *must* regret leaving us—but looking back I don't think he would have lasted anyway.

He was the right drummer for that phase of the band, but not for the sound we were moving toward.

Anyway, off he went to join the Panik and I barely saw him after that. He stayed around, because after the Panik he joined a band called V2. After V2 faded away, well, I went in a McDonald's about ten years ago, ordered a quarter pounder (no ketchup, no cheese) and medium fries, and the guy serving me went, "Hooky?"

And I went, "Yeah?"

He said, "Don't you remember me? Steve Brotherdale."

There he was. Let that be a lesson to you.

The next I heard of him was in 2009 in the *Manchester Evening News*, when he was banged up for stalking his ex-wife, sad to say.

Anyway—we needed a new drummer. What a ball-ache.

We placed more ads. Put one in Virgin Records in Piccadilly, where we used to buy our records, and Ian put one up in Jones Music Store in Macclesfield, which was where Steve saw it.

Steve was Stephen Morris. He contacted the number on the advert and arranged an audition, which took place in a classroom at the Abraham Moss Centre in Cheetham Hill, a community center we were using for rehearsals at the time.

The first thing we noticed about him was that he was dressed like a geography teacher, right down to the patches on the elbows of his jacket. The second thing: that he was nervous as hell. Smoking. Shaking. Me and Barney were looking at each other, like, *Oh my God, he's a shivering wreck.*

Still. After we'd shifted tables, we set up our gear and cranked up. You know exactly what I'm going to say now: he was mega, an absolute revelation. He had all that power that we were looking for but with a texture we hadn't heard before. Most drummers just hammer it out. Steve was *playing* the drums. You could tell he'd been playing with a jazz trio, because it was as though he'd somehow combined the feel and intricacy of jazz with the power and energy of rock and punk. We were over the moon. At last, we had a drummer: a drummer straight from the drummer genie who was not only brilliant but also had his own kit and his own car. Steve worked for his dad's plumbing firm, G Clifford Morris in Macclesfield, so he was on a good wage, and the car came with the job. He seemed a nice bloke, too, very witty and dry, and if it pissed him off that Barney's mate Dr. Silk called him Son of Forsyth because of his big chin—a nickname that stuck—well, he was gracious enough not to show it.

On the other hand, he was very closed-off. Musically we were fine: we clicked and went on to become one of the best rhythm sections in music history. But on the personal side I never got to know him properly, not in all the years we worked together. I'm very direct and he's not. I'm a working-class yobbo; he's an English eccentric. I like change; he doesn't.

It's quite funny really, because even at that early stage of the band we were all pretty distant from one another. Me and Barney—once best mates—had fallen out after a motor-biking holiday in the south of France we went on with Danny Lee and Stuart Houghton, when I'd ended up playing the middleman between the two sets of mates. That was bad enough, but the whole thing went tits-up when Stuart crashed his bike, spent all his money on medical bills, and then, when his bike finally expired, needed cash to get home. Let's just say that, when it came to helping out, Barney wasn't very helpful: "It's my holiday. Why should he spoil it?"

After that I couldn't really look at him the same way. When I got back I just hung out with Terry and Twinny—the roadies, in other words—because they were my mates. Twinny I'd met in the Flemish Weaver and got to know him over a beer. But then a couple of days later when I said hello at the bar he was really fucking rude, looked at me like I was off my head, and told me to fuck off. I went back to my corner moaning about it to Greg Wood, like, "That fucking Twinny's a weird one, isn't he? I had a good crack with him the other night and he'd just told me to do one."

"Why do you think he's called Twinny?" said Greg. "That's his twin, y'dickhead."

Ah . . .

He ended up being our roadie—the Karl Twinny did, while the Paul Twinny became a good friend once I got to know him—and mostly I hung around with him and Terry and Platty on the Precinct. Barney ended up becoming quite close to Ian—when he and Sue did eventually get married, in October 1978, they invited Ian and Debbie but not me and Iris, which goes to show how far we'd drifted apart by then—and Steve, well, he was Steve, an island of Steve. He was with his girlfriend Stephanie until he got together with Gillian, and then it was Steve and Gillian, "the other two." That was pretty much how the alliances went for the rest of our careers together. I mean, I loved them as bandmates—I *loved* the group—thought they were great musicians and we really clicked as songwriters. But as people? As friends? Not really. We were individuals, me, Steve, and Bernard. The glue that held us together, the driving force of the band, was Ian. Us three were concentrating on just our bits, with him holding it all together. That's why we never really looked at his lyrics until after he'd died. It was because we were all just concentrating on doing our bit. Three little musical islands with Ian pulling us all together.

The story of how New Order began is for another time, but it was hard to write songs without Ian because the spot we looked to for help was empty. Rob Gretton was our manager by then, so he became the glue that held us together—as people, at least—but when he died of a heart attack in 1999, well, that left nobody. And it's been downhill ever since—until, at the time of writing, it's as bad as it could possibly be.

Joy Division and then New Order were ships that needed captains, but our captains kept on dying on us.

· *Chapter 8* ·

"Apart from the odd pint pot in the gob it was a good gig"

So our first gig with Steve was at Eric's, Liverpool, supporting X-Ray Spex, which you'd have to say marked a new phase of the band: new drummer, getting out of Manchester more. I later found out that the audience was full of members of Liverpool bands: Jayne Casey from Big in Japan, Pete Wylie of the Mighty Wah!, Ian McCulloch from Echo & the Bunnymen, and Julian Cope from the Teardrop Explodes. It was there that we met Roger Eagle, a real legend in the northwest, who used to promote the Twisted Wheel club in Manchester and had gone on to run Eric's. It was his idea to put us on twice, first in the late afternoon—a matinee show for kids, which we were delighted about because we really did love to play in those days—and then again in the evening. What's more, Roger gave us a crate of Brown Ale, our first-ever rider. None of us liked Brown Ale, but still—the fact that we had a rider was fantastic.

So it was great, the beginning of a brilliant relationship with Roger, who we really got on with, and with Eric's, one of my favorite-ever venues.

The next gig was Middlesbrough. Put on by someone else who would have a big effect later on in our career. Bob Last, who, along with his label Fast Records, would become a great supporter. Now, back then, there was none of this, "Oh, bloody hell, not another gig." It was, "Yeah, let's go." Of course, we weren't used to playing outside Manchester, so were all out of bed at the crack of dawn with excitement, me having to run off the adrenaline as usual, and us turning up about midday only to find the venue shut up and locked till five. Great.

We waited around, got in, and did the sound check. Then later when the venue opened it began to fill up with skinheads, thousands of 'em. Well, probably only thirty, but at the time it seemed like more, all milling around swilling beer. Then just before we went on the DJ put on an Adam & the Ants record, which had some kind of weird, mad amphetamine-like effect on them, like a bunch of six-year-olds drinking Coca-Cola at a birthday party. No kidding, they went berserk. It was as if they wanted to get a full head of steam before the main event. Which was us, of course. As we came on and started playing, the skins surged to the front and immediately started slinging plastic pint pots at us. All of us apart from Steve were getting showered in plastic and beer (not much beer, mind—the pots were empty—but still) and I seemed to be getting the worse of it, with several bouncing off my head. One of these twats obviously had me right in his sights and I spent the whole night ducking. I was livid.

It didn't affect our playing, though. We were always the kind of band who performed best with the crowd against us. Apart from getting the odd plastic pint pot in the gob it was a good gig. Bob had been watching us play, and had seen this particular skinhead throwing pint pots at me all night, and afterward he dragged him by the ear backstage. But the dressing room was L-shaped and I was at the bottom of the L, so he spoke to Bernard.

"This is that bastard who was throwing pots at Hooky all night. I've brought him to apologize."

And Barney went, "Oh, don't worry about that. It's all right, let him go"—without telling me; I was just sitting at the back, oblivious to it all.

Next thing I knew Ian came back and said, "Oh fucking hell, Hooky, that skin who was throwing pint pots at you all night—he's just been dragged back by the promoter to apologize."

"Right, where is that *twat*? I'm going to rip his fucking head off." Full of the usual bravado.

"Oh, Barney told him it was all right and to let him go," says Ian. I went mad. Stormed up the dressing room and went off at Barney: "You fucking what?" Started having a massive row with him, which was probably our first-ever argument, after all those years. Even during the holiday in the south of France we'd never really argued; whenever he'd pissed me off I just used to seethe and bottle it all up. But that night, because my blood was up, I let rip at him and it opened the floodgates because from then we were *always* arguing, worse than a married couple.

In New Order he'd say, "If you ever hit me, it's all over. You'll never see me again." We never did come to blows. I sometimes wonder, though, if a good scrap might have been the answer, might have cleared the air.

Manchester's punk hub, the Electric Circus, no longer able to afford the big names and refused a food license—and thus a late license—by the council, was forced to shut in October. Among the bands performing on the final Saturday were Steel Pulse and the Drones. Warsaw opened the Sunday, while the Prefects, the Worst, and the Fall all played; Howard Devoto debuted three songs from his new band, Magazine; and the Buzzcocks headlined, the night ending with a stage invasion and a "Louie Louie" sing-along. Virgin Records sent a mobile studio to record the weekend for a ten-inch, Short Circuit: Live at the Electric Circus, *which was eventually released in June 1978. It featured "At a Later Date" by Warsaw (though credited to Joy Division, the band having changed their name by then), the performance beginning with Bernard Sumner calling out, "You all forgot Rudolf Hess."*

I don't know the reason for him saying that. One theory is that we'd just played "Warsaw," which was a song about Rudolf Hess. Well, it wasn't *about* Rudolf Hess as far as I know, but the lyrics quoted his prison number, 31G–350125, which Ian had used because Hess was in the news. A book had come out about him that Ian and Bernard had read, and there were people saying he should be let out because he'd served his time. It was very much a topical issue of the day. However, I don't know if we'd even written the song at that point, never mind played it.

Whatever the reason, Bernard must have been gearing himself up for it, and we got the shock of our lives when he did it because he didn't even have a microphone; he went over to grab Ian's mike to do it.

We'd regret all that later, of course. Because all it did was give more ammo—if you'll forgive the phrase—to those who said we were glorifying Nazis. But at the time we were just pleased to get on the record; whatever Barney said was nothing compared to that. We'd had a period of lying low a bit. There was the demo tape debacle, then Steve Brotherdale leaving, and Ian in particular was getting frustrated that we didn't seem to be getting anywhere.

Other bands—the Panik, the Nosebleeds, the Drones, Slaughter & the Dogs—seemed to be overtaking us, which wound him up no end because he felt we were much better than they were. All of which meant that we turned up for the last night of the Electric Circus absolutely determined to get on the bill.

Trouble was, so was everybody else, and there was loads of infighting and backbiting going on. We felt we were being excluded. We didn't even know it was being recorded.

We couldn't even get through the front door. We had to use a lot of harsh language and threats to argue our way in and onto the bill, and we found out later that the Drones told the promoter to leave us off the bill and we almost didn't get to play. It ended up with us going on first; and when we played there was a cock-up in the sound truck. The sound engineer for some reason started recording halfway through "Novelty," which is why only "At a Later Date" appeared on the record when all the other artists got two tracks. As I said, I can't remember what else we played. But it was another example of the utter chaos that reigned supreme that night. A fucking shambles, it was, most of it orchestrated by the Drones and Slaughter & the Dogs, the bastards. Another unpleasant aspect of this was our first brush with publishing and a "proper" publishing/record company. Virgin, Richard Branson's label, decided to sign the bands' publishing rights for the tracks featured on the record. Each band would get £200 advance on signing, a fortune then, and all bands would receive 10 percent of the publishing. Now, that didn't seem like a bad deal, 10 percent each—good old Virgin—and we couldn't sign fast enough. Afterward, though, we found out that what they meant was that *all bands* would receive 10 percent in total, as in 2 percent each. We got two pence on the pound for whatever Virgin earned on the sale of our track, signed away in perpetuity, as everything was in those days. If you're in a band, take my advice and get a lawyer, whatever stage you're at—in fact, it's even more important at the start. Don't ever sign your publishing away; you wrote the songs and they should always be yours. Those starting mistakes will haunt you till you die. (I have a ritual with my lawyer, Stephen Lea—lovely man. He shows me a piece of paper. I read it, say, "What fucking idiot would sign something like that, Stephen?" He turns it over and says . . . "It's you again, Hooky!")

The only joy where that record was concerned came after we got big, when it was reissued and stickered "Featuring Joy Division." Ah well, back to our tale.

Just our luck, we had to play with both bands again four days later, this time at Salford Technical College. Apparently this was the first time Martin Hannett saw us. All I remember was afterward chatting up this girl who lived near Langworthy Road, and then it all going off between the Wythenshawe lads, who were with Slaughter & the Dogs, and the Salford lot, who'd steamed in to get them, and me, like a knight in shining armor, protecting this girl from all the violence. My first groupie.

Of course if a band gets a reputation for trouble, then trouble's bound to follow; and when we played with Slaughter & the Dogs *again* the following night, that went off in a riot too, with all the Slaughter lot upstairs throwing bottles into the ruck downstairs. Later, after Rob became our manager, we got talking to him about that gig and he said, "Oh fucking hell, yeah, that was me fighting and throwing the bottles off the top balcony." He was their roadie for a while, of course, and no doubt loved all the mayhem that came with it. Their music, thankfully, wasn't built to last and it wasn't long before all that sped-up punky stuff sounded absolutely prehistoric and we finally said good-bye to Slaughter & the Dogs and the Drones.

· *Chapter 9* ·

"Even the shit ones were pretty good"

I suppose you could say we were getting a bit fed up with our lack of forward motion. We'd looked at other bands with records out and decided that the only way was to release one of our own: to go DIY. We'd started taking turns to manage and when it was Ian's go he worked out that for us to press a thousand or so records was going to cost about six hundred quid. So he borrowed the money from the bank. I think he told them he was going to buy furniture for his new house. I don't think he told Debbie straightaway, either. He saved that particular pleasure for later.

We booked the studio, which was Pennine in Oldham again, and Paul offered a one-stop-shop deal: you go into the studio, play, hand over the cash, and in return they give you a thousand singles, but with blank sleeves so you have to do the sleeve yourself—which of course Barney was going to do, being the graphic designer. Then you had to distribute the records.

In the meantime we got talking to Paul Morley one night. He was writing for *NME* and had covered the last night of the

Electric Circus for them, and we'd made his acquaintance around town, mainly at the Ranch. Although he had this strange art-band project called the Negatives, which annoyed us because we felt they were taking the piss, we asked if he fancied producing the EP for us. Couldn't hurt to have a prominent journalist on your side could it? He said yes so we arranged to meet him in town and take him up to Oldham. It just goes to show how green we were that it seemed like a good idea—he'd never produced a record before. The morning of the session we sat in St. Ann's Square, the four of us, waiting for him to come. For two hours we sat there and he never turned up. Turned out he'd got pissed the night before and couldn't get out of bed. I don't think Paul would have helped much, to be honest, which he freely admits, but he's gutted about it now. He'd love to say he produced our first record.

At Pennine the session went well, apart from sussing out that my guitar was out of tune and had been the whole time I'd been playing. The neck was warped so it wouldn't stay in tune. The guitar—my £35 first guitar—was fucked.

I've never been able to tune. I'm tone-deaf. Barney always did it for me, much to his delight. Like, if I knocked the guitar onstage and it went out of tune, he'd have to come over and retune it, with a big piss-take grin on his face, or I couldn't play. I'm telling you, the best moment in my musical life was when they invented a portable guitar tuner in a foot pedal. I went out and bought four. Fantastic, because you don't half feel like an idiot onstage when your band mate has to come over and tune your guitar for you.

But anyway, when we were recording the EP, I was greeted with the news that my guitar was out of tune, which immediately ruined it for me because I was shitting myself. But we struggled through. We did "No Love Lost," with Barney going, "Ooh, it sounds a bit out, doesn't it? Hooky's guitar . . ." and me getting wound up but having to grit my teeth and let him retune it each time. After that we did "Leaders of Men," "Failures," and "Warsaw," all of them Ian's songs—I'd pretty much given up on the songwriting by then. I knew when I was beat.

Listening back to the EP, you can really hear how we'd developed—although I'm still amazed how fast we played. Later on in our career I think we ended up playing some of the songs too slowly, funnily enough. Like on *Unknown Pleasures* "New Dawn Fades" is too slow, if you ask me, and when I play it live now I speed it up a bit. But back then we were definitely playing like our arses were on fire. Still had that punk thing going on.

Lyrically, I was struck by "No Love Lost," especially the spoken-word verse, an extract from *House of Dolls* (not the last time Ian found inspiration in that book, of course . . .). But like I say, I never paid too much attention to the lyrics at that time. I kind of knew that they were good, and that there was something really special about them, but mainly I just appreciated that they *sounded* good, and that Ian singing them *sounded* great and looked great. Which he did, he really did. I think you could point to that EP as being the moment that he truly began to find his feet in his writing and singing. All of the experiences he'd had with the band so far, watching other bands at work, reading, getting into Iggy and Throbbing Gristle, it was all coming together for him. It was shaping him into the writer that he became, which was arguably one of the best lyricists ever. His songs from that point were like having a conversation with a genius, sort of profound and impenetrable at the same time. I think that for a while he found it easy as well. The songs seemed to flow out of him and he didn't put a foot wrong after that point, didn't write a single bad lyric after *An Ideal for Living*, right up until his death. Whether we were feeding off him, or whether it was Steve joining or what, I don't know, but musically we were gelling so well too. The songs were flooding out of us. Any one of us would be playing and it'd be, "Oh, that's another great riff." Ian would either memorize it and go home and come back with some lyrics for it, or he'd pull out scraps of paper from a carrier bag and start adapting them on the spot—and we'd have a song. A good one. I'm not being big-headed; I'm happy to say if a song is bad. I've done a few bad songs in my time. But there weren't any in Joy Division. Even the shit ones were pretty good.

Which was why the session turned out to be so easy: because we had the material, and we were working well together, and we didn't know enough about the recording process for it to be difficult. All four tracks were played live and the vocals were overdubbed at the end. I think he did them in one take, and then we sang the backing vocals together, me and Ian, and that was it.

I have a feeling it took a day. The engineer did us a mix and sent it off to be pressed. We were too inexperienced to be pains in the arse about it. We didn't say, "Oh, it needs a bit more reverb on the snare drum," because we didn't know enough to ask. God, we must have been so easy to work with.

All we had to do then was wait a couple of weeks for the record, during which time, of course, Barney designed the sleeve. And what did he do? Used a picture of a Hitler Youth member banging a drum. *Yet again* something else that would come back to haunt us. Saying that, I did like the sleeve a lot. He did a thousand or so of them, printed on pieces of paper that we had to fold into four.

All we needed now were the records. The day they were delivered to the studio I drove to Oldham to pick them up, all one thousand of them, then sped back as fast as I could to play it. Got home. Rushed upstairs. I was still using the same Dansette, the one I got off Gresty. I'd played all my records on it and now I was going to play *my own* record on it. Excited doesn't cover it: I was nearly wetting myself. I put on the record to play.

It sounded awful.

I thought, *Oh God, there must be something wrong with this one. . . .*

So I whipped out another one and it was exactly the same. Got another one out: the same. Really, really quiet, like there was a wad of dust on the needle. I tried and failed with five of them before I gave up and rang Bernard.

"There's something wrong with the record," I wailed at him. "It just sounds fucking shit. It sounds terrible, really muffled and horrible."

He said, "Get on to the guy at Pennine, find out what's gone wrong."

I phoned up Paul at Pennine. "Hey, man, our record—it sounds shit. It's all muffled."

And he went, "Oh yes, it will do. You've made a mistake there."

"What do you mean we've made a mistake? What mistake?"

"Well," he said, "because you've put four tracks on the EP, long tracks, the amount of time makes the grooves really narrow, and when the grooves are really narrow, the sound quality's really bad."

I was like, "Why didn't you tell us? You're the fucking engineer; you're supposed to say, 'Don't put four tracks on, lads, it'll sound shit—just put two on.'"

He went, "Hey, hey, don't start fucking moaning at me, you dick."

I said, "Don't you fucking call me a dick. You're the dick. The fucking record sounds shit, you tosser."

He hung up. Put the phone down.

Me and Bernard were panicking and I think it was him who suggested that, while the record sounded shit on my old Dansette, it might sound good on a big system. So off we went to Pips Discotheque. When punk got big, Pips had started punk nights alongside the Roxy nights. One of my favorite stories was when Roxy Music were playing at Belle Vue in Manchester and Mr. Ferry, hearing about the infamous Roxy/Ferry room, decided to visit after the show, but when he got there the bouncers wouldn't let him in because he had jeans on. Me and Barney used to go quite a bit. One night they had a competition to win the Sex Pistols album and I won by correctly naming the lead singer. Still got the album at home.

The point was, they sort of knew our faces in Pips, so we thought there was a good chance they'd play our EP for us. We handed it over to the DJ, Dave Booth, and patiently waited to hear it, then watched horrified as it cleared the floor, sounding just as bad as, if not worse than, it had on my Dansette. The big system didn't hide the terrible sound, it just amplified it. He took it off and handed it back.

I felt sick, like you feel when you've lost a lot of money. Ian had lied to the bank to pay for a thousand singles that were virtually unplayable, and there was no question of dumping them because he needed to get the money back. We had to sell them. Going round to Steve's one night we found ourselves putting the vinyl into Barney's sleeves, knowing that we had to go out and flog a terrible-sounding record that would probably do us more harm than good. Knowing that people were going to buy it and not realize it was shit till they got home.

We were so demoralized that we barely even noticed how posh Steve's house was. He had a koi-carp pond in his drive and not one but *two* inside toilets, as well as central heating. Any other time we would have been ripping into him about it, but all we could do was sit there pushing the record into sleeves, putting the sleeves into plastic bags, having to be very quiet because his dad was having a nap. Steve's mum and dad were proper parents, like off the telly. I remember one night he had a cold, so his mum locked away his drum kit to stop him from coming to rehearsal. Of course he arrived anyway and ended up having to use Terry's kit, which kept falling apart as he was playing. He was forever stopping to put it back together again. Good practice for working with Martin, that was.

Anyway, we were sitting in his house, being dead quiet so as not to wake his dad, putting the crap record together. Every now and then one of us suggested that maybe we should drive up to Pennine and beat the shit out of the engineer because there was no doubt about it: he was the one to blame; he knew we were inexperienced. You can get only three or four minutes of great-sounding music on each side of a seven-inch single. That's why, when I'd listened to "Sebastian" by Cockney Rebel all those years ago, I'd had to turn the record over halfway through the song. I'd always thought it was a bit of a gimmick but suddenly I knew why—and why most hit singles were three minutes long. It's because that's the ideal length for good-sounding audio on a seven-inch single. If you go above that, the audio quality gets progressively worse until you end up with a record that sounds like ours did, which had more than six minutes on each side.

Faced with no other choice, we soldiered on and tried to sell it. Debbie was going to chop Ian's bollocks off if we didn't recoup the money, so we lugged it from shop to shop trying to offload it as quickly as we could before word spread about the abysmal sound. Knowing that promoters hardly ever played the tapes and records they were given, we used to leave it with them as a calling card, hoping that at least they'd be impressed with the sleeve. Our Nazi sleeve. Knowing that if they ever got round to playing it, it would do us no good at all.

In the end we were just giving them away, and weeks after delivery we still had hundreds left over. God knows what became of them—they're worth a mint now, of course. The *An Ideal for Living* EP is probably our most bootlegged item. I get kids coming up to me with a twelve-inch version with the seven-inch sleeve, swearing it's the genuine article.

"No, mate, never came out as a twelve-inch, not with that sleeve," I tell them. "Believe me, I wish it had."

If they still want me to sign it, I write: "This is a bootleg. Love, Peter Hook."

· *Chapter 10* ·

"I told him exactly where he could stick his vibrators"

In between recording the EP and Barney doing the sleeve we decided to change our name.

We were still sharing managerial duties at that time. When it was my turn I used to sit at work with *NME*, going through the live listings and phoning up trying to get a gig—like, "Hello, is that the Elephant & Castle? We're a band from Manchester and we're looking for a gig."

"What's your name?"

"Warsaw."

"Warsaw Pakt? Oh yeah, I've heard of you. . . ."

"No, just Warsaw."

They'd go, "Oh? Just Warsaw? Not Warsaw Pakt? Oh, right, not interested, mate. . . ."

The phone would go down and I'd be left wondering, *Who the hell are Warsaw Pakt?* Our group wasn't getting gigs because we weren't Warsaw Pakt. This was very puzzling. Not long after there was a big piece about them in *NME*, in which it sounded like they were a pretty shit punk band but with a good gimmick:

they'd made an album direct to disc. I think they'd recorded it in one take in a cutting plant, the idea being to cut out the tape stage or stick it to the man or something. I don't know. Who cared? All I knew was, they were stopping us from getting gigs.

Warsaw Pakt had links with Pink Fairies and Motörhead, and their album, Needle Time, *was notable for being recorded direct to acetate at Trident Studios, released within twenty-four hours and then deleted after a week. Despite the publicity, the band split up shortly afterward—but as far as the Manchester-based Warsaw were concerned, the damage had already been done.*

Even though we'd been using the name Warsaw for longer, they'd effectively taken it over. During the usual band meeting in the pub we decided to change ours, and so began the long conversations about what we should be instead. Obviously Ian had read *House of Dolls*. He'd already pilfered it for the spoken-word bit on "No Love Lost," and now he took Joy Division from it too—and thank God he did, because he saved us from the shame of being called Boys of Bondage or Slaves of Venus. Barney went off and started doing interesting typographical things to it. He gave it Germanic lettering for the *An Ideal for Living* EP, and an exclamation mark. And that was it, we were Joy Division.

Now, of course, it's a full-time job trying to safeguard the name. There's even a Joy Division in Germany that does marital aids, vibrators and stuff: "joy sticks." Which is pretty weird when you consider the origin of the name. I rang the guy up. I do that when I see people ripping us off: bootleggers, photographers, you name it. Normally they back down, meek as kittens. I get them to make a donation to the NSPCC, send me the receipt along with a T-shirt or whatever, and we part on good terms. But this guy wasn't having it. We ended up having a full-scale row and before I slammed the phone down I told him exactly where he could stick his vibrators. He's still selling them now as far as I know. Wanker.

Quite funny, really: I remember having an argument with Barry White about bootlegging. What he construed as bootlegging was someone copying his LP, selling it, and not paying him royalties, whereas I thought bootlegging was somebody recording you live and putting it out as a live LP. So I was arguing from one standpoint saying, "Well, it's a compliment, and it's good that the fans do it," and he was going, "Shut the fuck up, motherfucker, you don't know what you're talking about," because of course we were talking about totally two different things.

I suppose it all goes back to when we were investigated by the taxman because of the Haçienda and foolishly we went to meet them. You don't have to go, but our accountant let us. It wasn't a great meeting. The taxman tore us apart. Rob was shaking. One thing that did come out in the meeting was them saying, "We've looked through all your accounts and can't see any receipt of monies for Joy Division T-shirts. Why is that?"

We went to great lengths to explain ourselves: how we didn't believe in self-promotion; we didn't believe in ripping off our fans; we didn't do merchandise because we thought it was blatant profiteering, the work of the devil, et cetera, et cetera. He listened patiently then said, "How come wherever I go I see Joy Division T-shirts, then?"

We were stumped, struck dumb, and after what seemed like an eternity he said, "I don't believe you and I'm fining you accordingly."

The only band ever to get fined for not doing their own T-shirts—£20,000. Bang!

Anyway, after the name change, of course, the Nazi shit hit the fan. Changing our name to Joy Division, calling the EP *An Ideal for Living*, and having a picture of a Hitler Youth banging a drum on the front of it—well, looking at it now, I can see the problem. I mean, *An Ideal for Living*? It even sounds Nazi. Not to mention the way we dressed and Barney shouting out about Rudolf Hess on the *Short Circuit* record. Let's face it, there was quite a lot of evidence against us.

But there was nothing more to it than a bunch of lads—Barney and Ian in particular—who were a bit obsessed with the war. Everybody was back then. We'd grown up with bomb craters behind our houses. It was the time of the big epic war films like *A Bridge Too Far*, and of *Warlord* and *Commando* comics. Little kids played with toy soldiers and big kids read Sven Hassell books. Everybody was fixated by the war, and punks, being punks, focused on the most unpalatable, shocking side of it. This started with the Pistols, who often had swastikas on their clothes.

But it was about being shocking, not about ideology. We didn't have a political bone in our bodies—none of us did, not even Ian. Arty stuff was what he liked, not political. Yes, we were naïve and stupid and probably trying too hard to get up the noses of the older generation, but we weren't Nazis. Never have been and never will be.

Rock Against Racism had been formed in August 1976, in the wake of Eric Clapton's drunken comments supporting the National Front and a resurgence of interest in the far right. The Anti-Nazi League was another organization formed in opposition, and would go on to organize awareness-raising concerts featuring the Buzzcocks among many others. Thus Joy Division's flirtation with Nazi imagery went very much against the political tide, and the band members not only found themselves asked about it during many interviews but also began to lose local popularity. The Nazi imagery would turn off Tosh Ryan at Rabid Records, as well as Bob Last at Fast Product, both of whom passed on Joy Division, and in June Sounds *reviewed the* An Ideal for Living *EP with the headline "Another Fascism for Fun and Profit Mob."*

It followed us around for years. Me and Steve did an interview on French TV in 2004 and the first question was, "Why did you glorify Nazism with the name Joy Division?"

We thought, "Fucking hell, mate, you're talking about twenty-six *years* ago."

All of that was yet to come, of course, and in the meantime we tried to put the shit-record fiasco behind us and concentrate on rehearsing and writing songs. Steve was so creative on the drums that we were riffing off that, and for the first time it felt like the group was four people matched in ability and vision.

Having said that, Ian, who was by now our driving force, did go through a period of being unhappy with Bernard, and called a group meeting when he was on holiday. According to Ian, Barney wasn't playing enough rhythm guitar—it was all lead stuff—and the group was suffering. Ian wanted that Iggy Pop wall of sound, whereas Barney was into lightness and separation like the Velvet Underground. Though at the time we all agreed to get another rhythm guitarist in, at some point we must have come to our senses and realized that the band wasn't just about any one instrument, it was about all of us, and if we messed with that formula it was fucked. Thank God we did. Bernard's a brilliant guitarist. He knew exactly what he was doing, and that sparseness and space of his guitar lines was one of things that made Joy Division special.

Anyway, it was me who ended up providing the rhythm guitar, because it was around then that I started playing high on the bass, all because of a new speaker I'd bought. I already had my Sound City amp (for which my mother, bless her, had taken a loan from A1 on Oxford Road) but I still needed a speaker. Every night I read the "Articles for Sale: Musical Instruments" column in the *Manchester Evening News*, and finally came across an advert for "Bass Speaker £10" with a phone number. So I thought, *Great, it's in Salford*, and phoned up to say I was interested in it. "What kind of speaker is it, mate?"

He went, "Oh, it's a Celestion eighteen, two hundred watt."

I didn't know what he was on about, so I said, "Sounds good, I'll have it. I'm on my way now." Drove up there, knocked, and my old art teacher opened the door.

"Oh, all right, sir, Mr. Hubbard, sir?" I said.

"Peter, how are you? And you don't have to call me sir." And he invited me in.

"I didn't know you were a bass player, sir," I said. Funny habit that; I still call him sir now.

"Oh yeah," he said, "I'm the bassist with the Salford Jets." They were a very well-known band in Salford and Manchester—the first band I ever saw live, funnily enough, as Smiffy in their glam-rock phase at the Willows. Mike Sweeney, the lead singer, is a lovely guy. Anyway, I couldn't try it. He said it sounded great with his setup so I gave him the £10, got home, wired it up to my Sound City amp, and it sounded dreadful, absolutely fucking awful. When I played a low note it farted. It made me feel physically ill to hear it. For a while I struggled with it, playing my farty low notes, but it was just awful. I couldn't even hear it above Barney's amp, not unless I played high on the neck of the guitar, and it was Ian who said, "Oh, Hooky, when you play high, it sounds really good. We should work on that. Barney, you play the bar chords. Hooky, you play high and Steve do some of them jungle drums. . . ."

That was how we got it—the Joy Division sound. We developed it in our new practice room at TJ Davidson's. TJ's really became *our* place; we were one of the first bands in and nearly every other band in Manchester followed suit. We stayed there right up until the end of the group. It was where a lot of the famous Joy Division photographs were taken. Also where the "Love Will Tear Us Apart" video was shot. An old, disused mill on Little Peter Street, it was split into many rooms with a band taking each one. Sad Café was in there; the Buzzcocks, too. It had a great vibe—just right for our music—because everything had been ripped out then left. There was empty shelving everywhere, exposed pipes; the floorboards were filthy and covered in cigarette butts, and there was even an old mattress at one end of our room.

When we first got in there it was great because the boiler was working so it was dead warm and, like all the other bands, we'd come in and gone, "Oh, this is brilliant. We'll take a room for three weeks—no, a month." But then the oil in the boiler ran out and was never refilled, and from then on it was absolutely freezing. We had to buy a little heater from a secondhand shop; Ian used to sit on it all the time but it gave him piles because his arse was dead warm but the rest of him was freezing. The rest of us could never get near it, of course, because we were playing, so he hogged it—and paid for his selfishness in piles.

We used a storeroom in TJ's, too, which was decorated with cans of our piss because the toilet was miles away so we used to piss in empty cans then stack them on the shelves, where they were always getting knocked over. Very funny, that was, when some poor unsuspecting bastard knocked over our cans of piss. We shared the storeroom with a band called the Inadequates, Gillian's band—Gillian Gilbert, of course, who later joined New Order and ended up marrying Steve—and we occasionally "borrowed" their PA, like the night we played at the Oldham Tower Club.

It's a gig that never appears on any listings in books or on websites, but I'll never forget it. Sad Café had played there the month before and sold it out, which sounded encouraging to us. Plus we were getting thirty quid for the gig, which wasn't bad at all. So we borrowed the Inadequates' PA, got it to Oldham, had a good look round the venue, liked it, sound checked, all the time really looking forward to the gig, thinking it was going to be a great night.

Nobody came. Not a soul. By ten o'clock there was still no one in, not even bar staff, only the manager, an old black guy, who said to us, "You've got to go on. You've got to go on now. You've got to play."

"But there's nobody here."

"Well, tough. If you want the money, you've got to play."

Whether he was taking the piss or not, I don't know, but after our third song he started sweeping up, and when the next song finished, said, "Do you guys know any Hendrix?"

Ian said, "No, mate. Sorry, mate."

"Oh, shame, man. Shame," he said, shaking his head.

We played our next song. Finished that.

"Are you sure you don't know any Hendrix?" he said.

"No, mate. Sorry, mate."

"Oh, shame, man. Shame."

So, anyway, we got about halfway through the set when these two punk girls came in, quite attractive girls, and we bucked up a bit. Wahey. Couple of fit girls in. Played another tune, finished, and one of the girls went, "Hey?"

Ian went, "What?"

"Are you the Frantic Elevators?"

The Frantic Elevators. *Fucking Mick Hucknall's band.*

Ian said, "No. We are not the Frantic Elevators. We're Joy Division."

She turned to her mate and said, "See? I told you we was in the wrong club," and they both left. That was it. We played the last three songs to an empty room, finished, packed the gear up, got our £30 off the guy, and went home.

Because of that, the way I've always been is: if there's anybody there at all, I'll do the gig. I've had none at Oldham Tower club and 125,000 at Glastonbury, and with anything in between I'm happy. I accepted this DJing gig at Reading a while ago, but in the meantime got offered a mini-tour in Greece, which would have paid really well, so I phoned the promoter in Reading and said, "Look, I've been offered this tour but it clashes. Is there any way of postponing the gig?"

He was like, "Oh, sorry, Hooky, I can't. It's been advertised and everything. There's been loads of interest, lots of people coming."

Grr.

So I blew out the Greek tour, drove down, got to my hotel, which turned out to be a B&B, and when I tried to talk to the promoter about what time he wanted me at the club, he was being really cagey. First of all, I'd have to play for only half an hour, he said.

"Well that's not very long, mate," I said. "I could do with a bit more time. It's already half eight. What time do you open?"

And then he starts umming and ahhing and swerving the question.

Until in the end I almost lost it with him: "Look, why don't you tell me what's going on?"

"I've got a confession to make, Hooky."

"What?"

"There's no one here," he said, "but I'll pay you anyway, mate; I'll pay you anyway."

I said, "Look, it's only half eight. Why don't we give it a bit longer and see if anybody turns up?"

So we drove down to the club, and I cooled my heels in the car park while he went in and checked. Then he reappeared looking shamefaced. "No one in there. Look, I'll give you the money and take you back to the B&B."

"What?" I said. "So there's nobody there? No one? Not a soul?"

"Well, no, there's about eight people."

"Well, fuck it," I said. "If there's eight people there, we'll do it. At least the eight people have had the decency to come out. Let's go."

Lo and behold, we went and did it and I had the eight of them onstage with me, playing the tunes, dancing round. They were all New Order fans and it was brilliant, a really, really good night.

"Wow," the promoter said, "I can't believe it. I wouldn't have thought you would have done it."

"Listen, mate," I said, "I've played for no one before. Anything more than that is a bonus."

Anyway—back in 1977 and at least things were looking up for our next gig, which was a New Year's Eve party at the Swinging Apple in Liverpool. I took the seats out of my Mark 10 Jag to get the Inadequates' (again, "borrowed") PA in and take it to

Liverpool, where we discovered that the Swinging Apple wasn't really a venue so much as a club; but for some reason they'd decided to put a band on as a special New Year's thing, and we were that band. But it was brilliant, actually. Everybody was dancing all night and we were in a fantastic mood, firstly because gigs had been a bit hard to come by during that period and we were pleased to at least be playing, and secondly because we'd been given a crate of beer. I was driving, as I always was back then, but still. *A crate of beer.* We got paid a lot of money for the gig, too—about sixty quid, if I remember correctly. I even think we played our set twice.

So it was a good end to what had been an eventful year. We'd got the band going, found a drummer, and begun to really nail our style. Even so, we were waiting for something to happen. And we felt that something *needed* to happen. Something big.

TIMELINE TWO

JUNE 1976–DECEMBER 1977

SOLD TRANSIT VAN
REG NO V.R.J 242J, TO
PETER HOOK FOR THE
SUM OF £137-50,
DATED 25th MARCH 78

[illegible]

JUNE 4, 1976

The Sex Pistols play Lesser Free Trade Hall, Manchester. Peter Hook, Bernard Sumner, and Terry Mason decide to form a band.

JULY 20, 1976

The Sex Pistols play their second gig at Lesser Free Trade Hall, Manchester, with support from the Buzzcocks and Slaughter & the Dogs.

SEPTEMBER 4, 1976

The Sex Pistols make an infamous appearance on Tony Wilson's **So It Goes** ***for Granada TV. Peter Hook, Bernard Sumner, and Terry Mason make contact with Ian Curtis, who joins the band.***

One of our first practice rooms was above the Swan pub on Eccles New Road in Salford. Much later, around the time the Haçienda was taking off, Twinny started drinking in the Swan, so I ended up going back—back to our old rehearsal rooms. It did my head in, really freaked me out. It was exactly the same, apart from the fact that the pictures were missing from the wall and you could see where the wallpaper around them had faded. I was bawling like a baby that night, I'm telling you. It brought everything back. Ian. Joy Division. We never used to talk about it. The years that followed Ian's death were for getting on with New Order and the Haçienda, not for mourning and wallowing, but every now and then something like that would catch you unawares. You'd walk into a room you associated with Ian and suddenly you were poleaxed.

DECEMBER 1, 1976

The Sex Pistols make their notorious appearance on the* Today *program with Bill Grundy.

After this they embarked on their Anarchy tour. Public outrage in the wake of the Bill Grundy interview saw to it that most of the dates were canceled. However, they did manage to play Manchester twice, at the Electric Circus on Collyhurst Street.

JANUARY 29, 1977

The Buzzcocks'* Spiral Scratch *EP released. Produced by Martin Hannett, it becomes the third-ever UK punk single (after "New Rose" by the Damned and "Anarchy in the UK" by the Sex Pistols).

APRIL 1977

The Electric Circus begins to host regular punk nights on Sundays.

MAY 29, 1977

Billed as Stiff Kittens, Warsaw (later Joy Division) play their first-ever gig, the Electric Circus, Manchester, supporting the Buzzcocks and Penetration. Admission: £1.

> Stiff Kittens aka Warsaw aka whatever-they're-called-next-week rate zero even on my Mary Whitehouse odometer. The guitarist must be some refugee from a public school, the neat-

> est thing about the bassist is his headgear and the singer has no impact whatsoever. By the fifth number or so they can just about put together a coherent riff, but I don't think even the most demented headbanger could get off to this. Someone tells me it's their first gig. So let's pass over the rest. Next, please.
>
> Probably the band's first-ever review: from an unidentified source, reprinted in *Joy Division and New Order—A History in Cuttings 1977–1983*

Tony Wilson was in the audience. I can never remember anything if I'm nervous, and I must have been shitting myself about that gig because I can't remember a thing!

MAY 31, 1977

Warsaw plays Rafters, Manchester, supporting the Heartbreakers. Admission: £1 at the door or 75p in advance from Fagins' reception.

JUNE 1977

Slaughter & the Dogs' "Cranked Up Really High" released on Rabid Records. Produced by Hannett and partly financed by Rob Gretton, who produced the Slaughter & the Dogs fanzine.

JUNE 3, 1977

Warsaw plays the Squat, Manchester. Part of the Stuff the Jubilee festival; the bill also includes the Fall, the Drones, the Worst, and the Negatives, plus a new wave/punk disco. Warsaw are joined by John the Postman singing "Louie Louie." Admission: 50p.

JUNE 6, 1977

Warsaw plays the Guild Hall, Newcastle, supporting the Adverts, Penetration, and Harry Hack & the Big G. Admission: 75p.

This was the first appearance of Barney's sleeping bag. Having piles was a feature of being in Joy Division. Ian got them from sitting on the heater at TJ Davidson's and both Twinny and I got them from the van during the European tour in 1980. Terry Mason's would explode regularly. But you know what? As far as I know, Bernard never had piles, just a sore arse.

JUNE 16, 1977

Warsaw plays the Squat, Manchester, featuring last on the bill after Harpoon Gags, Bicycle Thieves, and Split Beans. The event is billed as "Time's Up" (in homage to the Buzzcocks bootleg) and held in aid of the "Windscale Festival," according to the flyers. Admission: 50p.

JUNE 25, 1977

Warsaw plays the Squat, Manchester.

This was Tony Tabac's last gig. We'd been introduced to the Squat by Pete Shelley. He said, "Oh, there's a place in Manchester where you can just turn up and play," which sounded great because it was really difficult to get gigs; the normal clubs just weren't into punk gigs at all. At the Squat there would be more people from bands than there was audience. It was very dingy. There were no lights and it was freezing. Everyone who went there remembers it though.

JUNE 30, 1977

Warsaw plays Rafters, Manchester.

This was Steve Brotherdale's first gig. A running-order squabble-fest with Fast Breeder led to us meeting a pre-Factory Alan Erasmus for the first time, as well as speaking to Martin Hannett by telephone.

JULY 1977

Warsaw enters "A Talent Contest," the Stocks, Walkden.

This was run by an agency from Bolton and the Stocks wasn't far from where I lived. The idea was that you just turned up and played and if you were good the agency would sign you up.

Perfect, we thought. *We can't go wrong.*

Things started to go wrong straightaway, though, when the proper old-school compere asked us how we'd like to be introduced. Result: blank faces all round.

After struggling to get anything out of four inarticulate punks, he blurted out, "Do you like Deep Purple?"

And with that he left for his build-up to a coachload of old ladies from the Farnworth Flower Arranging Club, during which he said the immortal lines: "If you like Deep Purple, you'll love these lads! Put your hands together for Warsaw!"

We trudged on and played but were too loud: our volume kept tripping the DB meter on stage, which then cut the power to our amps. Chaos. The old ladies all had their hands over their ears. We struggled through for a couple of numbers until Ian stormed off in disgust. When we went back into the dressing room to commiserate, he was buzzing.

"The female singer before us was changing when I came in," he said. "Saw her tits!"

With that we packed up and drove to the Ranch, where Foo Foo let us set up and play. Great gig; went down a storm. Those were the days. The Ranch was our regular haunt for ages, marred only by us getting chased by teddy boys occasionally. But it came to an abrupt end when the cloakroom gave Barney's leather jacket away one night—he went ballistic and we were barred.

JULY 18, 1977

The Warsaw demo session, Pennine Sound Studios, Oldham. Tracks recorded: "Inside the Line," "Gutz for Garters," "At a Later Date," "The Kill," "You're No Good for Me." These are the only recordings to feature Steve Brotherdale on drums.

JULY 20, 1977

Warsaw plays Tiffany's, Leicester, supporting Slaughter & the Dogs.

AUGUST 16, 1977

The Buzzcocks sign to United Artists on the bar of the Electric Circus. Elvis Presley dies.

AUGUST 27, 1977

Warsaw plays Eric's, Liverpool, supporting X-Ray Spex. This is the band's first gig with Steve Morris, comprising two slots at the legendary Liverpool venue: a matinee in the afternoon for children and then an evening show.

Roger Eagle was a really nice guy. It struck you straightaway, as soon as you met him, that he was different from other people. He was just a really nice bloke who loved music and looked after you.

SEPTEMBER 14, 1977

Warsaw plays the Rock Garden, Middlesbrough. Set list: "Reaction," "Inside the Line," "Leaders of Men," "Novelty," "At a Later Date," "Tension," "The Kill," "Lost."

Bob Last, the promoter, came into the dressing room after the gig. "Anyone want a tape?" he said.

No one but me replied, and this was the start of what was to become a collecting obsession. That tape he gave me is the only recording of us live as Warsaw and was the first time I'd ever been able to listen to the group. What a great revelation—we were really good. Warsaw "Live in Middlesboro," it was called: I treasured that tape for thirty years until it was stolen and bootlegged very recently.

SEPTEMBER 24, 1977

Warsaw plays the Electric Circus, Manchester, supporting the Rezillos.

The Rezillos' roadie/manager, Bob Last, was an early supporter of Warsaw but would eventually balk at signing them to his influential Fast Product label—legend has it because of the Nazi associations then dogging the band.

OCTOBER 2, 1977

Warsaw plays the Electric Circus, Manchester, on the second night of the club's final weekend. The gig is recorded by Virgin for the* Short Circuit *album to be released the following year. The recording includes "At a Later Date" and the release is later relabeled "Featuring Joy Division."

OCTOBER 7, 1977

Warsaw plays Salford College of Technology, supporting Slaughter & the Dogs, the Drones, Fast Breeder, and V2.

OCTOBER 8, 1977

Warsaw plays Manchester Polytechnic, supporting Slaughter & the Dogs.

OCTOBER 13, 1977

Warsaw plays Rafters, Manchester, supporting Yachts.

OCTOBER 19, 1977

Warsaw plays Pipers, Manchester, with the Distractions, Snyde, and Nervous Breakdown.

NOVEMBER 1977

The Panik's* It Won't Sell *EP released on Rob Gretton's Rainy Days records—the only release for both band and label.

NOVEMBER 24, 1977

Warsaw plays Rafters, Manchester, supporting the Heat and Accelerator.

DECEMBER 14, 1977

The* An Ideal for Living *EP sessions, Pennine Sound Studios, Oldham. Tracks recorded: "Warsaw," "No Love Lost," "Leaders of Men," "Failures (of the Modern Man)."

Not long ago I was DJing in Eden in Ibiza with this guy called Dave Booth from Garlands in Liverpool. On the flight home we got talking about places in Manchester and he mentioned that he DJed at Pips.

I went, "Pips? You're joking! Me and Barney took our first record to Pips for the DJ to play."

"Yeah," he said. "That was me. I was the one who put it on—cleared the fucking floor, it did."

Small world . . .

DECEMBER 31, 1977

Warsaw plays the Swinging Apple, Liverpool. This New Year's Eve gig is the last the band performs using the name Warsaw.

PART THREE

"TRANSMISSION"

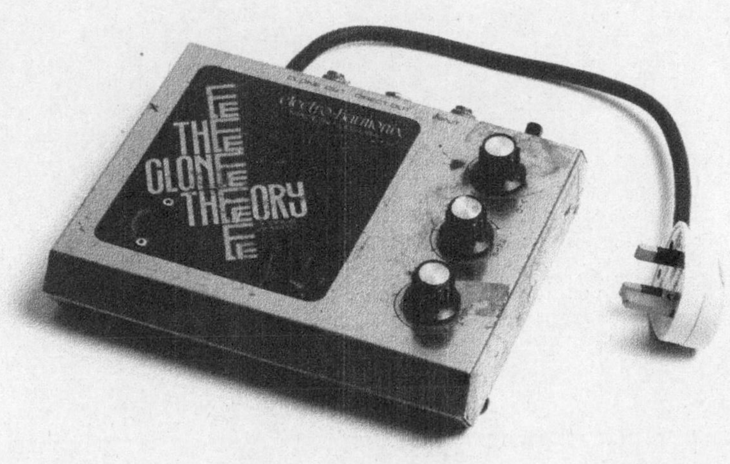

· *Chapter 11* ·

"It was like *The X Factor* for punks"

We played our first gig as Joy Division at Pips, as I've already said. After that . . . Nothing. Not for two long months.

It was my turn to manage the band. I was still working at the Ship Canal, and would phone up, say, Dougie James, who used to run Rafters on Oxford Road, hoping to get a support gig, *desperate* to get a gig. For us back then every minute without a gig felt like a week, like forever. So I was bugging the hell out of promoters, and especially Dougie, who was a nightmare to pin down.

I'd get him on the phone and he'd go, "I'll speak to you later, mate. Come and see me. Bring me a tape." Just fobbing me off. Always some excuse for not hearing me out. Twice I bussed it into town to try to catch him and speak to him face-to-face. Couldn't see him. On one occasion I went at dinnertime and had to walk back to work because I didn't have the money for a bus both ways. But I did eventually get to see Dougie, when I followed him into his office and more or less cornered him.

"All right, Dougie? I'm Peter Hook. We spoke on the phone. I was hoping to get a support gig for my band."

He was sighing like he'd heard it all a thousand times before and, to be fair, he probably had. "We haven't got any gigs. We've got no gigs. We've got loads of fucking supporting bands. We're all full up." Blah, blah, blah. It's quite funny, really, because naturally I'm a bit shy but when it came to the band I never was. I was so driven and so desperate for the group to do well that I was always dead pushy, like I was then in Dougie James's office: "Well, what about that Siouxsie & the Banshees gig you've got coming up? It's not even been advertised yet. You must need a support for that."

He sighed again. "Oh. Let me have a look. Let me have a look," and he flicked through his book, pretending to look. "Oh sorry, mate," he said at last, "I can't give you that one. Someone else is doing that."

My face fell. "Who?"

"Joy Division," he said. "Group called Joy Division are doing that; bad luck."

I said, "That's great because *we're* Joy Division."

You've never seen anyone backpedal like it. "Oh no, no, no. I mean, I mean . . . someone else is doing that. Look, fuck it, fucking don't bother me, all right. Get the fuck out." He threw me out. That was it. I walked back to work feeling very down and demoralized, which is a feeling you have to get used to when you're managing a band, any band, but definitely ours at that time. We were hurting for gigs, and we needed a manager to help us get them.

The Stiff Test/Chiswick Challenge, a touring talent show set up by the two labels, came to Manchester Rafters on April 14, 1978. Local groups affected to scorn the enterprise for its London-centric air, but twelve or thirteen turned up to play anyway, hoping to impress the label heads. They included an impatient Joy Division as well as a "joke" band, the Negatives, formed by journalist Paul Morley and photographer Kevin Cummins. Meanwhile, Ian Curtis barracked Tony Wilson for failing to feature Joy Division on So It Goes.

The Stiff/Chiswick night was like *The X Factor*. Except it was like *The X Factor* for punks, so a bit of a free-for-all and a very highly charged night indeed. The sight of our roadie, Platty, chasing Kevin Cummins out of Rafters, with him clutching his drum kit and screaming like a baby, is going to stay with me for the rest of my days—I hope.

It was Stiff we wanted to impress. They were *the* cool record label. They had Wreckless Eric and Kilburn & the High Roads—later to become Ian Dury & the Blockheads—and were run by a guy called Jake Riviera, a bit of a legend in the music business, who might sign you if he liked you. Needless to say we were dead keen to get on the bill, but the competition was fierce. Like the last night of the Electric Circus, everybody turned up and everybody wanted to play.

Having already been shafted by Fast Breeder, we knew that if we went on too late all the punters would have buggered off, so we were desperately trying to get on as early as we could. Trouble was, so were all the other bands. It was already dog-eat-dog, with everybody thinking that this could be their big chance and arguing about who was going to go on, when Morley turned up with Kevin Cummins and some others in tow, taking the piss with their made-up punk group. They thought it was going to be dead funny to audition as a band that couldn't play. What a hoot. Maybe it would have been funny—I mean, let's not get all no-sense-of-humor about it—maybe we would have seen the funny side if we hadn't been a group that *could* play and were deadly serious about what we were doing, desperate to get a gig and a contract. We weren't writers or photographers larking about to make some obscure arty point that nobody understood anyway. This was serious for us. Life or death.

Morley started by telling us that they were going on first. And we were saying, "Oh, fuck off, you're not fucking pissing about and pissing off the judges before we come on; you can fuck off."

"No, we're fucking going on."

"Fuck off are you."

Ian was livid. One thing I remember about that night is that Ian was pissed and angry the *whole* night. Which was why he'd gone up and had a go at Tony Wilson, of course. I wasn't there for any of that, but I know in Debbie's book she says he first wrote Tony a note calling him a twat and all sorts, then went up to him to have a go at him for not putting us on TV. Tony was apparently pretty good about it, but I don't think he knew much about us at that point. He said on the *Joy Division* film that we were next on his list, but I'm not so sure about that. I don't think we were really on his radar then—not until that night, in fact.

Anyway. Our argument with the Negatives escalated. I was threatening Paul Morley, Ian was threatening Paul Morley, Barney was under a piano, and Steve was hiding in the corner, and we finished by basically chasing the Negatives out, so they ended up not playing while we went on last, at about twenty past two in the morning, played about four or five songs and played our socks off. Being so angry gave us a bit of an edge—it always did—and it was probably one of our best performances.

Well, we thought so. But we never heard from Mr. Stiff, or Mr. Chiswick, come to that.

Sounds *writer Mick Wall called the band "Iggy imitators," while Paul Morley of* NME, *evidently putting aside the evening's rivalry, wrote that "with patience they could develop strongly and make some testing, worthwhile music."*

Even more impressed was Granada TV's Tony Wilson, who later said, "It took just twenty seconds of Joy Division's set to convince me that this really would be a band worth investing in," as well as Rafters' resident DJ, Rob Gretton, who, after his experiences with the Panik, was looking for a new band to manage. That night he decided he'd found one.

"[Joy Division] were blazing madmen," Gretton later said. "Best band I've ever seen. They sent a tingle up my spine. I was dancing all over [. . .] I went up telling them at the end, telling them how brilliant I thought it was [. . .] I went raving about them all next day."

There were further developments. For some time Ian Curtis had been a regular face at the northern promotional offices of RCA Records, where he had befriended manager Derek Brandwood and his assistant, Richard Searling, a noted northern-soul DJ in his own right. Curtis had given Brandwood a copy of the An Ideal for Living *EP; though Brandwood had been unimpressed, his teenage son had liked it. Not long afterward, Brandwood and Searling were asked by the owner of the American Swan Records, Bernie Binnick, if they knew of an English punk band available to do a cover of the northern-soul track by N. F. Porter "Keep On Keepin' On" . . .*

I think he'd come into contact with RCA thanks to a part-time job he'd had at Rare Records—which is quite funny, because when I'd worked at the Town Hall, I bought records from there, so I'd probably bought some off him. Anyway, he'd started hanging around their offices in Piccadilly Plaza. The guys who worked there used to give him records: Iggy Pop and Lou Reed. Trouble was, the other record they gave him was this N. F. Porter song called "Keep On Keepin' On" that they wanted us to cover—but in a punk style. God knows why. I think they thought that RCA was missing out on the Manchester punk scene and maybe thought we were their way in. Where the northern-soul connection came from I cannot imagine.

We listened to the record and hated it. We tried to learn it, but it changed into something completely different, which later became our song "Interzone," but we turned up our noses at the idea of doing a cover. Then, at a meeting with the RCA guys and John Anderson, who was going to produce it, Ian and Steve were offered a deal. They started to hear things like "advance of £20,000," "go and record in Paris," and "American tours," which made them jump around, even making Steve squeal "Paris" two octaves higher than normal, according to Ian. It all turned out to be a load of rubbish, though, because although we were impressed enough to take the deal we didn't get an advance and the studio wasn't in Paris. It was Arrow Studios in Deansgate, Manchester, and on the day we arrived there was a voiceover guy doing an advert for Littlewoods Lotteries that I can still remember now: "Littlewoods Lotteries. Things go better with Littlewoods. . . ." The guy kicked off proper when Ian walked in on him, tutting, "How unprofessional." We looked at one another—me, Barney, and Steve—and thought, *What have we got ourselves into here?*

But it was too late to back out and we ended up recording an album with John Anderson—and what a turkey it was. Everything he suggested ended up sounding cabaret and we were getting more and more frustrated, especially Ian, of course, who'd been thinking, *RCA: Lou Reed, Velvet Underground, Iggy Pop . . .* only to hear it come out like the most awful un-rock-'n'-roll, anti-punk, most conventional sound you can imagine. Nothing like Iggy. Nothing like the Velvets. We'd be doing, say, "Ice Age" and suggest having some wild feeding-back guitars on it, but John Anderson would scratch his chin and say, "I was thinking more along the lines of getting some girls in to do backing vocals . . ." Which we all know is the kiss of death.

Holy shit. It was awful. We ended up recording eleven or twelve songs with him, all the ones that ended up on the album, which—despite the fact that we were hoping it would never see the light of day, please, God—has since been bootlegged to death. Then we left the studio with our tails between our legs, feeling worse than ever.

We couldn't even get gigs. All the other groups in Manchester were trying to be a bit arty, like the Buzzcocks, but we weren't. We were just dead working-class and had no pretentions. Ian, I suppose you'd say, was the most pretentious of us, with his love of Burroughs and Kafka and whatever, but I think when other groups looked at us they saw a bunch of yobs. So we were getting pushed out; we felt like outsiders, and nobody wanted us to play.

Not long after that I remember being manager again. I phoned up the Elephant & Castle one day from work and in my best phone voice said, "Can I speak to the booker, please?"

And she went. "All right, darlin', I'll put you through to the booker." And then she went, "Hello, booker, Elephant & Castle."

And I said, "Oh, hello there. My name's Peter Hook. I play in a band called Joy Division and we're trying to get support gigs in London—"

She stopped me. "What was that? What was your name?"

"Joy Division."

"Listen darlin'," she said, "you'll never get a gig in London with a name like Joy Division," and hung up.

I didn't know what she meant but it didn't matter. I stared at the phone thinking, *Typical. Shit album. Shit single. No gigs.* We were at a very low ebb.

All I can say is: thank fuck Rob Gretton came along.

· Chapter 12 ·

"We need to get rid of this Nazi artwork"

Barney was out from work in one of the phone boxes by Spring Gardens Post Office, talking to Steve, when suddenly this guy yanked open the door. A big bloke with a beard, wearing glasses that he pushed up his nose before he spoke.

"Fucking hell. You're out of Joy Division, aren't you?"

It was Rob.

"I watched you at the Stiff /Chiswick night," he carried on. "I want to be your manager."

Christ, did we need a manager. Barney hung up on Steve, chatted to Rob, and invited him down to see us at TJ Davidson's.

Of course, Barney then promptly forgot and didn't tell any of us, did he? We were standing around playing when Rob came in, perched himself on the edge of a step, and sat there, nodding in time to the music.

Me, Steve, and Ian were looking at one another, like, *Who's this?*—with Barney off in his own little world, obviously. Then the song finished and there was an awkward silence as gradually we turned our attention to Rob, who looked at us, still nodding, as though he was pleased with what he'd heard. Until at last Barney said, "Oh, lads, I forget to mention. This is Rob Gretton. He's the DJ at Rafters. He saw us play the Stiff/Chiswick night. He wants to be our manager."

There was a collective sigh of relief. I wasn't the only one who hated managerial duties: Ian couldn't do it; Steve couldn't do it; Barney couldn't do it; Terry certainly couldn't do it, God bless him. But without one we were fucked, so this was like offering a straw to a drowning man. Plus, of course, we liked Rob straightaway; he seemed to know what he was talking about, probably because he'd already managed the Panik and had a lot of band experience working with Rabid and Slaughter & the Dogs. And, even though we hated Slaughter & the Dogs, and Rob had had precisely zero success with the Panik and in truth had the same managerial experience we all had, he seemed to say the right things.

The first being: "This record's shit." (Straight-talking would become his forte.)

He held up a copy of our *An Ideal for Living* EP.

"Yeah," we mumbled.

He pushed his glasses up his nose. "What we need to do is get it remastered. We need to make it into a twelve-inch."

He was already referring to us as "we," which I liked. This was someone who was on our side.

Next he pointed at the picture of the Hitler Youth drummer. "We need to get rid of this Nazi artwork, too."

Music to our ears and to Ian's, especially; he was desperate to recoup the money that he'd borrowed from the bank for his non-existent furniture—to get Debbie off his back as much anything.

So one of the first things Rob did was recover the masters and repress *An Ideal for Living* as a twelve-inch with a different cover, a picture of some scaffolding on King Street, solving both the sound and Nazi problems. Next he persuaded Tosh Ryan of Rabid Records, which was Slaughter & the Dogs' label, to buy and distribute the rest of the seven-inches along with the twelve-inches. Paying us upfront. The seven-inch ended up having an official release in June, the twelve-inch in October, and in one fell swoop Ian was paid off.

Now *that* is how you start off managing a group. We'd told him all about the Arrow Studios debacle and he cut a deal with John Anderson, offering him a grand for the master tapes. From then on any gig money we earned went into a pot managed by Rob, until we had enough to pay John Anderson and retrieve the tapes. (How, if we bought back the masters, did the record later appear as a bootleg, you might ask? That's a very good question, but one I can't answer here, because I've already given enough money to lawyers and have no desire to give them any more, thank you very much.)

By this time I'd sold the Jag and saved enough cash to buy an old petrol-blue Transit van. I was over the moon about that because I was sick of squeezing the gear in my car, or having to hire a van when we needed to take our own PA, which was a total ball-ache. I'd crashed a hired Bedford van when we did Pips. Only a little bit. It had a side hinge that jutted out from the door and I'd hit another car, taking the paint off and bending it a little bit. For that the rental place swiped my £20 deposit, but the rest of the group said it was my fault and refused to chip in. So having my own van was a massive relief. From then on, I drove it and all the gear; Terry and Twinny came with me, while all the rest of the group went in Steve's car. Having it made us more self-sufficient and meant that as long as Rob could get us gigs we could earn money. And he was good at getting us gigs.

In fact, from the moment he stepped on board things changed for us: because we couldn't organize shit and he could. You watch *Control* and the character comes into our lives like a whirlwind, with a big personality right from the start, but in real life it wasn't really like that. At first, he was calm, rational, quietly spoken and very logical, always scribbling away in his notebooks. Later he got more like his character in *Control*, when he became a very domineering, almost intimidating personality—he was a big guy and he used it. He could cut you dead and often did. He had a biting tongue. But in him we knew we had someone who shared our vision and had the same ideals, who wasn't going to suggest we hire backing singers or record northern-soul covers. He was like us, but a larger-than-life version of us, a more forthright us.

Things started to happen right off the bat. I mean, apart from what I've already mentioned, just look at the way we started to develop when he became our manager: the relationship with Tony Wilson began, and we all know where that led; he got us involved with the Musicians' Collective, so we started playing gigs regularly; and we began getting known among the promoters. All of that gave us confidence to grow, leaving Rob to go off and to do the shit we didn't like to do and us to concentrate on doing things we did. (Writing songs.)

We got better and better—we could tell, because a song like "Transmission" suddenly was stopping traffic. I remember the first time. It was at the Mayflower Club, Belle Vue on May 20, 1978, a gig we did with Emergency and the Risk. The Mayflower was a horrible hole with a pond of rainwater in front of the stage where the roof had gone and let all the water in like a moat. Normally we wouldn't have gone within a mile of the place but we did it as a favor to Emergency, who we knew very well. It was a bit of a you-scratch-my-back-and-we'll-scratch-yours setup: we used to borrow their PA for out-of-town gigs and in return would help them out when we could. At this particular gig at the Mayflower they were promoting themselves as headliners, so they wanted decent support; they asked us if we'd do it, knowing we'd bring a few people along.

Rob was there with us that night—his first gig in charge—and it was also when we first met Oz McCormick and Ed, from Oz PA, who did the gig on the night and ended up being our sound guys for years. Right through Joy Division and New Order, out-front and fold-back respectively.

Not only that, but we got plenty of time for a sound check, during which we played "Transmission." We'd recorded it for the awful Arrow album but we hated that version and we'd worked on it a lot since—so this was the first time anybody outside of our circle had heard it as we wanted it to be heard. The funny thing about writing a song—any song—is that you never know how good it is when you write it. The last one always seems the best. We were lucky in Joy Division that we wrote several songs that are regarded as absolute classics: "Digital," "Disorder," "Transmission," "Love Will Tear Us Apart," "Atmosphere," "Shadowplay," and "She's Lost Control." But we never thought, *This is a classic.* That isn't your place. We knew they were all right, mind you. But the best we hoped for was that they matched up to the caliber of the other stuff, the stuff we knew people liked. It was only when we played them live and gauged the reaction that we started to get an idea of how good they really were.

Playing "Transmission" there was probably the first time that we had a real stop-the-presses moment. I distinctly remember playing it at that sound check and the crew turning around, the guys in Emergency and the other support band, the Risk, coming front of stage to watch us; the PA guys, too, were watching us instead of getting on with stuff.

We were looking at one another, like, *What the fuck's going on here?* because we'd never experienced that kind of reaction before. Looking at one another we were thinking that, maybe, just maybe, we might be able to make a go of this, a living out of it. We might just be able to pull this off. It was a big moment for the band. A big confidence-booster.

The gig itself, well, it went off all right, apart from the Risk's bassist getting a hiding from some of the crowd. Poor bloke was wearing a T-shirt that said MY FISTS ARE MY SIDEARMS, and I can distinctly remember standing there during sound check, seeing this T-shirt and thinking, *That's a bold statement.* You've got to be fairly confident to carry off a T-shirt like that.

His band was a bit of a nuisance, to be honest: they spent the whole night arguing with us and Emergency. So I've got to say—and God strike me down for it—I wasn't that bothered when a section of the crowd took exception to his T-shirt, dragged him off the stage, and leathered him. Funnily enough, his fists weren't his side-arms.

Otherwise it was a great gig and as a band we were breathing one long, giant sigh of relief because Rob had parachuted in to take a whole load of pressure off us. Before, with managers—well, Terry, then each other—we'd always be looking over the shoulder of whoever was doing it, to make sure everything was being done properly, and then moaning accordingly. It was strange: when someone else was doing it you knew you could do it better, but when you did it everything went wrong. With Rob we didn't do that. He'd have told us to fuck off and kicked us if we'd dared.

Another of Gretton's managerial duties involved corresponding with Tony Wilson about his new protégés. On April 19, 1978, Wilson replied to his letter saying the band were the best thing he had heard in Manchester "for about six months." Nevertheless, Ian's desire for Joy Division to appear on So It Goes *was not to be. Wilson's music program had ended, and as a result he was looking for new ways to stay involved in the music business. At the same time his friend Alan Erasmus ended his association with Fast Breeder and the two cast about for ideas, taking on management of the fledgling Durutti Column. They looked into venues in the hope of featuring the band and settled on the Russell Club, which they booked for four Fridays over two months. Located on Royce Road in Hulme and run by colorful local character Don Tonay, the Russell Club had been used by drivers for the bus company SELNEC and was well placed to appeal to the nearby student population. Erasmus saw a sign saying* FACTORY CLEARANCE *and suggested Factory as a name for the club. To design a poster, Wilson hired the services of graphic designer Peter Saville, who had introduced himself to Wilson at a Patti Smith concert. Saville earned £20 for the design, which used the color scheme of the UK's National Car Parks and included a warning sign from his college workshop; he also misspelled the club's name as "Russel" (this error was repeated—perhaps intentionally—for the next two Factory club posters). Famously Saville delivered his poster—which was later given the catalog number FAC 1—two weeks into the four-week run.*

In the meantime, Tony Wilson had written to Gretton a second time, on May 9, reiterating how much he liked the An Ideal for Living *EP and inviting Joy Division to play at the new club. They did, on the fourth night of the initial run, June 9, 1978, supporting the Tiller Boys.*

The Tiller Boys were very wacky. They stood chairs up in front of them onstage so you couldn't see what they were doing and played tape loops, probably inspired by the Pop Group and Throbbing Gristle. Cabaret Voltaire without the songs, really, which is saying something. That's about all I remember about that gig, funnily enough, despite the fact that it was the first Factory event to involve us and that it marked the beginning of a period during which we started to play a lot more regularly, really honing our sound and getting the message out there.

Rob had got us to join the Manchester Musicians' Collective, which used to meet in a room above the Sawyers Arms pub in the city center. Dick Witts from the Passage was chairman and the idea was that all Manchester's musicians would get together and support one another, to stop some of the backbiting and treachery that generally went on between local bands. If truth be told, we reveled in the backbiting and treachery (would we have been as good at the Stiff/Chiswick night if the Negatives hadn't pissed us off? Probably not) but we wanted to get gigs. So despite that, and the fact that we secretly thought the whole thing was a bit poncey, we went along and listened. We'd heard they were going to put on a gig a month at the Band on the Wall, and we desperately wanted to play.

The collective was on to them. In the sleeve notes to the album Messthetics #106: The Manchester Musicians' Collective 1977–1982, *Kevin Eden of the Elite says, "Joy Division joined and there was initially some grumbling that they were trying to grab gigs, but they allowed MMC to use their gear when possible."*

So on the one hand we got to play more, but this did mean that every now and then we had to meet to discuss music, which I thought was a monumental drag because they were so earnest and arty about it all and frankly it was like being back at school—like in a society or something. Steve didn't go, as far as I can remember, but me, Ian and Barney had to. Ian thought it was all right, mind you. He liked anything arty.

Meanwhile, the *An Ideal for Living* twelve-inch EP came out, and at last we had a record we could be proud of. Then the *Short Circuit* album came out, and suddenly we looked like part of a movement. As well as playing loads of gigs around that time we had a go at promoting; one such instance was at Band on the Wall, where we got a bit more insight (pun intended) into Rob's character.

What he'd done was spend all our money on a big PA because he believed we should sound the best we could and present ourselves in the best possible way. Not a bad philosophy, of course—no one's going to argue with that. Got a gig, all sold out, lots of profit? Let's put it all into a bigger PA and more lights. Nobody I've ever met was as talented at spending money as Rob Gretton: he was the proverbial big spender—and that gig at the Band on the Wall saw the seeds of his philosophy being sown.

Only one of us noticed at the time, though: Ian. Before Rob came on board he was the one with the ideas. Musically he'd introduced us to loads of new stuff—Kraftwerk, Throbbing Gristle, Velvet Underground, the Doors, Can, and Faust—and when it came to the direction of the band he was always the most forthright. He had the plan and the rest of us were his tools to carry it out, if you like. Having someone new arrive with plans of his own—notebooks full of them, in fact—well, there were bound to be problems. The rest of us were going, "Yeah, yeah, do whatever you want, Rob." Might as well have had rings through our noses, we were that easily led. But not Ian. It didn't take long for the pair of them to bang heads, the two dominant personalities of the group fighting for control.

The other thing Ian had to deal with was Debbie being pregnant. Not that Ian ever announced it as such; the news just gradually leaked out, but there it was—soon he'd have another mouth to feed. So there was even more reason why Rob's grand gesture didn't go down too well. Ian was probably thinking, *My slice of that PA would have bought a pram.*

Tell you what, though: it was a good PA and we did sound amazing. So Rob was right, I suppose—particularly because it turned out to be one of those gigs that did wonders for our profile. We got two good reviews from that gig, one in *Sounds* and one in *NME*, from Paul Morley, our former mortal enemy, who was comparing us to Magazine and the Fall, the two big post-punk groups. Then—at last—we got on the telly.

Joy Division's first TV appearance was on Granada Reports What's On, *which was then in the habit of prerecording local bands to broadcast when news slots suddenly became vacant. So it was that on September 20, 1978, presenter Bob Greaves, speaking live, introduced Joy Division by saying, "We hope that we're launching them on a real 'joy ride' as we have so many other others, haven't we, Tony?" Then there was a cut to a prerecorded Tony Wilson, who said, "Seeing as how this is the program which previously brought you first television appearances from everything from the Beatles to the Buzzcocks, we do like to keep our hand in and keep you informed of the most interesting new sounds in the northwest. This, Joy Division, is the most interesting sound we've come across in the last six months. They're a Manchester band (with the exception of the guitarist, who comes from Salford—very important difference). They're called Joy Division and this number is 'Shadowplay.'"*

Fucking tosser—"the guitarist, who comes from Salford"? Two of us came from Salford. I was really annoyed. I was proud of my roots, whereas Bernard always played them down.

It was a momentous day, though. Rob again decided that we needed to invest in ourselves and took us to town shopping. We all got new shirts to wear on *Granada Reports*. Two pounds fifty each, they were, and we felt dead spoiled, like dogs with our bellies tickled: fantastic. But also another example of Rob's—what would you say?—"unique" managerial style, because he'd never just give you the money to go and get a shirt for yourself; oh no, he'd have to buy it for you. Me, Barney, and Steve: fine about that. We all lived with our parents; we were used to being mothered (it turned out Steve's mum bought all his clothes anyway) and were over the moon with our new shirts. Ian: not so fine. Whether it was Debbie bending his ear or what, I don't know, but he always took exception to things like that.

Later on, in New Order, Rob would behave the same, except the stakes were higher then, so it would be, "Look, here's two grand, give yourself a holiday." Or, "Here's money for a car." But it all started off with that blue shirt that I'm wearing to play "Shadowplay" on *Granada Reports*.

The other thing about that performance is that I had blond hair. The reason for that is that after we'd changed our name to Joy Division we thought we needed a gimmick; and, during a group meeting in a pub in Piccadilly, it was decided that we were all going to bleach our hair. The next day I bought a hair kit called Born Blonde. It cost £1.25, dead expensive. Got home, put the plastic cap on, bleached my hair, got a clip round the ear from my mum for it. She hated it—hated anything like that, God rest her soul. She kicked the shit out of me when I got my first tattoo, then didn't speak to me for three weeks. I was thirty-two!

Anyway, I'd dyed my hair, and next time I went to rehearsal was dead excited about seeing everyone else with their blond hair.

Except when I got there it turned out that I was the only one who'd done it—and them lot were laughing their arses off at me.

Those fuckers.

I went, "I thought we were all bleaching our hair blond!" And they just laughed. They'd stitched me up, the bastards.

Apart from that, it was a good performance, and I remember enjoying the day, being overwhelmed to be in Granada studios. Me, the big *Coronation Street* fan. Then recording it, and being really pleased with how it came out, because it was a good showcase for what we were about, really. I mean, you see Ian's dancing. Not nearly as full-on as it was when we played live but it's there; Bernard with his guitar high, picking out those dead-brittle guitar lines; Steve, like a machine; me with my bass starting to get low.

The low bass was an idea I got when I saw the Clash at Belle Vue and was fixated by Paul Simonon, who looked the dog's bollocks—one of the coolest men ever. Staring, I thought, *How come he looks so good compared to other bass players?* Then I realized it was the strap. He was playing the bass dead low. There and then I decided it was a long strap for me from then on.

Ah, but what I discovered when I got home was that that my playing style is nothing like Paul Simonon's, which is easy to play with a long strap. My kind of bass? Really hard to play with a long strap.

Didn't stop me though. Fuck it: I dropped my strap by about six inches and—typical of me, always taking everything to obsessive levels—carried on dropping it until I was physically bent double. All of which meant that I ended up playing the bass high, which is my sound, but with the lowest strap, because what happens is that the lower you play, the more you have to bend your hand over, to play the notes, and that's the hard bit, that bend. Which is also why I make so many bum notes. I'm renowned for them.

Sound-wise I was most influenced by Jean-Jacques Burnel of the Stranglers. I used to listen to his bass on "Peaches" and "5 Minutes" and think, *That's how I want to sound.* When I went to see them at the Bingley Hall in Stafford I wrote down his equipment, a Vox 2x15 cab and a Hi-Watt head, then went out and bought the lot, and it was magnificent, sounded wonderful. So, I got my sound from Jean-Jacques and my strap from Paul Simonon. I'm so pleased I never got into Level 42.

It was around about that time that we played a gig where one person turned up. The Coach House in Huddersfield on September 28, 1978. We'd borrowed the PA that night, either from the Inadequates or Emergency—one of the two, or both—and lugged it all the way up these really steep, winding stairs, only to get one person in the audience. A bloke who stood there for half the gig then left. I mentioned it in a newspaper interview and all the fans online were going, "What's Hooky talking about? What gig in Huddersfield?" It wasn't well advertised, which was the reason it had slipped through the net. Then not long after that piece was in the paper, a guy came up to me somewhere and said, "Hello. Do you remember me?"

"No, sorry," I said.

He said, "I'm the guy who came to see you in Huddersfield. It's me."

"No way!" said I.

Joy Division's relationship with Roger Eagle of Eric's in Liverpool was partly responsible for Eagle suggesting to Tony Wilson that they join forces and release a compilation album. Names suggested for the Manchester-Liverpool union included Joy Division, the Durutti Column, and Pink Military, but the project faltered at the negotiating stage when Eagle preferred a conventional twelve-inch format while Wilson, having dropped acid, had conjured an image of a double seven-inch pack. He had the money: a £5,000 inheritance from his mother, who had died in 1975; the idea was greeted favorably by Saville, Erasmus, and Hannett; and so the A Factory Sample *EP was conceived, with the release to feature contributions from Joy Division, the Durutti Column, John Dowie, and Cabaret Voltaire. Graduating from club night, Factory became Manchester's fourth independent label after Rabid, New Hormones, and Object (the label started by Steve Solamar, the Electric Circus DJ) and at the vanguard of independent labels in the UK.*

We weren't signed and didn't have a publishing deal, so when Rob told us that Tony Wilson wanted to meet us, and maybe put one of our songs on his EP, we were like, "Wow, yeah, sounds great."

Well, when I say that, what I mean is that me, Barney, and Steve sat there scratching our heads while Rob and Ian discussed it—and how it was an EP of bands that Tony Wilson, *Mr. Granada*, liked, the bands he'd picked up on and was championing, so it was also an establishment of loyalty between us and Factory as much as anything else.

Money never came into it, of course. That was one thing we never really talked about in the early days. "How much are we getting for doing it?" "What's the deal on the record?" "What's the split, man?" There was none of that, which was wonderful because it was just about going forward, working with people you liked, and trusting that the rewards would come. Now, having had more experience, I know that we should have done a deal. Or certainly Tony should have done a deal. The songs on the Factory sampler belonged to us, even though he'd paid for them to be recorded. No way would that happen now, and it happened then only because both parties were young and naïve and a bit too idealistic. I mean, looking back, we had "Digital" on the sampler, one of our best early songs and a possible hit in its own right. Yet we put it on the Factory sample, limited to five thousand copies. We were giving away the chance to have a hit single: not the cleverest move in the world, surely.

But we were all in the same boat and Tony was as naïve and idealistic as we were. We first met him in a pub, the Sawyer's Arms again, I think it was, and were bowled over by his enthusiasm. For whatever reason we hadn't had a lot to do with him when we did the *Granada Reports* recording, so this was our first opportunity to get the measure of him. We felt like we were in exalted company. He dressed much older than we did. He was still wearing all that tail-end-of-glam gear: velvet jackets, big collars, big kipper ties. He always wore a suit because of his job, whereas we were all punk, but I liked him straightaway. He made us feel very welcome and comfortable. He wasn't at all intimidating or threatening; even though intellectually he could run rings around us all day, he never made us feel like that. He wasn't one of those people you got to know well—he was never a close mate—but he was a colleague and he certainly had an aura and presence, and we were in awe of him right from the word go. I mean, he was on TV and you can't overestimate that. I was watching him every night at six o'clock, so to suddenly be sat next to him was wild. It felt like an amazing aspect to what we were doing, that we got to meet people like Tony Wilson. *The* Tony Wilson. Who liked our band, liked what we were doing, wanted to make a record and put us on it.

He and Ian hit it off most, of course, probably because Ian was more on his intellectual level as well as being a lot more worldly about music. The thing about Ian was that he was into the bands we all grew to love; he was into them first. Not only that but he could also talk in depth about them in a way that appealed to Tony. You could tell that Ian was pleased to have this equally knowledgeable guy around, and you could tell that Tony felt the same way. I doubt there were many people who worked at Granada who knew about Throbbing Gristle.

So that was it: it was decided that we'd do the EP with Tony; go into Cargo Studios in Rochdale, and record it with Martin Hannett.

Which brings me to Martin. I think we'd heard of Cargo Studios—it was the most famous punk studio in the north. I think the Gang of Four had done their record there, which was a great record, and John Brierley was renowned as an excellent engineer/producer. This was the "Damaged Goods"/"Love Like Anthrax"/"Armalite Rifle" single, recorded at Cargo for Fast Product with John Brierley as the engineer.

I've also since found out that John was a proposed original member of Factory. So when it first started out it was Tony, Alan Erasmus, Peter Saville, Martin Hannett, and John Brierley, with John putting the studio into the partnership. The idea was that Martin was going to produce the bands, Saville would do the sleeves, Tony would be the talking head, and Alan Erasmus would be the enforcer. Saying that, I don't think that from that day to this anyone has ever figured out exactly what Alan Erasmus did in Factory—he was just incredibly important in some way no one can seem to figure out. He always was, and remains, a complete mystery, a true enigma. The funny thing about Alan is that he always moans about his lack of presence in the Factory legacy but just you try coaxing him out of the woodwork to get involved. He was moaning to me about the Grant Gee Joy Division documentary, saying, "How come I'm not in it? Cheeky bastards never asked me."

So I said to him, "Look, I'm making a Factory documentary; why don't you come and meet me and you can be on it?" He said yes and came down. I stuck the microphone in his face and asked the first question. All of a sudden he spluttered, turned puce, then remembered a prior engagement and ran away. Literally ran away. So he's his own worst enemy without a shadow of a doubt. Big heart, though.

Anyway. Back to John Brierley. John sussed out pretty quick that the Factory lot were a bunch of amateur, disorganized lunatics, so he bailed. Pretty smart move. He just said, "Pay me as usual for the studio," and went on to being the engineer for the Factory sampler, with Martin as the producer. We went in with our two songs, which were "Digital" and "Glass," which I think were the two newest songs that we liked the best—as I said, it's always your most recent material that you rate the most highly. So in we went and met Martin Hannett for the first time. I'd seen him before; I saw him play bass in Greasy Bear once, in a clothes shop in Manchester. But this was the first proper meeting.

Prior to opening Cargo, John Brierley had worked at Granada. He'd built his own mobile recording truck in an ex-ambulance that had been used for recording bands on Tony Wilson's So It Goes, *and at the end of 1977 left Granada to open Cargo on Kenion Street in Rochdale, running it from 1978 until 1984. Gang of Four's arrival in 1977 paved the way for the post-punk bands who liked it for its "live" sound, while its most famous client was Martin Hannett, who recorded, among others, Joy Division, Orchestral Manoeuvres in the Dark, Durutti Column, Crispy Ambulance, A Certain Ratio, and Section 25 there. Hannett liked the sound of Cargo, while the reasonable rental rates gave him the freedom to experiment.*

"Whenever he was in for a session he would bring all this extra gear in," writes Brierley on cargostudios.co.uk, "his AMS Digital Delays, AMS Digital Reverbs, several synths and that along with all my Rebis delays and noise gates, Compressors, MXR delays, MXR harmonizers and echo plates, Roland chorus units, various analogue delays and effects [meant] he had a phenomenal amount of choices. Because he had so many choices it was inevitable that he would come up with some interesting effects, and many of his good sounds came about by accident. I was always impressed by his use of very fast delay on the snare drum, it did sound good and very punchy. His mixes were a combination of very obvious effects and a lot of very subtle effects, just a hint of delay here or a touch of reverb there. The result was often stunning."

Hannett, meanwhile, was counting his blessings. He loved the "space" in Joy Division's sound and was especially impressed with Steve Morris's drumming—not to mention the fact that the band never argued with him. "They were a gift to a producer," he said, "because they didn't have a clue."

Cargo was great. It was a converted warehouse that from the outside looked like a factory unit but inside was stuffed with gear. It had dry-stone and brick walls and thick hanging drapes everywhere, and we arrived to find Martin already ensconced in a vast black leather chair behind the desk, John Brierley running around and virtually no room for anyone else.

I think we all thought Martin was a bit bonkers, because he was a weird, larger-than-life character, no doubt about it, even at that stage before the drugs got hold of him. Thinking back my first impression of him was his big curly hair and the trampy, hippie look he had going on. That and the nonstop smoking—

dope and cigarettes—so that the atmosphere in the control room was like that of a wizard surrounded by smoke and in charge of his strange machines. A lunatic wizard who never used one word when he could use twenty-one, nineteen of which you couldn't understand.

John Brierley, on the other hand, was the opposite: a straightforward, very businesslike, quite formal bloke. Bit brusque, you might almost say, but I got on well with him.

We didn't realize it then, of course, being so green, but Martin and John, they were two of the best, certainly in the region, probably in the country, and Cargo, despite its size, was a great studio. For a start we were recording on a sixteen-track, which was for us—when you bear in mind that our demos were done on a four-track and the *An Ideal for Living* EP on an eight-track—a big step up. Cargo had a Cadey sixteen-track machine using two-inch tape. It was a valve recorder, making it really warm- and fat-sounding and frankly the best recording medium that you can ever use. Sounds immense. We were delighted about that. All of which made it an easy session. Tony and Alan were floating about that day, so the Factory lot was very much in attendance, and the atmosphere was good. The whole thing, in fact, was very, very straightforward, none of the fooling about with Martin that would come later. He put some sound effects on. You can hear them in "Digital" and "Glass," which both sound amazing—*easily* our best recording up to that point—but I don't remember him doing it while we were there. My main feeling was just, *yes*, because my parts sounded good. It's only when your work starts disappearing that you get fed up. So if you listen back you'll hear a happy me, because the bass on "Digital" is kicking it. As a musician your ego and self-confidence really grows if your part is getting used, whereas they can take a huge blow if your part is downplayed, which is what happened to me on "Atmosphere" later on. On that record Martin mixed the bass down, but when we played it live it was loud in the mix. During the session I was like, "No, no, make it louder," but Martin just grinned and told me I was outvoted. Now I listen to "Atmosphere" and I think it's . . . okay. But he must have been going off me because on *Closer* he mixed the bass right down. The guitar too, actually. Both Barney and I fell out with him on *Closer.*

Anyway, all that was still to come. During this particular session I was feeling pretty good about my contribution, but other than that I just kept myself to myself. You've got to remember that we were in the presence of some pretty big characters: Rob, Tony, Alan, Martin, so us lot just sat in the corner quaking.

After the session we did the sleeves. It was a double seven-inch and we got paid to put them together. I think we went to Alan's flat at Palatine Road. I seem to remember that it was in the scruffy hippie kitchen that we did it. Tony didn't have to pay us really, but me, Ian, and Barney got 50p for every hundred that we folded and put in the sleeves, five thousand altogether. Not for the last time, either. Later on, Factory released the Durutti Column's debut, *The Return of the Durutti Column*, which came in a sandpaper sleeve, and I got paid for sticking bits of sandpaper onto two thousand Durutti Column albums.

Inspired partly by Far Eastern record packaging and partly by the arty designs of Fast Product releases, Tony Wilson suggested a heat-sealed gatefold format for the A Factory Sample *package. Peter Saville's design echoed his poster for FAC 1, and the EP included a set of stickers, one to represent each band, with Joy Division being a sailor's marionette. Its intricacies, however, made it more difficult to assemble than anticipated and a Christmas Eve release had to be postponed. Tony had scheduled* A Factory Sample *for release in December 1978 but Peter Saville missed the deadline for completing the artwork, pushing the release date back to January 1979. Wilson, however, was determined to give copies of the EP as Christmas presents to all the musicians who had played on it. So on Christmas Eve he photocopied Peter Saville's design and made his own sleeves with careful use of paper and glue, putting in the already-pressed discs and delivering them himself, like a punk Santa Claus, to the homes of the twenty musicians, including Ian Curtis, Stephen Morris, Bernard Sumner, and Peter Hook.* A Factory Sample *eventually appeared in two batches in January and February.*

In the meantime we resumed playing live, still in the northwest and mainly in Manchester but elsewhere, too. On October 24, we played the Fan Club at Brannigan's in Leeds, a really nice club in a very dodgy area, the red-light district. It was a good gig; I didn't think too much of it until not long after, when I answered a knock at the door one night and there stood two plainclothes police officers on the doorstep, faces of stone.

"Yeah?" I said.

"Can we speak to the owner of a blue Transit, VRJ 242J?" said one of them.

(And that again, by the way, is the *actual* registration number of the van. How I can still remember it after all these years is beyond me, but I do. When I told Anton that detail for *Control*, he laughed; he thought I was mad.)

"Oh, yeah, that's me," I said. "I'm the owner." Thinking, *Aw, no, what's this all about? Tax? Insurance? Speeding?*

A lot worse than that, it would turn out.

"Right, we need to talk to you."

They came in. Still I thought it was motoring: I had a bent MOT on the van. I'd bought it for a tenner, couldn't afford to fix it. . . .

"Right," he said, when we were all sat down. "We've had reports that your van has been seen in the red-light districts of Bradford, Huddersfield, Leeds, Moss Side . . ." He looked at me. "Want to tell me why that is, son?"

For a moment my mind went blank. All I could think was: *Yorkshire Ripper.* This was during the time they were searching for him. He preyed on prostitutes in Leeds, Bradford, Manchester . . .

"Oh, hang on a minute," I said, "I'm in a group. I play bass in a group. Where you're saying, they're gigs we've played."

They looked at each other, all doubtful-like. "What's your group called?"

"Joy Division."

"Never heard of them."

Probably Level 42 fans.

"Really," I insisted. "I play bass and all the gigs that we play are in the red-light districts."

"Why's that, then?"

"Well, we're sort of a punk group and they're the kind of places punk groups play."

"Can you prove that, then?" he said.

"What, that we're a punk group?"

"No, that your group has played in those places."

"Oh, yeah, yeah, of course," I said. "Our manager's got all the dates written down. And proving it's no problem. We've had punters—I mean, audience—watching, you know. And we've been reviewed and stuff."

They seemed satisfied. "Well, in that case, we won't ask you to come to the station or anything, but you must bear in mind that you're appearing in all these areas where there have been Ripper killings, so you can consider yourself under investigation."

I was nodding like a bastard, pleased to be off the hook, as it were. "Yeah, yeah. I'll give you any help I can, anything you want."

And he went, "Right, okay, we'll leave it at that for now."

Off they went. And, though I breathed a sigh of relief, I chuckled a bit about it too.

The next day I got a call from Steve.

"All right, Hooky. Have you had the police round?" he said, voice trembling.

"Yeah," I said. "They came and asked me about the red-light district and all that. Did they come to you?"

"Yeah," he said. "They came round and I panicked and they arrested me."

Oh dear. He was so nervous they'd thought they had their man, dragged him off to the police station, cuffed him, locked him up and interviewed him. His mum had to come down and rescue him.

Oh, did we laugh. Not that it was particularly surprising. Poor old Steve. We used to call him Shakin' Steve, he was that nervous all the time. The police must have taken one look at him and thought, *Got him. We're looking promotion in the face.*

· *Chapter 13* ·

"The biggest rain of spit I've ever seen in my life"

In November we joined a tour with the Rezillos and the Undertones. A bit of an ill-fated tour, that one, because the Rezillos fell out following the first gig, after which it was just a matter of time before they split.

What's more, the Undertones were all very young, about fourteen and fifteen, and this was the first time they'd been away from home so they were really, really homesick. Us, though, Joy Division? We were okay. I mean, we thought it was a bit of an odd billing because they were a pair of power-pop bands and we were . . . what we were. But we were pleased to play, to get the gigs, to do the traveling. Plus we got to stay in hotels and B&Bs for the first time, which was pretty exciting. First time we'd stayed away from home for a gig.

But then of course the Rezillos had this big bust-up. We played Brunel the next night and I remember that well for two reasons. Firstly because the Rezillos' singer, Fay, got changed in front of us and our eyes were on stalks as we tried desperately not to look. She probably didn't have much choice, it being a shared dressing room and all, and being in a band I'm sure she was quite used to decking off in front of the other guys, but even so we were shocked. The second reason was that the crowd wouldn't stop spitting. There was a gap between the stage and the crowd, like a no-man's-land, and every now and then some twat would run into the space and gob at Ian as we were playing. So I started twatting them with my bass. It had this hook on top of the headstock, the Hondo, and every time one of these little fuckers darted through the crowd to gob at Ian I swiped him in the ear with the top of the bass. I got about ten of them that way, little bastards. There was a speaker stack in the way so they couldn't see me when they came running in. Got a nice surprise.

Even so, there were too many, and we called it a day after seven numbers and fucked off. It's horrible, spitting. I remember one awful night where the Buzzcocks were getting spat at, at the Electric Circus and it was happening so much that Pete Shelley ended a song early.

"Stop the gig, stop the gig, stop the gig," he squealed. "Listen, right, if you lot don't stop spitting, we're not going to play." The crowd stopped. It lasted for about three seconds before he was showered in the biggest rain of spit I've ever seen in my life. Everybody just spat at him all at once—and he shrugged and played on. Should have walked off. That was how Joe Strummer got hepatitis, from swallowing someone's spit. Disgusting.

Anyway, a couple of the gigs were canceled because the Rezillos had walked off the tour. Then when we turned up to the Locarno in Bristol to play, we were told that *we* were off the tour. We'd done the sound check only to be suddenly told that they'd brought Chelsea in instead, and John Otway. Fuck me, we had a massive row with them. Gene October, Chelsea's singer, was such a twat and was being so fucking arrogant that Ian wanted to kill him, to bottle him. Rob was freaking too. It went the way all fights between gobby Cockneys and gobby Mancs go:

"You fucking Manc bastards, I'll have you."

"You bunch of Cockney twats. We'll fucking do you."

Ian started throwing punches, and the Chelsea guys were hitting back. We were just so fucked off because we really wanted to play. I mean, I still don't know why the Rezillos leaving the tour meant that we had to leave the tour too; why didn't they just put us and the Undertones on? But in the end we were actually physically ejected, chased out of the building.

It was not long after that we had our first gig in London, at the Hope & Anchor. Bernard's sleeping bag made another appearance. That night we discovered that there was something wrong with Ian. Something really wrong.

First off, it was a really big thing for us to play London. We were dead excited and nervous about doing it, as though the whole of London would be there to look at us. In reality the gig was in the basement of the pub. The Hope & Anchor is a legendary venue, don't get me wrong, but still: it was hardly the Marquee. It was a nightmare journey into London to get there. The others hadn't turned up yet, so it was left to me and Twinny to unload and set up the gear. We had to load it down the beer chute into the basement, which was cold and damp, pretty horrible, if I'm honest. Meanwhile, the rest of them—Steve, Ian, Bernard, Rob, and I think Gillian was there too—had been lost because Steve was a rotten driver, a terrible driver. He collects tanks these days, of course, and all I can say is that I hope he never takes them for a spin because he is the world's worst. He held some kind of Macclesfield record for having the most driving lessons and tests. Something like four hundred driving lessons and twenty-five tests. He was so nervous. Insisted on driving with a cigarette in his hand so he'd only ever have one hand on the wheel.

"Put both hands on the wheel!" they'd scream. Whenever he followed the van in the Cortina he'd always drive way too close. So close that I'd have to stop and say to him, "Steve, listen, you're driving too close, mate; you've got to back off, 'cause if I have to brake you're going to kill us all!"

Also, we had this sort of flimsy "no girlfriend" rule, one of Rob's ideas: it was okay to bring your girlfriend along to a gig in Manchester but not to away gigs. There wasn't any sleazy reason for it; it was just logistics, really. You've got your band, your crew, your gear. There isn't really the room for girlfriends; it made sense. But not to Steve—Steve would always bring his girlfriend along. First it was Stephanie, and because there was no room for her she'd have to sit on someone's knee all the way to Sheffield or Aberdeen or wherever. Then, of course, when he started going out with Gillian he began taking her along to every gig too.

I can't say for sure whether she was with him that night. What I do remember is them all turning up expecting to get warm, then coming into the basement of the Hope & Anchor and their faces falling when they discovered that it was freezing down there. This was especially bad news for Bernard, of course, who had the flu. We had to literally drag him from his sickbed just so he could make our first big London gig, only to find that it was in this cold basement—no heaters or radiators. Probably didn't have a toilet either. Honestly, kids in bands these days, they don't know they're born. (And yes: I know I sound like an old fart, but fuck it, it's my book.) They don't. With their sound men and stage managers, and overproud parents, poncing in and expecting everything laid out for them. You go to a gig now, like at the Academy or something, and it's got toilets with paper in them, and central heating and everyone gets a rider and coffee and clean towels and all that. Not in 1978, you didn't. Most gigs were like this one: complete chaos: "There's the stage; set up and shut up."

Most times you managed to muddle on through and a mixture of good luck, better songs, and the love of it all magically created a great gig. But we didn't have luck on our side that night; we were fresh out of the love of it all and even the songs sounded diabolical and there was no fucker there. I tell a lie: there were twenty people there. Got us our first bad review, too: "Joy Division were grim but I grinned." Cheeky bastard. Afterward I did the sums: it had cost us £28.50 in petrol to do the gig and we'd earned £27.50 from the door, so we'd lost a quid doing it. When it was all over, we packed up our stuff and drove home.

We were driving down the motorway together, me checking in my rearview mirror occasionally. Obviously I'd warned Steve to back off because he was scaring the shit out of me; and I was pleased to see that he was taking notice at last when all of a sudden they disappeared. My heart sinking, I pulled over on the hard shoulder and we waited—and waited.

Don't forget that in those days there was no traffic. You could be stopped on the hard shoulder of the M1 for an hour and not see another car. So we sat there in the freezing cold. We couldn't keep the heater running, of course, because it was a waste of petrol, so we just shivered in the cab of the van, rubbing our hands together to keep warm, moaning about them. Like, maybe they'd broken down. Maybe they'd stopped for something to eat. It would be just like them to stop off for a fry-up. But then again, no. Bernard, the last I saw of him, had looked like something out of *Night of the Living Dead*, he was that full of the flu. They were potless anyway, plus I hadn't seen any services open along the way. No, they couldn't have stopped.

So maybe they'd broken down. Well, if they'd broken down they'd be all right because Steve was in the AA. I wasn't even sure I had enough petrol left to go back for them *and* get home anyway. We had no room in the van anyway. So in the end we made a decision: we'd go home. Which is what we did, and it was only the next day at work that I phoned somebody and they told me what had happened. I just remember thinking, *Oh shit. There's something wrong with Ian.*

During the return journey from the gig there had been a minor altercation in the car. Disconsolate about the evening's performance, Ian had been talking about leaving the band and then pulled flu-ridden Bernard's sleeping bag from him. Having wrapped it around his head, he began lashing out at the doors and windows: he was having a seizure. The others pulled the car over on the motorway and laid Ian down to restrain him on the hard shoulder. This event culminated with a shaken Steve Morris taking the cigarettes out of Ian's pocket, as immortalized in 24 Hour Party People. *Then they drove him to the nearest hospital, Luton and Dunstable, where he was given pills and referred to his doctor. Ian was dropped home to a worried Debbie by Steve and Gillian, and was given an appointment to see a specialist. In the meantime he began having more fits—three or four a week—until on January 23, 1979, at Macclesfield District and General Hospital he was officially diagnosed with epilepsy and prescribed more pills.*

TIMELINE THREE

JANUARY 1978–DECEMBER 1978

VIRGIN RECORDS LIMITED

ARTIST ROYALTY STATEMENT ARTIST Joy Division

Period 1st January 1979 to 30th June 1979

Balance at 31st December 1978 £ ......74.86...... ~~DR~~/CR

Add Advances to date £

28.2.79 De Cross-Collateralisation of Publishing Royalties 136.19

£ .....136.19..........

Less Royalties for period

28.2.79 Publishing Royalties for period ended 31.12.78 36.19

30.6.79 Recording Royalties 17.44

30.6.79 Publishing Royalties 28.50

£ 82.13

BALANCE DUE/~~OWED~~

£ 20.80

JANUARY 24, 1978

Tony Wilson and Alan Erasmus devise their "management project," the Movement of the 24th January (or M24J for short), formed to oversee the career of the Durutti Column. They later launch the Factory club to provide the band with a live outlet and go on to start Factory records.

JANUARY 25, 1978

Joy Division plays Pips Discotheque, Manchester. This is the band's first gig under the new name.

APRIL 14, 1978

The Stiff Test/Chiswick Challenge Battle of the Bands, Rafters, Manchester.

Having been confronted by Ian Curtis earlier in the evening, Tony Wilson was impressed by Joy Division when they went on at two fifteen a.m., following an argument with the Negatives, and delivered a suitably fired-up performance. Rob Gretton also saw the light that evening; and soon he and Wilson, who were already friends from Rafters, were comparing notes.

MAY 1978

Rob Gretton visits the band, and they accept his offer to become their manager.

MAY 3–4, 1978

The unreleased-album sessions, Arrow Studios, Manchester. Tracks recorded: "The Drawback (All of This for You)," "Leaders of Men," "They Walked in Line," "Failures," "Novelty," "No Love Lost," "Transmission," "Ice Age," "Interzone," "Warsaw," "Shadowplay."

MAY 20, 1978

Joy Division plays the Mayflower Club, Manchester, with Emergency and the Risk.

JUNE 3, 1978

An Ideal for Living *seven-inch EP officially released as part of a distribution deal with Rabid. (Enigma PSS 139.) Photography by Gareth Davy. Cover design by Bernard Albrecht. Track list: "Warsaw," "No Love Lost," "Leaders of Men," "Failures."*

JUNE 9, 1978

The* Short Circuit—Live at the Electric Circus *ten-inch LP (Virgin Records VCL 5003) is released, featuring "At a Later Date," credited to Joy Division (though the band was called Warsaw when it was recorded on October 2, 1977). Other bands featured are the Fall, Steel Pulse, the Drones, John Cooper Clarke, and the Buzzcocks. Produced by Mike Howlett. Design/artwork and typography by Russell Mills.

JUNE 9, 1978

Joy Division plays the Factory, Russell Club, Manchester, supporting the Tiller Boys as part of the Factory club's opening concerts. Admission: £1.

JULY 12, 1978

Joy Division plays Band on the Wall, Manchester, a Manchester Musicians' Collective gig.

JULY 15, 1978

Joy Division plays Eric's, Liverpool (matinee and evening shows), supporting the Rich Kids.

They wouldn't talk to us, and wouldn't even let us in the dressing room. The only one of them who was nice was Midge Ure. He actually spoke to us.

JULY 27, 1978

Joy Division plays Roots Club, Leeds, supporting the Durutti Column.

We went for a meal before the gig and that was where I first noticed how sickly and delicate Vini Reilly was. You know when you look at someone and think, *Fucking hell, it's going to be tough on you, mate?* We went to an Indian restaurant in Leeds for something to eat before the gig; I remember Vini asked for Heinz tomato soup. In an Indian restaurant in Leeds. Because of his constitution he couldn't eat anything else.

Also, I can't say for sure but I think the third support was the Fairbrass brothers, who later became Right Said Fred. Years later I was at a Skin Two fetish party in London that ended with an unrepeatable story involving them, lots of naughties, and Cleo Rocos. Earlier that night one of them had said to me, "We supported you in Leeds in 1978 as Joy Division," and gave me a big hug. The next time I saw him was through the roof of one of those huge stretch limos, and he was . . . Well, let's just leave it there.

JULY 28, 1978

Joy Division plays the Factory, Russell Club, Manchester, supporting Suicide with the Actors. Admission: "A quid at the door."

Ian and Steve were really thrilled about this gig because Suicide were a pretty avant-garde group and those two, being the most musically forward-thinking of us all, loved them. I got into a lot of music through Ian, and Suicide was one of the bands he introduced me to. I love how all their songs sound like intros.

AUGUST 29, 1978

Joy Division plays Band on the Wall, Manchester, with Stage 2 and the Elite.

SEPTEMBER 4, 1978

Joy Division plays Band on the Wall, Manchester. The gig is promoted by Rob Gretton, who also designed the poster.

SEPTEMBER 9, 1978

Joy Division plays Eric's, Liverpool, supporting Tanz Der Youth. (Andy Colquhoun of Warsaw Pakt was a member of Tanz Der Youth for a time.) Admission: 60p members; 90p guests.

SEPTEMBER 10, 1978

Joy Division plays the Royal Standard, Bradford, supported by Emergency "and disco." Admission: 80p in advance; £1 at the door.

It was full of National Front skinheads. That was a terrifying evening. We had to pretend to be Nazis to get out alive. How ironic.

SEPTEMBER 20, 1978

***Joy Division appears on* Granada Reports*, introduced by Tony Wilson; they play "Shadowplay," overlaid with negative offcuts from* World in Action.**

They put those cars on it because they thought we were boring to look at, but that was what Tony liked about us—that we were reserved. Maybe Ian took it to heart, I don't know, but it was around then that he started doing his dancing more often, which became his trademark.

SEPTEMBER 22, 1978

Joy Division plays the Coach House, Huddersfield.

One person turned up. It was diabolical.

SEPTEMBER 26, 1978

Joy Division plays Band on the Wall, Manchester, with Dust and A Certain Ratio.

ACR had a guitarist whose hair was like a chunk of cheese. So we used to call him Cheesehead.

OCTOBER 2, 1978

Joy Division plays the Institute of Technology, Bolton, supported by the Curbs.

I remember going to that gig, because I remember parking outside (which is always handy). I don't remember anything else about it, though.

OCTOBER 10, 1978

The An Ideal for Living *twelve-inch EP (Anonymous ANON1) is released. This is a twelve-inch reissue, two thousand copies only. Recorded at Pennine Sound Studios, December 1977. Cover design by*

Steve McGarry. Photography by D. B. Glen. Track list: "Warsaw," "No Love Lost," "Leaders of Men," "Failures."

OCTOBER 11, 1978

The* A Factory Sample *session, Cargo Studios, Rochdale. Produced by Martin Hannett. Engineered by John Brierley. Tracks recorded: "Digital" and "Glass."

OCTOBER 12, 1978

Joy Division plays Kelly's, Manchester, with the Risk, for Rock Against Racism. Admission: £1 at the door.

This was in aid of a great cause. We were proud to support it.

OCTOBER 20, 1978

Joy Division plays the Factory, Manchester, supporting Cabaret Voltaire and the Tiller Boys. Admission: £1.

> The intensity, the passion of this music completely eclipsed anything the audience had seen in a long, long time.
>
> Mick Middlehurst, writing in *The Face*, 1980

The poster for the event was given the catalogue number FAC 3 (FAC 1 was Peter Saville's Factory-club poster and FAC 2 was the A Factory Sample *EP, not yet released).*

The first time we played at the Factory there were, like, fifteen or twenty people there but by this stage we had two or three hundred turning up. It was great to play with Cabaret Voltaire, too. Mal and Richard, lovely lads. And it was a great poster. I still have a lot of the posters, but people borrow them for exhibitions and whatever and never give me them back. I've lost loads.

OCTOBER 24, 1978

Joy Division plays the Fan Club, Brannigan's, Leeds, supporting Cabaret Voltaire.

Come to think of it, I don't think any of the Cabs were under investigation for being the Yorkshire Ripper. Hm . . .

OCTOBER 26, 1978

Joy Division plays Band on the Wall, Manchester (possibly a Manchester Musicians' Collective gig).

NOVEMBER 4, 1978

Joy Division plays Eric's, Liverpool (matinee and evening shows), supporting Ded Byrds and John Cooper Clarke.

Ded Byrds had a female saxophonist, and Terry and Ian did something to the reed on her saxophone that I can't possibly repeat here. I'm sorry, but I'm just going to have to leave it to your imagination—but judging by her face it tasted vile! Meanwhile, Barney and Twinny were also up to something unrepeatable round the back of the car park. An action-packed gig, that one, onstage and off.

NOVEMBER 14, 1978

Joy Division plays the Odeon, Canterbury, as part of their tour with the Rezillos and the Undertones.

The Undertones—they were so young. They'd bought an air pistol and were having target practice backstage, shooting cans off the stairs. Then someone brought in letters from home because they'd been away touring for a while, and next thing they were all crying in the dressing room reading letters from their mums. Me and Ian were looking at each other like, *Aw, isn't that sweet?*

NOVEMBER 15, 1978

Joy Division plays Brunel University, Uxbridge.

Unfortunately the set was cut very short; there can't have been any more than four or five numbers. The reason being that a part of the audience was still into the spitting thing and took a big dislike to Ian. They covered the poor man from head to foot. At the end of "Digital," Ian had clearly had enough and said quite politely to the audience, "I see you are not educated down south," and promptly walked off. He was quickly followed by Sumner and Hook. Steve Morris realized it was over and scrambled from his drums, unfortunately he had to walk past the front of them to exit the stage and he tripped on a speaker cable, the crowed jeered and heckled him, he picked himself up, hurled some obscenities and walked off.

Martin (fan), on joydiv.org

NOVEMBER 19, 1978

Joy Division sound checks but doesn't play Locarno, Bristol.

The last time I saw Joy Division was at the Locarno in Bristol. They'd travelled down from Manchester to be told that the Rezillos had split up and instead John Otway and Chelsea were to headline that night, with us onstage first. No room on the bill for Joy Division. That's show business, that is.

Mickey Bradley, bassist, the Undertones

NOVEMBER 20, 1978

Joy Division plays the Check Inn, Altrincham, supported by Surgical Supports and Bidet Boys. Admission: £1.

> Joy Division were okay and could well prove to be to next year what The Fall have been to Manchester this year and what Buzzcocks were to last year.
>
> *Record Mirror*

We'd been told all the posh girls lived in Altrincham and Hale, and we thought, *Wow: yes!* for that reason. Otherwise we had the feeling that the Check Inn wasn't going to be very wild and (lo and behold) when we played it, it wasn't. It was a dreadful gig and a dreadful audience, no girls at all. The only redeeming factor was that we didn't have far to go home.

NOVEMBER 26, 1978

Joy Division plays the New Electric Circus, Manchester, supported by the Passage.

This was an Alan Wise promotion, I think, but I don't remember the gig. It's nice to say that we'd eclipsed the Passage by then, though.

DECEMBER 1, 1978

Joy Division plays the Salford College of Technology; they are second on the bill, with Ed Banger (Ed Garrity) headlining and Fast Cars (with Steve Brotherdale on drums). Admission: £1.

DECEMBER 22, 1978

Joy Division plays the Revolution Club, York, supported by Cabaret Voltaire.

DECEMBER 27, 1978

Joy Division plays the Hope & Anchor, London. Admission: 60p.

This was, I suppose, the first time that we thought, *It's not all perfect.*

Nick Tester's Sounds *review of the Hope & Anchor gig was scathing:*

> Joy Division try to be a grim group, but I just grinned. This retracted grimness is alienating, but not for intended provocative or creative reasons. I found Joy Division's "tedium" a blunt, hollow medium, comical in its superfluous angst [. . .] They may have gathered a tight following in home town Manchester but they failed to ignite a similar impression in front of a new (though not necessarily more objective) audience. An off-night maybe, but Joy Division's lack of an enlivening approach could be improved by an all-round sharper articulate stance and musical method. Joy Division could be a good band if they placed more emphasis on poise than pose.

PART FOUR

"LOVE WILL TEAR US APART"

BUZZCOCKS / JOY DIVISION

PETER

FROM: New Hormones (Management) - May 1979

TO: All relevant departments - Liberty-United Records (UK) Ltd

ITEM: BUZZCOCKS Autumn Tour - UK/Ireland 1979 - projected dates

Month	Date	Town	Venue
OCTOBER	2	Liverpool	~~Empire~~ Mountford Hall (SU)
	3	~~Hull~~ Leeds SU	~~City Hall~~
	4	Newcastle	City Hall
	5	Edinburgh	Odeon
	6	Glasgow	Apollo
	7	Aberdeen	Capitol
	8	Dundee	Caird Hall
	9	DAY OFF/Travel	
	10	~~Portrush~~	~~Kelly's~~
	11	~~Belfast~~	~~Ulster Hall~~
	12	~~Dublin~~	~~Dominion/Olympia (TBA)~~
	13	~~Cork~~	~~City Hall~~
	14	DAY OFF/Travel	
	15) 16) 17)	BRUSSELS	
	18) 19) 20)	DAYS OFF	
	21	Sheffield	Top Rank
	22	Derby	Assembly Rooms
	23	Blackburn	King George's Hall
	24	Birmingham	Odeon
	25	Bradford	St George's Hall
	26	~~DAY OFF~~ ELECTRIC BALLROOM	
	27) 28)	Manchester	Apollo
	29	Leicester	De Montfort
	30	Oxford	New Theatre
	31	DAY OFF	
NOVEMBER	1	Guildford	Civic Hall
	2	Bournemouth	Winter Gardens
	3	Cardiff	Sofia Gardens
	4	Bristol	Colston Hall
	5	Hemel Hempstead	Pavilion
	6	DAY OFF	
	7	West Runton	Pavilion
	8	London	Marquee (Fan Club only).
	9) 10)	London	Rainbow

It will be appreciated that the above details are NOT FOR RELEASE to press or public at the moment.
Please circulate to sales/promotional staff in order that promotional activities (radio/TV/press/personal appearances/etc) may be organised well in advance.

· *Chapter 14* ·

"Peter's fell off his chair again"

I hated being the one who drove the van. Apart from making me a suspected serial killer, it meant I had to load and unload the gear all the time. And what do most bands do after gigs? They get pissed and chase girls. Not me. When a gig finished and everybody ran off to the bar I was left to pack the bloody gear. Twinny and Terry might lend a hand if I could collar them before they got a pint in their hands, but they weren't getting paid so it wasn't like I could insist. As for the rest of the band, well, Steve would occasionally lend a hand, bless him, but Barney and Ian were always too busy chasing skirt/meeting the fans. I used to have to literally drag them away. Oh God, it used to wind me up so much. Drove me mental! I was always saying to them, "Let's just get the gear done and *then* go to the bar," but it always fell on deaf ears.

As a group you've got to have responsibility for your gear: let's face it, without it you're useless. But that fact was lost on those two. Even Ian still had a PA to shift. I'm sure they thought it got in the van by magic.

"Well, that's what we've got roadies for, isn't it?" Bernard would say with a sneer.

"Listen, they're my mates. They don't get fucking paid to shift your shit. They don't get fucking paid at all. Do your own fucking shifting or get your own fucking friends to move it."

The fact was that Terry and Twinny would do the carrying in the afternoon, no problem. Set it up, sort the sound check, look after it till the doors opened, no problem. But that was because there were no distractions in the afternoon. At night? Forget it. No one wants to do the gear at the end of the night. The only one doing it was the daft bastard driving the van, yours truly.

Some mornings I'd come home from a gig, change into my suit then drive straight to work. There was a pelican crossing outside the docks, right opposite work, where I always used to fall asleep. There was something about reaching that point, eight o'clock in the morning, feeling knackered but nice and warm in the van, and just . . . feeling . . . sleepy . . . My snoozing hotspot, that was.

My work mates would bang on the window to wake me up, laughing. I'd get to work and try to keep going, but after a really late night I'd have to go hide in the file room and fall asleep on the floor. Either that or risk it at my desk, but I'd just black out and go . . .

Thump.

"Oh look, Peter's fell off his chair again."

So I was tired. Exhausted, actually.

And I didn't have epilepsy.

There's a lot that's been written about the effect it had on Ian. How he felt embarrassed about the condition, and how the drugs affected him. We saw bits of that: his mood changed a bit; he was quieter, less ready to laugh and more introverted than before, which was understandable. Otherwise he just soldiered on. So instead of taking time off for Ian to rest, and instead of getting together and working out how to adapt to our lead singer's epilepsy, we buried our heads in the sand, all of us, Ian included, and—and you'll be hearing this a lot throughout the rest of the book—we just carried on.

Meanwhile, far from slowing, the pace began to pick up.

Rob had jacked in his job at Eagle Star Insurance on Princess Street. His base was his attic flat in Chorlton and with plenty of time to devote to management work he'd come to us with gig offers all the time. We never said no. Wherever it was, whatever it was, we'd agree.

Christ, it must have been exhausting for Ian. (After we found out I eased off getting on at him about not moving his amp, so at least that was one advantage of being epileptic—every cloud and all that.)

But seriously. I mean, if I was that knackered I was nodding off at the pelican and sliding off my chair at work, how did he feel? But because Ian was Ian and didn't want to let us down, he allowed us to keep on going like nothing had happened, and nobody—not us, Tony, Rob, Debbie, his parents, doctors, or specialists—stepped in to say he should do anything different. All of which suited us fine, I hate to admit, because the discovery of Ian's epilepsy coincided with a period when the band was really beginning to take off.

Having the *An Ideal for Living* EP out as twelve-inch had made promotion so much easier. We didn't have to apologize for it the way we'd had to with the seven-inch. With the twelve-inch out, both Rob and the band had something great to work with—something that represented us really well.

God knows how much time Rob spent in phone boxes. He must have used them like an office, phoning round for gigs and reactions on the records then phoning us. We were easily reachable, so Rob would just grab a load of coins, go to the phone box and ring us up. I'd pick up the phone at work, probably exhausted from a gig the night before.

"All right, Hooky. It's Rob."

"All right, Rob."

"John Peel likes the record. He wants us in for a session."

I'd put down the phone and I wouldn't think, *Aw, that's going to be stressful for poor old Ian*; I'd think, *Fucking hell, we're going to do a session for John Peel!* and go for a run.

We were totally in awe of John Peel and his program, and he'd already played tracks off the EP. Somewhere I've still got the tape with the places marked in pen where John introduces our tracks, can still remember listening to it in the car, freezing, taping off the car radio on one of those portable cassette players. Doing the session was mind-blowing. For a start, when you work for the BBC you get paid personally: the money comes to you, not to the group. (Later, in New Order, I used to love doing *Top of the Pops* because I got a check for £280 when I was getting nothing off the group.) But it was also mind-blowing because John Peel was a hero, a true musical hero. His was the only show on radio for people like us to listen to, so to be offered a session, well, that was like getting a chart placing back then, only better. We didn't give a shit about chart placings. Right then, success for us was about playing the music we wanted to play: that was that. For us, in Joy Division and New Order, it was always about playing without compromising your music. Doing that was the only success.

When you did a Peel session there was no messing about. It started at two, finished at four, and there was no overrun. Hours overdubbing? Forget it. "Hey, why don't we try some synth here?" None of that. You were in and out.

Which suited me down to the ground. A great way to do things, if you ask me. Nowadays you're so spoiled by technology you can spend hours and days and months on the computer perfecting every tiny detail. Of course there's some great music being made that way. But is it greater than the music being made back then? No.

· *Chapter 15* ·

"Fuck, Martin's got a boot full of stolen car radios"

We were still at TJ Davidson's, where we were being very productive. From two rehearsals—one on a weeknight, for an hour or an hour and a half, which cost us £1.50, then three hours on Sundays, which was £3—we'd get an idea a week and write two to three songs a month; and I'd say that from the time we wrote "Transmission" onward they just flowed like rain. I mean, writing songs is easy when you're just starting out. It gets a lot harder and takes longer when you've written two or three hundred. You get overdrawn at the riff bank. But back then we couldn't stop writing them.

All four of us had ideas. One of us would have been listening to Kraftwerk and suggest using that sound as the basis for a song. We'd all chip in and by the time the song was finished, even though the seed of the song had been Kraftwerk, it wouldn't sound like Kraftwerk at all. That was the art. It sounded like Joy Division. In this particular case it sounded like "Digital," in fact.

"Shadowplay" happened in a similar way: Bernard had been listening to "Ocean" by Velvet Underground and wanted to write a track like that, with the surf sound, a rolling feeling in it. So we started jamming and that's how we came up with "Shadowplay." You wouldn't say it sounded anything like Velvet Underground, but once you know you can hear the root.

That was the thing about Joy Division: writing the songs was dead easy because the group was really balanced; we had a great guitarist, a great drummer, a great bass player, a great singer. As soon as Ian died it became difficult. He had an ear for us, a great ear, and all bands need one of those. You could tell he would have been a great guitar player too. His guitars of choice were the Vox Peardrop and the Vox Teardrop, very idiosyncratic; the Teardrop had some wild built-in effects that he loved. He'd picked the guitar up late, starting around the time we were writing the songs that would become *Closer.* Maybe Barney's playing was still bugging him, but a more likely explanation was that we were featuring more keyboards and Barney was switching between the two. Maybe Ian thought he'd fill in. He played on the video for "Love Will Tear Us Apart" and was obviously quite a rudimentary player, but you could tell he would have gotten so much better because he had that ear—he thought like a musician. The way it worked was that he'd listen to us jamming, and then direct the song until it was . . . a song. He stood there like a conductor and picked out the best bits.

Which was why, when we lost him, it made everything so difficult. It was like driving a great car that had only three wheels. The loss of Ian had opened up a hole in us and we had to learn to write in a different way. It was hard, that period, just starting New Order, and we suddenly found it very difficult to adjust. We felt like we'd been cheated. It had been so easy, so good when it was the four of us. We were so tight, as a group, we didn't even use a tape recorder half the time. Didn't need one. We had the odd one, of course, but they never lasted or the quality was so poor as to make them virtually useless. But it didn't matter because we could do most things from memory. Everything up to and including *Unknown Pleasures* really existed only when the four of us were in a room together playing it. Not written down, not recorded, just from memory.

Peter Saville has a wonderful theory that musicians stop writing great music when they learn about the formal process of making music. Why? Because then they won't take any chances. When you're young, you go, "G, B. Oh yeah, man, that fucking takes your head off, that! Weird but sounds great!"

Then, when you get older and you know a lot more about how music is *supposed* to sound, you go, "Oh, that G, B, that jars a little doesn't it? Oh no, try E flat. That's better," and the edge is gone. I agree with him. The more proficient you become at writing music the fewer chances you take because you become aware of all the rules and theories that may well be the proper way to do things but end up constricting you, throttling all the creativity out of what you've got. No more risk-taking. Back then we didn't know rules or theory. We had our ear, Ian, who listened and picked out the melodies. Then at some point his lyrics would appear. He always had his scraps of paper that he'd written things down on and he'd go through his plastic bag. "Oh, I've got something that might suit that." And the next thing you knew he'd be standing there with a piece of paper in one hand, wrapped around the microphone stand, with his head down, making the melodies work. We'd never hear what he was singing about in rehearsal because the equipment was so shit. In his case it didn't matter because he delivered the vocal with such a huge amount of passion and aggression, like he really fucking meant it. It was great. Who cared what he was saying as long as he said it like that.

When we were mixing, Rob Gretton always used to say, "Make it go WOOOMPH!" and Ian always did.

Later, of course, I'd listen to the lyrics and try to pick them apart, but for two years in the rehearsal room all I really heard was a scream and that was what was important to me. I just thought, "The guy means it." It doesn't matter what you're saying really, as long as you mean it.

It was only after we recorded *Unknown Pleasures* that I could hear and begin to take note of the words, and it was quite startling then to see how they changed between that album, where they were still quite detached and aggressive, to *Closer*, which is even darker and not detached at all but really introspective and quite frightening—especially of course when you listen to it in light of what later happened.

Still, we hadn't yet even made an album, but because we were being so productive talk turned to making one. There was a feeling that we had enough material—enough *good* material—to do it, and to be perfectly frank with you, we weren't that fussy about who we made it with. As far as we were concerned, there were a lot of record companies out there and they all did pretty much the same thing, which was got records out.

Despite the fact that none of us had a fondness for London—as a place or for the record labels—we all assumed we'd end up following that well-worn path and going there. Which seemed perfectly natural to us—desirable, really—because we were in a band. Nobody starts a band so they can stay in their hometown. You yearn for London and Paris and America and all that—all the freedom that comes with it. We weren't really loyal to any Manchester scene. We'd always been a bit outside it anyway.

Out of all of us it was Rob, of course, who was much more pro-Manchester. Everywhere was important, not just London, he said: "Fuck London"—that was one of his favorite catchphrases. We'll do what we do here, build up a following in Manchester. We were resistant at first but he worked his magic on us (in other words, he browbeat us until we would have said anything just to make him stop, but the idea did grow on us). Lucky it did, because in retrospect he was right—absolutely right.

So Rob went into talks with Tony about doing our record with him. The deal was a 50-50 split with the label to pay for recording and manufacture. (In actual fact, the deal was a mistake for Tony and Factory. He'd forgotten about what we call "mechanical royalties." So for reasons that are too boring to go into, it meant that the deal was 58 percent to 42 percent in our favor: a bone of contention for years.) The deal was great on the one hand, but had a drawback: there would be no advance, so we couldn't give up our jobs. Rob didn't have a job, of course, but he knew that us giving up our jobs would be best for the band, giving us the freedom and time to concentrate on making music. So with the Factory offer on the table he started fishing around, making inquiries. One of the bites he had was from Genetic, a part of Radar Records, which in turn was a part of Stiff Records. They had a good reputation. They offered us a multi-album deal and a £70,000 advance. That was so much money it was hard to comprehend.

We were like, "Whoa, whoa, whoa, yes!"

Okay: me, Bernard, and Steve were like, "Whoa, yes!" Rob, being nothing if not a man of many contradictions, had a sudden change of heart and decided he didn't like the idea of an advance. They were like loans, he said. Fuck loans.

"If you take this advance, you'll be signed to them for five albums and if you don't like them and they don't work, it's going to be a problem for your next four, isn't it?"

Which was absolutely true, and the £70,000 would have included recording costs as well; split between the five of us it maybe wasn't such a great deal after all. He convinced us of this, probably in his normal intimidating way, and he did it every time we came to do our publishing deals too, insisting: no advance. Ian would be screaming at him, and me and Barney would be screaming at him, and Steve would probably whisper something as well, but he'd never budge. He'd push his glasses up his nose and go, "We're better off getting a bigger deal at the back end."

Of course he hated London. From the day he was born till the day he died, he hated London. So naturally it really appealed to him to stay in Manchester and have control, because Tony was offering more or less complete freedom musically. We could do what we wanted.

So poor old Rob at this point—it must have done his head in: Genetic was in London offering an advance, and he hated London and distrusted the advance, *but* . . . his band could give up their jobs. Factory was in Manchester and was offering the split, and he loved Manchester and thought the split was best in the long-term, *but* . . . his band would have to stay working.

His band, don't forget, with the lead singer who suffered from epilepsy, who really needed as much rest as possible.

So there was plenty of umming and ahhing. In the meantime Martin Rushent invited us down to the studio to record some demos, just to see if we were going to gel. He'd produced the Buzzcocks and the Stranglers by this point, so we were very excited by the prospect and went down there.

Rushent was based in offices above the Blitz Club on Great Queen Street, where he'd been monitoring the early appearances of the major players in the burgeoning New Romantic scene. His assistant, Anne Roseberry, had seen Joy Division in Manchester and told Rushent about it; Rushent in turn saw them and said, "My jaw hit the floor." Keen to try them out for his own label, Genetic, he invited them to his Berkshire studio, Eden.

When we got there, we saw that Martin Rushent had a brand-new Jaguar XJS—and as it happened I'd been reading this article about how nine out of ten Jag owners don't lock the boot of their car.

So I thought, *I wonder if that's true* . . . Tried his boot and, lo and behold, it was unlocked. When I looked inside it was full of stolen car radios; you could tell they were stolen by the way the wires were dangling off from where they'd been ripped out.

Me and Terry were looking at each other, thinking, *Fuck, Martin's got a boot full of stolen car radios*. And then, *Wonder if he'd miss a couple* . . .

All day, actually, whenever there was a break in the recording, we'd be daring one another to go back in his boot and nick one each for our cars—because they were proper high-end stereos—but I was going, "Oh no, we can't, because he might be our record company. We can't nick fucking cassette players off our record company."

So we didn't take any. Christ knows what he was doing with them, though. We never asked him, and anyway he was too busy moaning about the boil on his bum. It was giving him real gyp and he was in agony with it. So much that he couldn't sleep in his bed and had to sleep in his car instead—couldn't get comfortable otherwise.

He went on about that a lot, his boil, and it meant he kept having to get up to walk around and ease the pain, but otherwise the session was great. It was a really nice studio and he worked well with Ian on the vocals, did a few overdubs and stuff, nothing wild, very low key. The tracks were "Glass," "Transmission," "Ice Age," "Insight," and "Digital." He was a nice guy; we got on well. He was a lot better than Martin Hannett in one respect: he spoke English and you could understand what he said. But he was nowhere near as exciting or unpredictable and, to be honest, once I'd heard the results I much preferred Hannett's production to his.

I got offered the tape of that session back, recently. Eden Studios was taken over by a firm of solicitors, and left in a storeroom, hidden in the bowels of it, were the Joy Division master tapes. One of the staff found them. He got in touch with me through a third party to offer me the tape. He wanted £50,000 for it and I just thought, *Oh, fuck off.* This was in 2006 or something. Even then there was no way on earth you could make a record and hope to recoup fifty grand. I offered him a finder's fee, two grand, but he said no and I've never heard from him since; it's never appeared, so I don't know what's happened to that one. They used monitor mixes for the Eden versions on the *Heart and Soul* box set, but I was offered the twenty-four-track master tapes, so it could have been remixed. Shame, because as far as I know the only Joy Division multi-track that still exists is for "Love Will Tear Us Apart."

Ah well. It's a funny thing, people trying to sell you back bits of your own past, but I'm getting used to it, to be honest. We have the same problem even with studio staff. When Strawberry Studios closed, someone spirited a load of master tapes straight from the trash to their parents' loft. I caught them hawking the tapes round a few Joy Division collectors. They wanted £20,000. I patiently explained how you can't make any money these days, what with illegal downloading and so on, and offered the usual £2,000 finder's fee. They sneered, "I'd rather deal with Steve and Gillian!" I instigated legal proceedings on that one. But lo and behold, one day, as we were negotiating, their car got broken into and all the tapes and digital copies got stolen. They even had the police-report number. Ah well, the ones that got away. Although in this day and age I challenge any thief to even recognize thirty-year-old recording tapes, let alone know what to do with them. They are huge. Strangely enough, they were hawking the same tapes around again a few months later. The thief must have returned them.

· *Chapter 16* ·

"It sounds like a fucking helicopter"

Pleased with the demos he'd recorded with Joy Division, Martin Rushent brought them to the attention of Genetic's owner, Warner Bros., who were less impressed, reportedly telling him to forget about Joy Division and the New Romantic groups and concentrate instead on finding the new Angelic Upstarts. History was to prove Rushent correct, not only in the case of Joy Division but also with Visage, Ultravox, and Spandau Ballet, and he would go on to produce the Human League's masterpiece, Dare. *Either way, Joy Division had decided not to join Genetic, wanting the greater artistic freedom of their relationship with Factory as well as preferring the financial terms offered. During Joy Division's gig at Band on the Wall on March 13, Gretton and Wilson agreed that Joy Division would record their debut album with Factory, with all concerned assuming that the band would make just one album with the label before moving on to a major.*

So what actually happened was that we were presented with two very different scenarios: London plus advance and small profit split or Manchester with no advance but great profit split. We all plumped for the latter. We thought that as long as we were able to stay at home and play the songs we were writing, that was enough. Everything else would be a bonus. In the end it was an easy decision to make. We met with Tony and told him our decision. He was delighted and must have thought, *Fuck this is a great band, we need to get them on a record and get it out right away.* He was absolutely right.

Even so, it was a bit of a wrench because we still had in our minds the idea that if we had a contract with an advance, and could give up our day jobs, everything would be fine and dandy. Follow the Yellow Brick Road. But what Rob and Tony were suggesting was *not* giving up our jobs, taking an independent-label deal, which meant that you had to put a lot more work in and there was no safety net and all the things that you normally do in a group full-time you had to do at the same time as you were working. You'd still be doing the gigs, coming home sometimes at six in the morning and then having to go to work at seven. Which was, like I say, exhausting.

But Rob convinced us it was the best thing to do. The deal was great—probably the best deal a band had ever had, actually. For us to make any money, though, we had to make a great record that sold well. So the pressure was on. We prepared for the sessions with two storming gigs. The first was at Bowdon Vale Youth Club, where we were being filmed by Malcolm Whitehead as part of his short film about Joy Division. It was a cracking gig and one I really remember because I felt at the time that we were very nearly the finished article. For a start, we looked like a great group. If you see the film, I'm getting the swagger on and Bernard's more into himself, doing his not moving-type thing, which made a nice contrast. We sounded good too. Personally speaking I was really pleased with the bass sound pretty much from then on. I'm sure Ian wouldn't mind me saying that a lot of the vocal lines were guided by the bass and I was coming up with some good riffs. I mean, going down the set list for the Bowdon Vale gig, just look at the bass lines: "Exercise One," "She's Lost Control," "Shadowplay," "Insight," "Disorder," "Glass," "Digital," "Transmission," "I Remember Nothing." You stand and fall on your riffs and I was just amazingly, sickeningly lucky in that I was coming up with them. To write something like "She's Lost Control" and have the whole song based around it. That's one of our most famous songs, really personal to Ian, and for him to base those lyrics around my riff was so fucking cool. As a player I was being featured very highly, was an integral part of the sound of the band, which was great for me, a wonderful platform. To be a part of something like that when I was (a) tone-deaf and (b) self-taught was amazing.

It wasn't all roses, though. I still had to drive the fucking van. That kept my feet firmly on the ground as well as causing me no end of problems, not least of which was paying for the maintenance. Because you might think that if something went wrong with the van then paying for it would come out of the group purse. You might think that. You'd be wrong. Anything like the clutch going, a puncture, a flat tire, and I had to pay for it. I'd go to Rob and say, "Listen, I've had to pay for this tire."

And he'd go, "Well? What's that fucking got to do with me? I'm not paying for your fucking van; you fucking pay for it."

On our way to our next gig, in Walthamstow, we were driving down the motorway when the van's top hose split and water blew on the distributor cap. It backfired and peeled the exhaust like a banana.

We pulled over.

"What are we going to do?"

"We've got to fucking go," said Rob. "We've got a fucking gig."

I said, "Fuck off. I can't drive through London like that, with no exhaust. It sounds like a fucking helicopter."

He was going, "No, no, it's fine, fine—we'll fix it when we get to Dave Pils's house."

They all piled back in the Cortina and we had to drive all the way down the motorway, which wasn't too bad, actually, apart from the fact that me, Terry, and Twinny were completely deaf by the time we got there. We drove through North London to Walthamstow, parked up, and I said to Dave, "Listen, we're going to have to get it fixed."

"Kwik Fit round the corner," he said.

I didn't have any money, of course, and looked at Rob, who said, "Well, I'll lend you the money to fix the van."

"*Lend* us the money? I can't afford to pay for the fucking thing myself."

So he gave me the cash and I went to Kwik Fit and got it sorted—£13 for a new exhaust—and while I was out they'd had a group meeting at Dave Pils's house. Waited till I was out, the rotten bastards, and had a group vote. This would become a habbit.

"We've decided that we're not paying for it," said Rob when I got back. "We'll lend it to you but you've got to give us the money back."

I said, "Right, from now on you can hire a van because I'm not fucking paying to drive you twats about when you're keeping the gig money and I have to fork out. Fuck off, the lot of you."

I stormed out, didn't I. Went for a walk round the block, calmed down and when I got back to Dave Pils's house they were all sat in the living room.

Rob said, "It's all right, Hooky, we're going to pay for it." So it was sorted. I didn't have to pay back the money. I was still pissed off, and would pretty much stay pissed off until August 13, when . . . Well, we'll come to that.

In the meantime, we had an album to record. Sheesh!

• *Chapter 17* •

"He was looking for that spark"

Strawberry Studios in Stockport is offices now, but for years it was the major studio in the northwest. If you go to where it is on Waterloo Road they have one of those blue plaques up with a list of all the legendary artists who recorded there: Paul McCartney, Neil Sedaka, Stone Roses, and the Syd Lawrence Orchestra.

No mention of us, the bastards. Even though that was where we went in April 1979 to record our debut album (and, later, to record "Transmission" and "Love Will Tear Us Apart," among others). Tony Wilson always gave massive credit to 10CC for putting Strawberry in Stockport. The way he saw it, they'd reinvested the money they made from their music back into Manchester. He was right. Thanks to them we had one of the country's best studios on our doorstep, and we were pretty excited about it: our first foray into twenty-four-track recording, with the ability to overdub, in four-star luxury. We were once again being produced by Martin Hannett, who was using all sorts of great gear. The AMS, of course, as well as the Marshall Time Modulators (Marshall Time Wasters, the engineers called them), which he used a lot on the guitar, especially on some of Bernard's more . . . *economical* playing, shall we say. So to be honest it felt like such a thrill. Like taking the next big step up. We were all raring to go and happy and had enthusiasm to burn.

If only I'd known then what I know now, I'd have savored making our first album—because by the time we got to the second one there were already divisions beginning to form and we were very worried about Ian. Martin was having a hard time with the drugs so it got very fraught and very stressful. Then, on *Movement*, the first New Order album—well, we were fucked from that album on as far as I'm concerned. Whatever record we were making from that point on, there was always some elephant in the room. Whether it was Ian's death, or business matters, personal disputes, the Haçienda sucking the life out of us, or Factory going to the wall, there was always something. Always an elephant. Should have given it a catalog number.

There was no elephant on *Unknown Pleasures*, though. It turned out to be the only album we made where we were focused and relaxed and enjoyed the wonderfulness of being young and in a band and going in to record your debut album on your new label with a producer who had mad hair and looked like a wizard and spoke in riddles.

He told us we needed forty minutes' worth of music for the album so we presented him with a batch of songs. Of those we recorded sixteen, ten of which were used on the album, all recorded on the weekend. We all had jobs during the week. No advance, remember. And it was cheaper on weekends. Even cheaper if we worked at night, which suited Martin down to the ground, of course, because he liked to work at night. So the band would arrive at the studio straight after work on Friday, record until seven in the morning, then return later in the evening on the

Saturday and work until seven in the morning. We'd be going home at seven on Monday morning, trying to escape before the cleaner arrived and started hoovering. Even now the sound of a Hoover goes right through me. We recorded for the first two weekends and Martin mixed the third weekend. So that was two days to record *Unknown Pleasures*. *Closer* took three weeks. *Movement* took about two months and *Waiting for the Siren's Call*, New Order's last, took three years.

Usually when a band went into the studio, back in the late '70s anyway, you'd have one eye on the clock and be concentrating on not messing around. The accepted way of doing this was to get the band in the studio and get them sounding as live as possible. There was no such thing as click tracks or backing tracks in those days. It was all recorded live. So for the most part what we used to do was go in and run through all of the tracks in one go, with Ian in the room—he'd do the vocal in isolation later, when we had the take. Now, normally when you record a band you have a microphone on each of the instruments, and each records to a track on the master tape, but you get a bit of leakage from one microphone to another, so you'll get a bit of the bass down the guitar mike and so on. If you want to feature, say, the guitar more prominently, then you turn up the guitar track, but because of the sound spill the other instruments come up too. Martin hated that.

Martin, being Martin, wanted the live feel of the band playing but without sacrificing the clarity of the instruments. So he set us up to get maximum separation, and the way he did that was to record us separately, especially the drums. Martin wanted them isolated so he could work on the drum sound, which of course he ended up doing a lot, creating that very clean, precise-sounding, almost clinical drum sound that became his trademark.

Of course, it was only much later, when we heard the finished product, that we knew what he was going on about. What we heard at the time was Martin and Chris Nagle, his engineer, constantly going on and on about keeping everything clean and separate, right from the start, the very opposite of what we wanted. The first song we played him was "She's Lost Control." He loved the drums on it, he said; then said it would be great if they were separate. Next thing we knew he was getting Steve to take his kit apart. Off came the snare and the toms. Martin wanted zero spill from the mikes, so he had to record each drum individually. Of course that meant that Steve was rarely playing his whole kit. He was allowed to play only one drum at a time and ghosted the others. So what happened was that we ran through "She's Lost Control" live, then Martin recorded the drum track, we took the kit apart, and Steve played his parts again—one drum at a time. It made everything very laborious and really hard for Steve, because he didn't have a click track to keep time to, so he kept speeding up and slowing down. Steve had to learn how to play the kit, but play it like a drum machine. He once said that his ambition wasn't to be a drum machine but Martin demanded the separation. It even got to the point where Martin was taking the drums themselves apart, taking the tightening springs out, because he said they squeaked. Only he could hear it.

Of course it had to be done in a matter of hours. If you went into the studio now and wanted to re-create the sound of *Unknown Pleasures*, it would probably take you years. But we were young and Martin was pushing us, and it had to be done double-quick, so it was a constant battle between Martin's desire to experiment and the time we had left in the studio. We worked very quickly. None of that farting about—all that happened later. For *Unknown Pleasures* we'd go in with our list of songs. We'd set up the instruments, sound check, "Right, 'Disorder.'"

We'd play "Disorder."

"Is that all right, Martin?"

"No, didn't like it. Try it slower but faster. Meaner but kinder."

We'd look at each other like, *Oh, do fuck off.*

We'd play "Disorder" again.

"How was that, Martin?"

"That was better, yeah, a bit on the buttery side but fine; we'll go with that one."

So then we had our master. Ten backing tracks, ready for editing, manipulating, and adding to. Next Martin would record the drums, and often he'd get Barney to put some heavier guitar on top too; he was a big fan of layering the recordings. He'd do the vocals last, right at the end, so they were clean without any spill from the instruments. When it came to the vocals Tony suddenly became very involved, suggesting strongly that Ian listen to Frank Sinatra's *Greatest Hits* so he could incorporate a bit of Frank's crooner style into the vocal lines. This made us all laugh and, while I didn't hear a direct influence on Ian's vocal style, I was quite surprised to see a few references to Frank's songs in the lyrics. Notably "I Remember Nothing" with its "We were strangers" refrain. Strangers in the night, anyone?

The band had its first studio row, actually, the first of many over the years, because Barney insisted on using infrared headphones and adjusting the levels to fit them, even though it fucked up the levels for the rest of us, plus we fell out a couple of times over songs that he didn't like and was reluctant to play. Martin had encouraged us to write a couple more in the studio so we had a better choice for the LP. Me and Steve jammed out "From Safety to Where" and "Candidate." Ian then worked on vocals. Barney didn't like that song either and his reluctance to play on it was marked. Martin had to turn the tape over so the songs were backward. He liked them then and played. Martin spun it over so the tracks had backward guitars and a few fed-up-sounding *EEEKs.* Apart from that, it was a pretty peaceful atmosphere, which was mainly down to Martin, of course, because he wasn't yet the tyrant he later became.

Back then he smoked a bit of dope but he wasn't into heroin, as far as I know. To be honest, I don't think he had the money for it. His drug problem really only became a problem for us when it came to *Movement*, when he refused to start the session until we brought him a gram of coke. "Where the fuck are we going to get a gram of coke from?" We'd never even seen cocaine. (At that point, I mean. We'd certainly put that right later.)

"I'm not fucking starting until you bring me a gram of Colombia's finest," he insisted, and then sat there for hours with his arms folded while the rest of us tried to persuade him to begin the session. After phoning God knows how many people, Rob laid his hands on some and brought it into the studio.

"Right," said Martin, handing it over to Chris Nagle, "You sort that out, Christopher, and I'll get started."

What a twat, we thought. All that fucking time wasted. Never is the saying "time is money" truer than when you're in the studio. The average cost then was £1 per recording track per hour (so, for example, twenty-four-track: £24 per hour). Fair enough, I suppose; he was struggling. It's a well-known fact that he took Ian's death hard. I mean, recording "Ceremony" and "In a Lonely Place" was easier because Ian had left the lyrics and the vocal lines for those two, so it was only our vocal efforts that amused and frustrated him. But doing *Movement* he found the album tough going from the start, and he let us know it. It was like that great car with the wonky wheel again. Martin was constantly having to fix New Order and he wasn't in good enough physical or mental shape to do it. He was off his peak. We all were.

He hated that we used to bug the shit out of him, me and Bernard especially. One on either side. Always on his case. Questioning everything. "Why are you doing that?" "Isn't it too quiet?" "Isn't it too loud?" "More bass!" "More guitar!" "More everything." Ian was much more easygoing, and perhaps that's why he was Martin's favorite. But maybe Ian was more easygoing because there was only so much Martin could do to the vocals, whereas he could do a lot to the instruments. And he did a lot to the instruments. Which was, after all, what he was there to do. As a sound manipulator Martin was in a class of his own, and the atmosphere, clarity, and depth he gave to the songs is still astonishing.

He was lucky, though. Like I know myself, when you're producing a band and they come in with great songs you rub your hands with glee, because you can have such fun with a great song. But when someone brings you a poor or average song, you have to start changing it and you're thinking, *Can we write a better middle eight? Can we improve the chorus?* That's not as much fun. It can be really hard work.

Martin had fun with Joy Division because the songs were so fantastic. He didn't have as much fun with *Movement* because, while the music was fantastic, we were lacking confidence on the lyrics and vocals. Struggling to do them to his satisfaction. We were feeling our way in the dark. He knew that and it pissed him off. And, along with fires and infestations of rats, the one thing you don't want in a studio is a pissed-off Martin Hannett because he was ruthless, a right dictator at times. Derek Brandwood, who ended up managing him toward the end of his career, once said that you could put him in a studio with a band who'd been the best of friends for forty years and within five minutes Martin would have them at each other's throats. So true.

His bag was winding people up. I remember he made Bernard sing "Cries & Whispers" by New Order forty-three times. He wanted a complete take and if there was one error, or what Martin *thought* was an error, he made Bernard do it again. Barney was totally pissed off with it all, and quite rightly so, but Martin fed off that. You could see the look in his eyes, like, *This'll get him*. He was looking for that spark, something intangible. But to him always a catalytic spark.

Did he get it? Well, it would be great if this particular anecdote ended with Bernard doing the performance of his life and "Cries & Whispers" becoming one of our greatest songs, but it doesn't because we told Martin to fuck off and stormed out. So no, he didn't get it. What he got was band and producer at each other's throats, which was all part of his divide-and-conquer ethic. And if you were looking for any support from Chris Nagle you might as well forget it: Martin's big thing was that the group should do their bit and then piss off, and Chris was very much his right-hand man on that. Even though he was our age he always took Martin's side against the group and the pair of them would visibly gang up on you, sniggering together like schoolgirls if you suggested anything.

I'd go, "Can we turn up the hi-hat, Martin, please?" and the pair of them would look at each other and dissolve into giggles.

I'd be like, "What's so fucking funny about that? What's so fucking funny about turning up the hi-hat?" But the pair of them would sit there sniggering like bastards. Infuriating.

If that failed, they would try to freeze us out. They sat at the desk in the middle of the room, where it was warm, while we had to sit at the back under the air-conditioning that they'd jammed on full to get rid of us. Barney had to produce the sleeping bag yet again. It wouldn't have been so bad if 10CC had kept the heating on at night, the tight bastards. But you literally had icicles hanging off your nose.

When we'd finished recording, we had to decide what songs were going on the album and in what order. Looking back now at the tracks we recorded, I'd say that "Exercise One," "Only Mistake," "They Walked in Line," and "The Kill" were a bit punkier than the tracks we ended up picking, and maybe didn't fit in with the album so well. "Exercise One" is the best one. "Only Mistake" is a good song as well. "They Walked in Line" and "The Kill" are a bit too punky, a bit throwaway.

Once we'd decided what was going to make the cut, Martin tuned it so that each song was in a sympathetic key, so it didn't jar but instead sounds like a smooth, ear-pleasing progression rather than a harsh transition, like harmonic mixing—so "Disorder" into "Day of the Lords" was in tune and so on and so on. Martin introduced us to all that. Very, very clever.

Then we could hear it, of course.

I can't remember if we were there for the mixing. Maybe not. As I said, Martin hated us hanging around when we weren't playing, getting on his nerves. "Get these fucking musicians out of here," he'd scream.

He used to say "musicians" like it was a swearword. What difference it would have made to the finished article if we'd been sitting on his shoulder while he mixed it I couldn't say. Back then we didn't know enough about the process to have much of an opinion. All we saw was him pressing buttons. He could have been releasing squadrons of bats for all we knew. So whether we were there or not, Martin mixed *Unknown Pleasures* his way.

Ian and Steve loved it. Me and Barney hated it. We thought

it was too weak. We wanted it to be miles heavier. We wanted it to go *RARRGH!* And instead it went *ptish.* All the things I now love about the album—the spacey, echoey ambient sound of it—were all the things I hated about it when I first heard it.

I was properly upset about it too. The kind of upset you get when you're in the minority—because when Tony and Rob heard it they loved it as well, so it was a fait accompli, mate. That was the end of it.

For me it was almost like the *An Ideal for Living* moment, when I got the record home and put it on only to hear that it was absolutely shit. *Unknown Pleasures* sort of had the same effect. To make us sound so . . . weedy. It made me feel sick. *Oh my God, he's taken all the guts out of it. All the balls. How could he do that?*

Now, of course, I can see the error of my ways. Now I can see that what Martin gave us, which was the greatest gift any producer can give any band. He gave us timelessness. Because *Unknown Pleasures* is just one of those things: it's a truly ageless album. Think of the millions of albums influenced by *Unknown Pleasures* that *have* aged, while *Unknown Pleasures* hasn't. That was his gift to us. We gave him the brilliant songs and he put them in little capsules so they'd stay brilliant forever.

Bernard had of course done a great job on the *An Ideal for Living* cover. And I'm not being sarcastic: I really think he did. He was always on the lookout for images to put on our stuff; and looking through a book, *The Cambridge Encyclopaedia of Astronomy*, he saw a diagram of a pulsar, showed it to Peter Saville, and that was it. Bernard doesn't get nearly enough credit for that, because he couldn't have made a better choice: that image is now forever associated with Joy Division and *Unknown Pleasures* the record. Speaking of which, I can't remember who came up with the title. Ian again? Either way Peter went off, applied his magic, and turned it into *Unknown Pleasures,* putting all his great little touches on it: the textured paper, the text on the reverse, and the light and shade of having the outer sleeve black and the inner sleeve white. To be honest, I wasn't that interested in the art. I was just pleased that they didn't intend to feature the band. We'd seen too many punk bands standing there scowling in black and white, their name sprayed on the wall behind them. We were all behind playing down the personality. Our image was a kind of anti-image, about anonymity and being chilly and gray and buttoned-up against the cold. In lots of our pictures we're hunched up or have our backs turned, which was a mixture of being cold and not giving a fuck about the whole business of image, really. We didn't want it to be about us. We certainly didn't want it to be about our looks, 'cause we were such a bunch of ugly bastards. We wanted it all to be about the music.

It was the same with journalists. Right from the early days Rob had been dead against us giving interviews—especially me and Bernard, because we just used to sit there and say stupid things. Taking the piss.

Rob's response was, "Right, you two. You don't speak. At all. Just sit there and look menacing." He didn't do it to create a mystique around the band but because he thought we were a couple of cretins. The result was that it created a mystique around the band. Absolute genius.

Anyway, we finished the album in April and, despite me and Barney protesting that we wanted to sound like the Sex Pistols, the master went off to the pressing plant and they pressed ten thousand of them.

One night Rob phoned me up and said, "Come on, we've got to go and pick the record up."

"Fucking hell," I said, "Ten thousand of them. Isn't anybody else coming?"

"No, just me and you."

I rented a van from Salford Van Hire and had to tell them I was moving house (they had a sign on the wall refusing to hire to "musicians, hawkers, and gypsies"). Then we drove down to London to pick up the records from the plant. Loading the van took an age, then we drove them back up to Manchester, thinking the axle was going to snap any second, taking it slow so we didn't fuck up the van. At Manchester we went straight to Palatine Road and started handballing them up the three flights of stairs to Alan's flat. Margox was there. That's Margi Clarke, the actress from *Letter To Brezhnev* and *Corrie*, of course, but back then she was called Margox and she did bits of singing and TV presenting and she was there at 86a with Alan's flatmate.

This was about seven p.m. and she said, "Oh, what you got there, love? Is this your record, like? Can I have one?" We ignored her and they disappeared off into the bedroom. Sure enough, as we loaded the records in we did it to a background noise of them having very noisy orgasms, thinking, *Fucking hell, could this be any fucking worse?*

She came floating out much later, when me and Rob were sitting there dripping in sweat from having carried ten thousand copies of *Unknown Pleasures* up the stairs.

"Can I have a record?" she said.

Seems a bit mean now, but it was just the culmination of a bad day; I'm ashamed to say that Rob told her to fuck right off again.

Quite funny, really, because at our very next gig, at Eric's in May, who should be there as our support? Only Margox again. She did this act where she sang over other people's records—Kraftwerk, Sex Pistols and stuff—just shrieking over the top of them. Absolutely awful, it was, and I'm sure she'd be the first to agree. Still, we loved her. How can you not love Margi Clarke? That really earthy, rude character you see onscreen is like a toned-down version of the real one. What you see is what you get there, let me tell you. She is wonderful. So when we were in the dressing room before the show, and Twinny winked at us before saying to her, "Show us your tits, love," I don't know why we were surprised when she went, "Here y'go, la," lifted up her top, and showed us them in all their glory.

We went bright red and stayed bright red when she didn't put them away. Just waited until we were at maximum discomfort, our faces burning so hot you could fry eggs on them and silently plotting revenge on Twinny and his big mouth, until at last she put us out of our misery, saying, "That taught you a lesson, lads?"

"Yes," we mumbled like naughty schoolboys.

Top down, she left the room pissing herself laughing. She'd played us at our own game and won hands down. She was wild—a great girl—and I was chuffed when she started on *Coronation Street* years later. Like I say, it's one of those programs that I always feel is inextricably linked with my life, right from listening to the theme tune at the top of the stairs with our Chris, to Margi Clarke, and then to Tony Wilson telling us how he'd started its most famous siren, Pat Phoenix, on drugs. He'd got her into dope, or so he said, and once she was into it she wouldn't leave him alone. She became a proper spliff-head.

"Where's that Tony Wilson with my drugs?" she used to scream in the office. "Come on, where is he? Tony! Where's my fucking drugs?" Tony would be hiding under the desk to try to get away from her. He'd created a monster. It's funny because I remember, just before I started the group, being in Kendals Department Store in town and I looked up and she was there, Elsie

Tanner, and I went, "Oh, hiya," and she glared at me like looks could kill and went, "Oh, fuck off, will you?" and stormed past. My first brush with celebrity.

One of Manchester's most famous sirens telling me to fuck right off. Two years later Margi Clarke telling me to fuck off too—the Peter Hook curse of *Coronation Street*.

· Chapter 18 ·

"Not that I'd change anything"

Unknown Pleasures *was released to great critical acclaim, with* NME *hailing it as an "English rock masterwork" and* Melody Maker *as one of the year's best debuts. Though initial sales failed to match the acclaim, word began to spread and Factory soon sold around fifteen thousand copies, earning the label between £40,000 and £50,000 profit inside six months.*

Our next job was a session for Piccadilly Radio, where we recorded our first version of "Atmosphere," which was called "Chance" at that point, along with "Atrocity Exhibition," which went on to become the opening track on the next album, *Closer*, except in a Hannett slowed-down, stripped-down, effect-heavy version.

To be honest, I always preferred it sounding like the version we did first—or better still when we did it live. "Chance," on the other hand, improved a lot when we rerecorded it. The version we recorded during the session had an organ on it, an old one that Barney had borrowed from his gran. She'd bought it from

Woolworths in the 1950s and it was made of old, hard plastic that had gone brittle by the time we got our hands on it. Had a wild sound, though. We liked it straightaway, thought it sounded immense and would be great on "Chance." Pleased with the way it sounded, we decided to play the song at our next gig, at the F Club in Leeds with the Durutti Column, and took the organ along. There was no case for it but we stowed it on top of the gear, until Vini came along, put his guitar on top of the stack, and knocked the Woolies organ off. All that brittle plastic just shattered when it hit the floor. Gutted. We loved that organ.

Ah well, onward and upward. *Unknown Pleasures* came out in June and got fantastic reviews. The distribution wasn't great, of course—that's what you get for being independent—but our stock was rising; we were in demand. We became like a touring machine.

Me, Bernard, and Steve found it exhausting juggling the late nights with work, and we weren't married. For us, home was a sanctuary. For Ian, once he got out of Steve's Cortina at night, he was stepping straight into another world of problems: a wife who was uncertain about how she fit into her husband's new life, and who felt excluded from it, a victim of Rob's no-girlfriends policy. An unhappy wife, in other words. And, of course, a new baby. . . .

Natalie had been born while we were recording *Unknown Pleasures*, and the fact that I can remember so little about it says less for my memory and more for the fact that Ian hardly mentioned it. There was no big announcement. No session down the pub to wet the baby's head. I don't think he would have said anything at all apart from the fact that he'd fainted at the sight of Debbie giving birth—falling, splitting his head open, and leaving Debbie to give birth alone while the nurses looked after him. We asked him more about the cut. In *Touching from a Distance* Debbie says that Ian had had a fit and cut his head, so what the truth of the matter is I'm not completely sure. All I know is that's how we found out Ian had become a dad.

Why didn't he announce it? I don't know. A mixture of things, I suppose. A desire to keep band and family separate, which was always Rob's philosophy, and a sign of the times, when men didn't go dotty about their kids like we do now. All wrong, of course, and it must have made things more difficult for him having to keep wife, kid, *and* the group all happy. Trying to follow his dreams at the same time. With the benefit of hindsight you can see how damaging it would have been and I'm pleased to say that I've learned from it: since New Order's split in 1993 I've always gone out of my way to make sure that family and friends of all the band members aren't excluded but very much *included*.

Great thing, isn't it, hindsight?

In July we went to Central Sound Studios in Manchester for the first of the "Transmission" sessions. The tunes were pouring out thick and fast. "Atmosphere," "Dead Souls," and "Atrocity Exhibition" all came during this period. I think if it hadn't been for the great reception at the Mayflower we wouldn't have bothered with "Transmission" as a single, to be honest. But the Mayflower had been the first of a series of occasions where "Transmission" had blown people away live. We'd begun to think maybe we had something a bit special on our hands—so special we should leave it off the album and release it as a single.

It's one of our songs that should have been a hit—and probably would have been if we'd been on a major, or even if Factory had done things differently. If we'd done things the way normal groups do them, in other words, and released "Digital" as a single, which would have been big. Then "Disorder" should have been a single, and that would have been bigger. By then we'd have had the kind of foundations we needed to make "Transmission" a monster, and by the time we got to "Love Will Tear Us Apart," we'd have been ready to take over the world.

But we didn't do it the normal way, of course. We did it the Factory way.

Not that I'd change anything, mind you. I'd stop Ian from hanging himself, obviously. But otherwise I really wouldn't change anything. I wouldn't change the fact that we downplayed the singles or that we left singles off the albums that we didn't promote. Because in many ways it's made us who we are. Besides, the way we did it seemed better than doing what a lot of bands had done. Siouxsie & the Banshees, for instance, had signed to a major and had to sell something like fifty times as many albums to make the same money we did, plus had less freedom and control and had to play the game, the awful game, which is all about selling albums. For us, the punk ethic that had brought us into it molded the whole way we behaved, and we had a manager who fervently believed in the same ideals, who let us grow and develop at our own pace, without A&R men breathing down our necks, without having to do loads of press we didn't want to do. We would have had to if we'd been on the dreaded major.

So the first session for the "Transmission" single was at Central Sound Studios, right next to the Odeon in the center of Manchester and right next to the best kebab shop in town. We got the shock of our lives when we realized where the studio was. We'd been going to that kebab shop for years, never knowing that there was a recording studio next door. What a bonus. The kebab shop, I mean.

It was a cheaper studio, not like Strawberry, but was good for demoing the songs before we went to record them properly. We did "Transmission," obviously, and it was a good run-through. Plus "Novelty," despite the fact that it was one of our really early, raw ones, one that I'd written, actually, that Ian had been generous enough to take and mold and make into a song. But for whatever reason Rob really liked it, so we just agreed and recorded it. Badgered into it, probably, because comparing it to the others it sounds very young—a young song from a young band learning their craft. "Something Must Break" was left off the single because there was no room and Rob didn't want to compromise the sound quality of "Novelty" because he loved it so much. It was an interesting song for us, though, being the first time the band had used a synthesizer. Martin had used them, of course, but the thing about us in Joy Division—especially me, Bernard, and Steve—was that we were sponges constantly learning off Martin. So you'd have this situation where on *Unknown Pleasures* me and Barney were moaning about Martin using a synth, then a couple of sessions down the line we were using it ourselves. Bernard would embrace all that more than me, and on "Something Must Break" he used a synthesizer instead of the guitar; there's no guitar on it. It's the same technique we used to write "Love Will Tear Us Apart," actually. There was no guitar on that when we first wrote it, just Bernard playing the synth, me on bass, Steve on drums, and Ian's vocals. Even live when we used to play it there was no guitar on it, which gave it a different, unusual sound. It was still a fantastic song and the melody was a great one. Later, when Ian mastered the guitar a little, he played on both.

With *Unknown Pleasures* out and "Transmission" in the can, it really felt like we were taking off: drawing ahead of the competition a bit. That meant we had to do more interviews, of course, which was a downside. But again, the fact that we were on an independent meant that we could be awkward bastards if we wanted to be. In fact Tony and Rob encouraged us to be—and, believe me, we did want to be awkward bastards. I mean, we'd all been reading *NME* and *Melody Maker* for years but, being the kind of contrary types that we were, rather than embrace the music press we kicked against it. The way we saw it, looking at most band interviews, was that if you took the name of the band off they were all exactly the same. Amazing that *NME* and *Melody Maker* got away with it week after week, because most people said the same thing. Then there was the fact that people kept bringing up the Nazi thing. Once we'd answered that but kept being asked about it, and once it had been made plain that the band didn't have Nazi sympathies but people still went on about it, well, it was bound to piss us off. So we insulated ourselves against it by being awkward bastards right from the beginning of any interview.

"Tell us about your new album."

"No."

I used to love that. I once did an interview with John Peel's producer, John Waters. It was for the first Peel session and he said, "So, tell us how the session's going?"

"It's all right."

And he went, "Oh right. Would you like to tell us about your plans?"

"No."

"Oh, right."

Afterward he said it was the most difficult interview he'd ever done, which of course I thought was hilarious. But it wasn't really a plan. Being bloody-minded just amused me—and when it became part of our persona and one of those things that got us remembered, that suited us fine. We were lucky. We had the luxury of being awkward because we were coming out with great music. We didn't really care if we pissed off any journalist. The way we looked at them was, *Where were you when we were playing to an empty room?* It's one of the eternal frustrations of being in a group. One minute you're playing to a handful of people yawning their heads off, then six months or eight months later you're playing the exact same material to a packed audience all going bonkers and you think, *Where the fuck were you when we played at Oldham Tower Club?*

What was good about our rise was that we were well managed by Rob, who kept our feet on the ground, kept us level-headed and focused on the music; because, even when we had *Unknown Pleasures* out and *NME* was saying it was brilliant, and we had "Transmission" coming out and a buzz around us, gigs coming out of our ears, he kept our feet firmly on the ground. The beauty of Joy Division is that we never made much money while the band existed so there was nothing to sully it—no piles of drugs or cases of booze in the dressing room. We went everywhere in a convoy of knackered van and Steve's Cortina and stayed with friends—no hotels for us, just the odd B&B. Even when we went to London to record *Closer* we stayed in a quite scruffy pair of flats with £1.50 per diem: you could spend how you wished, dinner or a couple of pints but not both. We didn't yet have any money from the record. (Publishing, as in who wrote what in the songs, brings nearly all bands down. I remember the immortal quote from the Happy Mondays: "Why is the one playing the maracas getting as much as me who writes the songs?" Ironically, Bez is now as important as all the songwriters, if not more. How the world turns.)

There was one memorable occasion with Ian putting a drum case on his head and marching round TJ's, screaming at Rob about money, so maybe we had the odd fallout, but nothing major. The gigs we were doing weren't big payers anyway. We just kept on doing our thing, which was playing, recording, winding up journalists, and in late July appearing on Granada TV's *What's On.*

Now, that was excellent and we were very excited to do it—even more so when we went to the subsidized canteen and found it full of Roman soldiers. Rob was following me and Twinny going, "Don't you nick anything. Don't you fucking nick anything, you pair of bastards."

In those days, Granada was very unionized. It was a very old-fashioned union; you had to be a member to work there. It was very powerful. You had to adhere to very strict rules. When we came to set up there was a light that somebody had taken down from the ceiling and put in the middle of the stage, and we said to the sound guys, "Do you mind if we move this light, mate?"

They all shook their heads. "Oh, don't touch that; that's Lighting. We're Sound. They're Camera. That's Lighting. You can't touch that."

"Okay, but we need to move it, mate, to play."

"You can't touch it."

We were like, "You what? What are you talking about? We've got to have a sound check."

They were going, "No, don't touch it."

They stuck tape around it to mark it out of bounds.

Our mouths were hanging open. "We can't sound check."

"You'll just have to wait."

Rob wasn't having that. He went to grab at the light and one of the guys started shouting at him, "Oh no, don't touch that. Touch that and we're going out on strike, the lot of us. That light belongs to the Lighting Union."

Rob was in his face. "You fucking what, mate?" but they weren't budging. Someone called Lighting, who said they'd send someone over, and we all looked at one another in disbelief then sat around to wait, Rob with steam coming out of his ears. Finally, an hour and a half later, this Lighting guy ambled into the studio and picked up the light—"Sorry about that; must have left it there when I did *Granada Reports*"—and buggered off again.

Brilliant. We leapt up ready to sound check—*at last*—only to watch gobsmacked as the lot of them turned on their heels and marched out. Not on strike, thank fuck for small mercies, but to have dinner. By the time they returned it was to tap their watches and say, "Right, you've got half an hour to film it. Better get a move on, lads. . . ."

They were rewarded with a slightly nervy and shell-shocked performance of "She's Lost Control" that was broadcast over the end credits of *What's On*. Best thing was that I was wearing the blue shirt that I'd worn on Tony's program. Very, very fond of that shirt, I was, right up until it got ripped when we were playing with Dexys Midnight Runners.

· *Chapter 19* ·

"Stop fucking moaning, Hooky"

Talking of Mick Hucknall (which we weren't), his band the Frantic Elevators used to practice in TJ Davidson's. They also put music out on his label, T. J. M. Records. Come to think of it, he was the butt of a few of our japes, too, as were a lot of the bands in there. I think we reached our peak with the stinky toilet we found loose somewhere, tied a rope to, and lowered gently from our window on the top floor, swinging it to and fro until it crashed right through into V2's rehearsal room. When the Buzzcocks' tour came along, Rob treated us to brand-new flight cases courtesy of Bulldog Cases in London, and we terrorized the whole place, locking people in the cases—usually one of a young bunch of fans from Chorley, led by our soon-to-be-roadie Rex Sargeant, who used to hang round watching us practice. We'd push them down the stairs, over and over again. It was a good testing ground. Sometimes Ian would have a ride but only with Barney's crash helmet and gloves on because he was allergic to foam. We used to take him for a spin round the car park too.

We liked Tony Davidson, actually. We'd asked him to be our

manager before Rob came on the scene and he turned us down. He already managed the Distractions, V2, the Frantic Elevators—nearly all of the people who used his rehearsal rooms—but he passed on Joy Division; I don't think he got the music. He was absolutely devastated about it later. As soon as we started making it Tony was like, "Come back, I'll manage you now!" But Rob saw him off. Little tug-of-love between managers there. But again it was one of those funny things that starts happening when you see a bit of success, like the press suddenly becoming interested. A manager who turned you down suddenly knocking on your door.

That's what happens. We were still the same band, still doing the same things we'd always been doing: Ian had been doing his dance virtually since the beginning; the music was always there. Maybe we had a bit more swagger about us now—speaking for myself: yeah, definitely, of course—but otherwise the look hadn't changed. What we had was confidence and belief. Staying in Manchester and staying with Factory meant that we were staying with people who'd believed in us right from the beginning—who didn't like us just because we'd had some success, who would have liked us if we'd been successful or not—and that made us different and them special. After our next gig, which was at the YMCA on Tottenham Court Road, the guy from *NME* wrote that we were "un-cramped by commercial pressure" and he hit the nail on the head. Thanks to Tony and Rob there was no pressure: no pressure to promote, to sell, to kiss the right arse. The only condition was to keep on writing great songs. We were more than happy to oblige. Had we gone down a different route, there definitely would have been that pressure. Like I say, the Banshees had it; the Psychedelic Furs, the Cure, they all had it. We didn't.

That gig, though, at Tottenham Court Road, when we played with Echo & the Bunnymen and Teardrop Explodes . . . I remember I drove down in the van, as usual (and yes, it's another poor-old-me-in-the-van story coming up, but it's my book), and we parked in central London.

"Right, you wait here in case the promoter comes," said Rob to me. "We'll go get something to eat." "We" meaning him, Bernard, Ian, Steve, Dave, Terry, and Twinny, leaving me all alone with the van.

I said, "Well, what about me having something to eat, you bunch of bastards?"

They were like, "Stop fucking moaning, Hooky," then buggered off, and I sat there behind the wheel of the parked van, seething, thinking, *What a bunch of rotten bastards. Why do I drive the van? Why do I always get left behind?* The usual. Then I looked across and saw another van parked opposite me, a Transit with a guy in the driving seat, sitting muttering away to himself. A bloke in a group, you could tell.

I crossed the road to him and went, "All right, mate?"

He went, "All right, la."

"Who are you with, then?"

"Oh," he said, "I'm Les. I'm the bass player from Echo & the Bunnymen."

I said, "You what? You drive the van as well?"

"Yeah."

"Have they all fucked off and left you here to do the loading?"

"Yeah."

We became great mates after that, me and Les, both of us the bass player and van driver for our bands. But I was jealous because he had a double-wheel Transit: bigger load capacity and a more powerful engine, you see. On the other hand, my single-wheel was cheaper to run, and the band was saving quite a lot of money in travel and van-rental costs because of it. I still hated it, though, because it was me who had to drive and maintain the bloody thing—and even pay for it, remember. There were times I wished we'd never had it.

Well, they do say that you should be careful what you wish for. . .

· *Chapter 20* ·

"I just went for a piss"

London was still a big and sexy place to us, so it was always a bit of a thrill to play there, and to get a gig at the Nashville Rooms was extra-special. After all, that was where the Pistols had their famous concert that got them in *Melody Maker* that I saw in the car park at Newquay, which inspired me to go to see them, et cetera, et cetera.

It turned out to be one of those brilliant gigs, because this this was the first time I remember seeing the audience mouthing along with the words—and that is a really *Whoa* moment when you're in a band. Quite an odd sensation, really, when you think of where the song has come from—the four of you freezing your arses off in TJ Davidson's—to see that it's traveled all that way. It's sort of thrilling and embarrassing at the same time.

So it was a storming gig, apart from the fact that halfway through a guy climbed out of the audience—a punk who got up onstage. We thought, *This guy's come up to have a dance or whatever,* and kept on playing, but he sauntered right past us and went back to where the dressing room was.

We were looking at one another, like, *What the fuck's he playing at?* but still playing, when a couple of minutes later he reappeared and went to climb down off the stage back into the crowd. I stopped him. Still playing, I said, "Where the fuck have you been?"

"Oh, I just went for a piss," he said.

I said, "In our fucking dressing room? You cheeky get," and kicked him right offstage.

Fast-forward to about twenty years later, and this guy comes up to me, can't remember where it was, and says, "Hello."

"All right, mate,"

He said, "I saw you when you were Joy Division, at the Nashville Rooms in London. I was with my friend, who got up onstage and went for a piss in the dressing room, and you kicked him offstage."

"Yeah, I remember him," I said. "The cheeky bastard."

He said, "Yeah, well, he ended up hanging himself."

I went, "Oh. Fuck. He didn't hang himself because of that, did he?"

"Oh, no, not because of that. It was a few years after that."

I said, "Well thank fuck for that!" Which I realize wasn't the most sensitive response but I just had this image, you know?

Anyway, back to the gig. What used to happen when we packed the van after a gig was that Twinny would arrange all the gear so he could lie on the bass cab in a sleeping bag (not Barney's) and sleep all the way home. He wasn't there for that particular gig, though, which he was absolutely gutted about because it was one of the first gigs he'd ever missed. But we managed without him and, after the gig, packed the van and set off, me ahead of Steve, who had strict instructions to stay behind me because I was worried about the van not making the journey.

Knackered, it was, the van. We'd lost the petrol cap and

someone—not me—had replaced it with a rag to stop the petrol from evaporating. Trouble was, the rag had fallen in the tank and was merrily disintegrating. Every so often the fibres would block the filter on the main jet of the carburettor and stop it working. I could always tell when it was going to happen because the van started to slow down gradually, which it had been doing on the way to London that day. There was no power in it at all. And I knew that when I got home I'd have to take the air filter off, take the carburetor off, take it apart, renew all the gaskets, clean the main jet, put it back together again, put fucking everything back on, and then it would work fine for a while. What a job.

But first I needed to get home, and I was seriously doubting the van would make the trip. It was going really slowly, about thirty miles an hour top speed. We were pottering home. Next to me Terry fell asleep. I looked in my mirror and could see Steve but he'd dropped quite far behind; there was just me and him on the motorway, as it often was in those days, especially in the early hours of the morning.

We'd just joined the M5 when I started to feel sleepy. Terry was snoring away beside me and I couldn't see Steve in the mirror anymore. The next thing I knew there was this huge bang and the van suddenly shot forward so hard that my head hit the divider and for a second I was seeing stars, just barely aware of thinking that the carb must have suddenly cleared because our speed suddenly increased, at the same time feeling the van spin around and the pain. That and a massive squealing of tires.

I must have been dazed. Because when I got my vision back we were sitting on the hard shoulder, facing the right way, and I thought I was dreaming because a forty-foot lorry was sliding down the motorway past me, sideways on, its tires screeching as it drew to a stop right across the motorway, blocking all three lanes.

The next thing I saw was Ian Curtis running down the motorway chasing a drum that was rolling away—a drum that should have been in the back of my van.

My head was still clearing when Ian arrived at the window carrying the tom.

"Are you all right, Hooky? Are you all right?"

"What's happened?" I said, completely befuddled by the whole thing.

Terry was the same, looking around him in a complete daze. Turned out the forty-footer had hit us at about seventy miles an hour, shunting us and sending us spinning in two complete 360s; it had taken out the back of the van, snapping the back axle and flattening the rear doors. My bass cab had come shooting out the back like a comedy coffin, straight under the wheels of the forty-footer.

Thank God Twinny hadn't been sleeping on it.

I spent the rest of the night being held back from punching the lorry driver, who was from Manchester but wouldn't give us a lift back there. We cleared up our gear from the motorway, worrying that the coppers would find out about my bent MOT. I watched as it was towed away. It wasn't really until the next morning—well, it was the afternoon by the time I woke up—that the reality of it all hit me: the van was history. It was an ex-van. It had ceased to be. No more driving the van for me. From then on either Terry, Twinny, or Dave Pils drove a rented van, and every night after a gig I lived it up with the rest of the band in the bar, boozing and trying to pull girls.

On the one hand, it was absolutely magnificent. On the other hand, I ended up an alcoholic.

· Chapter 21 ·

"You shouldn't trust a word I say"

It was at the Nashville Rooms gig that Annik Honoré came into Joy Division's orbit. She and her friend Isabelle, having traveled from Belgium to see the band, approached the sound engineer at the venue, and then spoke to Rob Gretton, who agreed to an interview for Belgian fanzine En Attendant *[We're Waiting] on August 22, after the band's gig at Walthamstow Youth Club.*

I don't remember Annik at the Nashville Rooms, and only very vaguely recall the interview on August 22. But, looking at the dates and knowing the way that things played out and the relationship she and Ian started, well, it must have been a slow-burning thing. There was the small matter of the distance between them, for a start. Not to mention the fact that he was married and probably didn't want the complications of falling in love again. After all, he had enough on his plate.

I liked Annik, though, and still do. Years later we talked about that interview she did at Dave Pils's flat. It was featured in *Control* and my character's sitting there saying dopey things about the name "Buzzcocks," which I hated when I saw it. Made me look a right twat. I told Annik I would never have said anything so daft and she said to me, "Ah, but I have the tape, 'Ooky, and zat is exactly what you said."

So there you go. You shouldn't trust a word I say. Both Bernard and I had a go at bagging Annik, actually, but she got the measure of us straightaway and we were both a bit pissed off when Ian got her. Not that they were ever lovers. I suppose he couldn't because of all the pills he was on, or maybe didn't want to . . . How romantic. It was just another one of those things—something else that maybe used to gnaw at him.

Even so, he still used to cop off. He got caught with a girl in one of the riggers' caravans at the Futurama festival in Leeds (I've read that Annik was also there that day, which suggests that they hadn't quite got it together by then). But he'd always be complaining that he couldn't get a hard-on. It was hardly surprising he couldn't get it up, really; he was on that many pills it's a wonder he didn't rattle. We used to take the piss: "How come you're still copping off when you can't even get a hard-on? Stealing them off us?" But I think he did it just because he could. I mean, there you are, you're the front man of a band and girls always go for the front man. For ages nobody gave a fuck and no girls wanted to sleep with us. But suddenly they did give a fuck and did want to sleep with us. This sort of thing doesn't get talked about a lot, because it's a bit unsavory and it's not a part of Ian's character that anybody wants to dwell on, but he was no angel in that regard. No shrinking violet. He was poetic and romantic and soulful—of course he was—but he was still a guy in a band and he liked to do what guys in bands do. Which is to cop off with girls and have a laugh. I do think that's why God gave us bands—so ugly blokes can cop off.

What gets me sometimes about the deification of Ian is that it suggests a real division between Ian and the rest of the band that in reality wasn't there. I've no doubt he was different with us from how he was with Debbie and Annik, because that was the people pleaser in him. The Ian who was with Debbie is the one she talks about in her book; he's the one in *Control*, and you see the Annik-Ian there too. But what you don't see—and what's never really come out—is the Ian we saw in the band. That's because it doesn't fit neatly into the myth, which prefers the idea that Ian existed on another plane from the rest of us. But he didn't. He loved the lifestyle and would have indulged way, way more if it hadn't been for his epilepsy. He loved the music, and he loved the group. He was our mate. When Terry discovered this unusual-looking turd that somebody had left in the toilets at the Leigh Open Air Festival, and made us all look at it because it was so massive—like a pile of Swiss rolls, the most unbelievable turd I've ever seen in my life—Ian didn't go scurrying off to bury his head in a Dostoyevsky, much as he'd have liked Annik or Debbie to think that's how he'd have reacted. No, he was laughing just as hard and was just as grossed-out as all of us. Just like one of the lads.

I think in that sense we definitely had the best of him and you have to spare a thought for Debbie. We'd deliver Ian home and he'd be fucked. That's what you do as a group: you pick them up, take them away, drop them back off, and let someone else pick up the pieces. With Ian being married, an epileptic, and a new father, that wasn't easy. They argued. Ian and Debbie argued like cat and dog, actually. They had a car, a Morris Traveller, the one with wood on the sides; it was only ever Debbie who drove it and to be honest we always avoided getting in it with them because they'd always be shouting at each other. Following them in Steve's Cortina we'd see them ripping into each other, all the hand movements that go with it, car swerving all over the road: both screaming, both as bad as each other. You've got to look at it from both sides. It must have been hard for them. For him, the eternal people pleaser, trying to juggle his two lives. For her, always having to pick up the pieces and probably having nothing to show for it. After all, it wasn't like he was bringing home much money as a sweetener.

He hid a lot of the bad stuff from us. The domestic problems, the fits—he had many more fits at home than he did with the band, apparently, which would have been something else to contend with. I really do feel sorry for Debbie, having to put up with all of that. Especially when we got the nice bloke, the good-lad Ian, who was coming on leaps and bounds, his confidence growing all the time, the adulation building, and she got the exhausted, coming-down Ian, who probably wanted nothing to do with nappies and bills and all of that. Who just wanted to be back on the road with his group, playing music and soaking up all the worship.

You could see how much we were coming along when you see the *Something Else* footage. We were feeling very confident by this point, and even had a backdrop. Rob had paid a hundred quid for it, wanting us to look good for our first-ever national-TV spot. The Jam was on that day, too, and I remember waiting to go on and Paul Weller coming up to me and saying, "Are you the support band?"

I thought, "You cheeky bastard."

I once told that story at an awards ceremony, funnily enough, and it went over like a lead balloon, but it was true: that's exactly what he did—just assumed that every band appearing with the Jam was "the support." Wrong, mate, we're Joy Division.

They did a short interview with Tony and Steve. Me and Barney wanted to appear but Rob wouldn't let us. The words "two thick bastards" were used. Then we played "She's Lost Control" and "Transmission," and you can see how much stronger we were by then. Ian seems to be channeling the music. I can only begin to imagine what it must have been like for television viewers to switch on and see this dancing dervish on their screens. The impression he must have made.

Barney had this mate called Doctor Silk, who I think he worked with, or knew through work or something. Strange boy. He was a magician. When you spoke to him he'd be doing things with his hands and would suddenly do a trick. It was all very impressive the first few times he did it, but became tiring really quickly; by the fourth or fifth time you just wanted him to disappear. He had a very strange haircut and he didn't drink, which for some reason annoyed me and Twinny. Maybe I annoy people now that I don't drink. I don't know. Maybe he just had an annoying way of not drinking.

But anyway, because he was always doing stupid tricks and had this irritating not-drinking thing going on, me and Twinny made it our mission to get him pissed. We were doing this gig at the Factory, so after we'd sound checked in the afternoon we took Doctor Silk down the pub and started plying him with booze.

"Come on, mate, have another tomato juice! Have another!" By now we were putting double vodkas in his Bloody Mary but none in our own, thinking, *Ha, this'll get him.*

When he didn't seem to be getting at all pissed we started putting triple and quadruple vodkas in his drinks. Until, after a while, we realized that we were both pissed as farts and Doctor Silk as sober as a magician who had seen right through us, knew exactly what we were up to, and had been swapping the drinks round all night—giving us the spiked ones and supping the alcohol-free ones himself—which was exactly what we deserved.

Oh dear. By the time we staggered back to the Factory for the gig we were shitfaced. I found out later that Ian had had a fit in the dressing room, before the gig, but if I was told about it on the night, it didn't register—sorry, Ian—because I was so drunk. The rest of the band were giving me the evil eye, like, *Look at you, you're so pissed*, and I was giving it all that, like, *Pissed? I've never felt better. Bring it on, man, bring it on.*

So we were playing. Me arseholed, the other three sober as judges. We did the gig, the place going absolutely wild, and mid-song I was saying to Steve, "Faster, mate, faster."

Steve just looked at me from under his fringe, going, "Fuck off, Hooky. I can't go any faster." But I was forcing him to keep up with me, really pushing the songs forward so that each one was flying past and we were whipping the audience into a frenzy. A huge, messy mosh pit had developed at the front, a right melee, even more brutal than usual. And there was this one kid—a real fan, you could tell, because he was by himself and he was mouthing the words to the songs and had lots of badges on his jacket—when suddenly, *Bok*.

Some guy had nutted him on the back of the head. For no reason at all that I could see. No provocation. This guy had just stepped forward, grabbed the fan by the hair, and struck. Really vicious, it was, and the fan dropped like all the air had been let out of him.

Straightaway I saw red, pulled my guitar off, held it by the neck, and swung it at the boot boy, all in one movement. Trouble was, I was pissed. I don't think I even connected. Instead what happened was the weight of the bass pulled me offstage and into the audience where the same kid and his mates descended on me. Swarmed all over, like those little dinosaurs in *Jurassic Park*, and held me down. Then the kicks started landing.

I thought, *This is it. I'm going to die.*

Did the band stop? Did, Barney, Steve, and Ian wade in to help their mate getting battered by the boot boys? No, they didn't. They played on. It was Twinny who leapt from the stage, twatted one of the kids, grabbed me, pulled me up, punched another, and then took the original thug by the scruff of the neck and together we dragged him all the way back to the mixing desk and started leathering him.

Suddenly the kid was going, "I'm a fan. I'm a fan!" We looked down and he was covered in Joy Division badges: this was just some other poor kid we'd picked up on the way and we'd been beating up the wrong guy. By this time people were dragging us off and I'd hardly had time to apologize before he was gone. Still the band was playing and I was throwing insults at them. I'd climbed back up on the stage and was calling them miserable twats for not helping me—"I was getting my head kicked in, y'bastards!"—calling them all the names as they played "Atrocity Exhibition" like nothing had happened. Like I hadn't just almost been ripped apart in the audience. Then I stormed off into the dressing room, picked up a bottle, and threw it at the wall—just as Ian came in.

It just missed him, luckily. "You're such a yobbo," he said.

"You're such a fucking poof!" I screamed back at him. Bernard, Steve, and Rob then arrived. "I only decked off to help one of our fans. I didn't see any of you bastards wading in."

(Of course, I didn't mention that we had accidentally beaten up a fan. You don't want to let a little thing like that get in the way of your righteous indignation, do you?)

"I tell you what," I was still shouting, "you fucking wait until you're getting the shit kicked out of you. I'm fucking leaving you there!"

Twinny resigned on the spot, calling them all the names under the sun, and stormed off, only to be grabbed outside by Mike Nolan, the Buzzcocks' tour manager, who was very impressed by his onstage actions and asked if he would do stage security for them, for extra money, on the upcoming tour. Twinny came straight back in the dressing room and withdrew his resignation.

The next day we had a band meeting. Of course I'd sobered up by then.

"Why did do you do that, Hooky?"

"You really upset Ian."

"Sorry, Ian."

"You almost hit Ian with a bottle."

"Oh God, sorry, Ian."

"He'd had a fit earlier."

"Oh, fuck, I'm so sorry, Ian, it won't happen again."

It was lucky for me that the bass was integral to so many of the songs: otherwise they would have kicked me out for sure. In the end they settled for Rob giving me a telling-off, although he must secretly have been pleased because we got a lot of publicity out of it. As far as I was concerned it was the beginning of a reputation that I've been trying to live down ever since. Everyone started gunning for me from then on: "Let's get that fucking twat Hooky because he'll kick off."

And for a long time, of course, I was only too happy to oblige.

· *Chapter 22* ·

"Bring it on"

Next, Joy Division embarked on a British tour supporting the Buzzcocks, who were promoting their third album, A Different Kind of Tension, *and by all accounts struggling to maintain their edge. Quite apart from the prestige of the tour—and the fact that an on-form Joy Division is widely believed to have overshadowed the Buzzcocks almost every night—this meant the band members could leave their jobs to finally go professional.*

Now, this was a bit more like it. We were a proper band now. On £12 a week—£15 for Ian, with a week in hand because he had a family to feed and Debbie had kicked off proper. Rob kept a tally so he could pay back the extra later. Only on £1.50 per diem still, but it didn't matter. We were professional musicians. The first thing we did when we arrived for the opening date in Liverpool was to look up our old friends the Buzzcocks, who we hadn't seen for about a year.

Our dressing room was the kind of dressing room you'd expect for a band on the bones of their arses: some plastic chairs and a couple of wire coat hangers. But the Buzzcocks' dressing room was a completely different proposition. They had the luxury version and, looking at the activity there, we were rubbing our hands together with glee. All kinds of crates and trolleys were being loaded in: beer, sweets, sarnies, piles of clean towels, the works. Earlier, one of their crew had been flashing a bagful of interesting-looking pills, one color to get you up, another color to get you down, just like in *Quadrophenia*, not to mention a huge block of dope, as if to say, *This, lads, is the rock-'n'-roll lifestyle. Get ready to party. . . .*

We were as ready as we'd ever be. Bring it on. They even had a huge tattooed guy with thick chains around his neck standing guard at their dressing-room door to keep out all the undesirables. Perfect.

"Where are you going, dickhead?" he said as we rolled up ready to become reacquainted with the Buzzcocks and partake of their beer, sweets, and sarnies.

"We come to see our mates, the Buzzcocks," I replied. "We started with them in 1976. Very good friends with them, we are."

"Fuck off," he said, and stepped in front of the door with his arms folded across his chest.

"Oi, you can't do that!" I said.

He could and did. This was Sarge, and he went on to become one of my best mates—he still is. And if Sarge says you're not going in a dressing room, then you're not going in it.

So we skulked off, denied entry. Always guarded by Sarge, the dressing room became a source of fascination for us, the door a portal to another world, a Narnia filled with clean towels, crisps, and groupies. If the Buzzcocks were onstage and Sarge went for a piss we'd be straight in there, helping ourselves to beer and biscuits. Or we'd loiter around until the end of the night when they'd all buggered off, move in, and hoover up the dregs.

Otherwise they'd be in it, and the only times we saw much of them during the tour was on the night of the gigs, when one of them—Pete Shelley, usually—would tell us what a wonderful time they were having at whichever five-star hotel they were staying at.

"I've had lobster Thermidor," he said to us one night, like Little Lord Fauntleroy. Back in our dressing room with its torn-up seats and wire coat hangers we called them a bunch of bastards who'd forgotten their roots. We were like, "Lobster Thermidor? What the fuck is lobster Thermidor?" I thought they were a local band.

I think the Buzzcocks thought of us as their rough cousins, to whom they couldn't say no in case they caused trouble, which we were a bit, I suppose. It might seem strange now, but at the time they were the middle-class arty types and we were the working-class yobbos. I mean, they had a new bass player, Steve Garvey, who used to change his strings every night. *Every night?* I changed mine when I broke one, and in between times I boiled them in vinegar to get the finger fat off. That's how different we were then.

Thing is, they had too much of the good life. They were trying to do something new with the album they were touring, *A Different Kind of Tension*, which had a more adult-oriented rock sound, and they'd gotten fat and bloated—musically and physically. Meanwhile we were at the top of our game, playing a tight half hour or so of great music every night, and every night—apart from in Manchester, where they had a very loyal audience—we blew them offstage. A lesson there: never have a support band who are at the top of their game. As New Order we had OutKast supporting us once. Big mistake that was.

So that was good, anyway; it was satisfying to feel like we were at the top of our game, even eclipsing the mighty Buzzcocks. Plus it was luxury for us to not have to get up for work in the morning. I was living with Iris and she'd get upset because I'd still be in bed when she left for work. She hated it so much she used to deliberately miss the bus so I'd have to get out of bed and drive her into the Co-Op in town. I'd have got in at three in the morning, something daft, but she'd insist I drive her in. I found out years later she never really missed the bus, just let it go past. Women. Still beat going in to work, though. All I'd do was hang around until the afternoon, wait for Steve to come and get me, then go on to the next venue, wherever it was, meet Twinny, Terry, and Dave Pils and listen to them regaling me with tales of whatever they'd got up to the night before.

The reason? Our crew was traveling with their crew on the tour bus, staying in the same hotels as the band. It was always going to be good. Jammy bastards. They had to be there to set up our gear for the early sound checks.

"All right, lads, what did you do last night?"

"Fucking great night, mate. We were up till half five boozing with the band, all doing blueys and smoking dope and chatting up these girls. It was fucking excellent, mate."

They rubbed it in. God, did they rub it in. We were the band and we were snuggled up in bed at night while our crew was living the rock-'n'-roll lifestyle. What a swizz. Me, Steve and Bernard were dead jealous.

But not Ian, of course. Outwardly Ian was the same as he'd always been. One of the lads. But with the benefit of hindsight you can begin to appreciate some of the pressure he was under: his attraction to Annik and the side effects of the pills; the responsibility he felt to both band and home. This was the period during which Debbie was most on his case about money (understandably, mind: they had a new baby); we knew that Debbie was on Ian's case because she was also on Rob's case. Debbie was the one who took against Rob's "no partners" rule the most and she'd be coming in to rehearsal wanting to have it out with him, mostly over money. There's no doubt she was a force to be reckoned with, and you'd have to say that if she was like that with us then she was possibly twice as forceful at home. Maybe because of that pressure, or perhaps just a general worsening of his condition, or the fact that he was spending more time with the band and was less able to hide it, Ian began having more seizures, often during the gigs themselves. Rob used to have mega fights with lighting men at the venues, telling them not to flash the lights; the flashing would always set Ian off. But the lighting men must have either thought, *Fuck off, y'Manc bastard, telling me what to do*, or got carried away, or forgot, because they'd start a light going off on the snare, then on the sides. We'd notice but too late: by then Ian would have stopped singing and gone into a trance, and then he'd either fall over into the drum kit or go ape shit onstage. We started using these washes of lights, which became our trademark—yet another of those things that unintentionally ended up defining us—and which we carried through into New Order. But sometimes he'd just go anyway. Ian had excellent microphone craft—you only have to look at the pictures to see how natural he was on the microphone—and of course he had the dance as well. Mesmerizing. Trouble was, it would set him off. He'd work himself up into a frenzy and go. It was like he couldn't help himself, and we'd end up having to carry him off the stage.

There was a bad one on the second date of the tour, at Leeds, when I had to hold him down backstage. Holding his tongue, I thought he wasn't going to come out of it—that he was going to die. After that he should have rested, of course. (And why didn't we insist? Because he said he was all right, that's why. And because it suited us to take his word for it.) But the next night he was playing Newcastle and the night after that we were in Scotland, where we were staying away from home and behaving like pigs at a trough.

Now, there's a story. It all started at the Hilton in Glasgow, the first time we got to stay out with the Buzzcocks. The bands and our crew were all in this hotel, drinking in the bar. Drinking like mad things, charging the drinks to other people's rooms, getting absolutely arseholed. Us lot were crowded round Sarge, who was of great interest to us because he'd been in the Hells Angels—a former sergeant-at-arms, which accounted for his nickname. The sergeant-at-arms is the guy who does all the enforcing. He polices the Angels, and one of Sarge's jobs was to preside over the initiations, which he was telling us about, one of them being that the new guys have to drink a pint of piss.

We were like, "How fucking disgusting is that?" and Sarge just shrugged.

So Ian said, "Go on then, you drink a pint of piss."

"All right," said Sarge, "You get a pint of piss and I'll drink it. But it's going to cost you a fiver."

That was it. Us lot were running around scabbing money off people to pay him to drink the piss, and once we'd got enough we set about filling the pint pot—Terry mainly, whose piss was like treacle it was that thick and brown.

We handed our warm pint pot of thick, treacle piss to Sarge and put it on the table, watching as he looked at it then dipped his hand in it then put it in his mouth.

He went, "It's warm. I want a tenner."

We raised more, gave it to him, then watched as he downed the pint in one, banged the glass down, and said, "Right, shit sandwich for twenty quid."

Shit sandwich. We needed some bread for a shit sandwich.

Disaster—we couldn't find any bread. Next thing you know, the whole lot of us were tearing around the hotel trying to find bread. Me and Dave Pils ran down a corridor and came across this breakfast trolley that had all the stuff in it you could wish for, so we started rooting around in it and then, for no good reason—apart from that I was pissed and it seemed like a good idea at the time—I turned the trolley over on Dave and pinned him to the floor. Lying there covered in knives and forks, and little pots of marmalade and sachets of brown sauce, he was laughing, calling me a bastard, then he shoved off the trolley and came at me, grabbed a huge plant out of a pot, and began swinging it at me.

One messy plant-pot fight later and we got back to the bar, only to find it had been closed because we were getting so rowdy. We weren't having that. They're supposed to leave it open all night if you want. So, even though it was four o'clock in the morning and we were as pissed as bastards—or more likely *because* it was four o'clock in the morning and we were as pissed as bastards—one of the Buzzcocks' lighting crew ripped the shutters off the bar and we all dived in. Midway through that session somebody shouted that the cops were on their way—they weren't; it was just somebody being a bastard—and we all scarpered. Never has a bar emptied of people so quickly. Then we all passed out in our beds.

I woke up the next morning to discover two things: first, that I'd slept with my arm out of the bed; and second, that the police really were on their way. The theft/vandalism/whatever you want to call it in the bar had been discovered and Joy Division was being blamed. For about half an hour we ran about like headless chickens, Rob grabbing our clothes for us and shoving them into bags, desperately trying to get us out of the hotel before the police arrived. The Buzzcocks' management could sort it out later. We just needed to concentrate on not being taken into custody and risk missing that night's gig in Edinburgh.

We made it. Just. Left behind our wreckage and traveled on to Edinburgh, all of us except Steve nursing terrible hangovers and me wondering about my arm sticking out of the bed like that—and this is the funny thing, because ever since that night I've always had to sleep with one arm hanging out of the bed.

We kept our noses clean until we got to Dundee, where we decided that Twinny was getting too big for his boots, because he was always sniding off with the Buzzcocks, so we decided to jape his room.

First order of business was to get all his clothes and tie them to a flagpole outside the hotel. Then we took the bed out of his room and replaced it with a baby's cot we found in the corridor and then, because Twinny's dead superstitious, we took out all the lightbulbs, tied a bit of string around the coat hangers in his room, and fed it through the connecting door, where we waited, giggling.

And waited. Five o'clock in the morning, when Twinny finally got back to his room, pissed as a fart, and we'd long since stopped giggling. But still, we felt extra-justified now that he'd spent all night living it up with the Buzzcocks again! So when he got into the room and we heard him flicking the light switch to no avail, we started rattling the coat hangers. He freaked. Shouted something about the room being haunted and tried to escape. But because he was pissed and the room was pitch-black he fell over, right into the cot, which smashed to pieces.

He passed out and the next morning was furious, demanding we give him his clothes. We just pointed him in the direction of the flagpole and told him it served him right.

· *Chapter 23* ·

"Turned out to be horse meat"

We had a break from the Buzzcocks tour to do our next gig, which was at Plan K in Brussels, a big arty happening with a William Burroughs reading, screenings of films, Joy Division, and Cabaret Voltaire. We were almost late getting there because Terry was driving the van. The thing was, Terry, Twinny, and Dave Pils got on really badly sometimes, always bickering, and it was only me that kept them from battering each other. But now that we were a proper professional band with paid road crew (in other words, them) I didn't drive the van anymore so I didn't travel with the crew; I went in Steve's Cortina. Luxury. But it did mean that the Three Stooges didn't have anyone to keep them apart; and on the day we left for Brussels they must have had some massive fallout because Terry was in a bad mood, and because he was in a bad mood he was driving at Miss Daisy speeds down the motorway and kept pulling over. Never the most competent of drivers, he was telling me that he couldn't get the van to go over thirty miles an hour and I ended up replacing him in the driver's seat and flooring it down the motorway rather than risk missing the ferry. I got it up to eighty, though, and we made it to Brussels, which was dead exciting—the first time we'd traveled outside the UK.

Somehow we found Michel Duval, the organizer, who took us to the hotel and we were buzzing—even more so at the thought of the luxurious Brussels hotel he was bound to have chosen for us.

Except when we got there it wasn't a hotel. It wasn't even a B&B. It was a youth hostel. Instead of having rooms with two sharing, which is what we were used to, we had to sleep in this huge dormitory. We grabbed the best beds. Steve, being too slow, got one with a big lump in it where the springs had broken and when he lay on it he was all bent over; Barney was already complaining that he wouldn't be able to get any kip, being such a light sleeper, even though it had never seemed to bother him before; while Ian took one look at the setup and went off to try to wangle a bed elsewhere—which he did, with Cabaret Voltaire in their normal, nice room, before returning to rub our noses in it.

With our sleeping arrangements sorted we went to the gig, which was at this huge, amazing "art space," I suppose you'd have to say. We did our bit and it was really good gig, and afterward me, Ian, and Barney went along to see William Burroughs then stood around as he sat at a table signing books.

Ian was a bit awestruck, but poor, so he couldn't afford to buy one of the books William Burroughs was signing. "I'm going over to ask him if I can have a book," he said, after standing there for ages looking over at the table like a kid eyeing up a plate of warm pies or something.

Me and Barney thought this was hilarious. I mean, looking at William Burroughs, how grizzled and world-weary he looked, he didn't seem like the kind of guy who was in the habit of handing out freebies to oiks from Macclesfield. Still, Ian had sunk a couple of Duvels and was feeling brave and we were winding him up something rotten. So when there was a lull in visitors to William Burroughs's table he strolled over, ignoring us two, who went and hid behind a pillar nearby, sniggering.

"Oh hello, Mr. Burroughs," he said, "I'm a big fan of yours, and . . ."

William Burroughs looked at him and growled. "Yeah, kid, yeah. Whatever."

He'd probably been hearing that all night—from people who were at least buying his books.

"Well, I'm in the band Joy Division who played tonight . . ."

"Yeah, kid, yeah. Whatever," growled William Burroughs.

"Well, I was wondering if I could have a book?"

"*Have* a book?" snapped William Burroughs.

"Yeah."

He looked at Ian. "Fuck off, kid," he said, and Ian slunk away, tail between his legs, as we wet ourselves laughing. We then spent the rest of the night growling, "Fuck off, kid," at Ian—whose response was to get really, really pissed.

He wasn't the only one. Twinny: also absolutely pissed. I found him outside and instead of loading our gear into the back of the van he'd raided the bar and had stacked the van full of stolen beer. We made him put it all back so we could get the gear in, so we could return to the youth hostel. When we got there, it was absolute carnage. Back in the dorm, Twinny discovered this Belgian guy asleep in his bed.

"Oi, you, fuck off!" he was shouting, just hollering at the bloke, who in return looked terrified, like a rabbit in the headlights. Twinny was advancing on him and would probably have grabbed the guy if I hadn't stepped between them.

"Twinny," I said, "he can't understand you, y'daft bastard. He's a Belgian. You'll have to speak French to him."

Twinny looked at me, nodded, and went to the guy, "Oi, you. *Fucky offy.*"

Poor bloke just got out of bed and legged it, by which time the lot of us were in absolute hysterics and there was no stopping us. Ian was laughing because he was going off for a good night's kip in Cabaret Voltaire's room and it was obvious that things in our dorm were only going to get more out of control. Barney was moaning about something then started having a fight with Twinny, but Twinny got carried away and upended Barney's bed, with him on it, so Barney came flying off and hit his head on a radiator. That completely enraged him, so he picked up a bottle of orange squash, smashed the end off on the radiator, and poured it all over Twinny's bed. Twinny's response was to smash open two bottles of Duvel and pour them on Barney's bed, by which point we were telling them both to calm the fuck down before someone got hurt. Just then Ian got his knob out and started pissing in our ashtray—one of those tall freestanding ashtrays, it was—thinking it was hilarious, looking back over his shoulder going, "Ha, you wankers, I'm pissing in your room! Ha-ha, pissing in your room!" It was one of those pisses that just seemed to go on and on forever, like a donkey's, and we were calling him a dirty bastard when a caretaker walked into the room flanked by two security goons.

The guy went berserk. Ian wasn't smiling anymore. He was trying to stuff his cock back into his trousers and at the same time pacify the caretaker, who was turning all shades of purple, calling Ian in French what we'd just been calling him in English, except that now Ian didn't think it was at all funny.

"I don't understand French," he was saying. "I'm sorry. I don't understand French. Just tell me what you want me to do and I'll do it."

Whatever it was he did to calm the caretaker down, I don't

know, but he did, and the festivities continued and next thing I passed out, one arm hanging out of the bed.

Next morning we woke up in this wreckage of a dorm, with orange and Duvel and Ian's piss everywhere, hungover to shit, desperately needing something to eat and ending up in what we thought was a burger bar. There we spent the last of our money on seven burgers, which they handed us to eat raw. Turned out to be horse meat, and of course none of us could eat it so we went hungry.

Which served us all right, I suppose.

That was our Belgium jaunt. On our return home we went straight back on tour with the Buzzcocks, but somewhere in the middle of all that madness we found time to record what would go on to become one of our best-known tracks, "Atmosphere," which we did for *Licht und Blindheit*, a French-territory-only EP. Who puts one of their best songs on a limited-edition single available only in France? Us, that's who.

"Atmosphere" is a massive song. A lot of people say it's their favorite Joy Division song, but it's not mine; it reminds me too much of Ian, like it's his death march or something, and it figures that it's one of the most popular songs to play at funerals: Robbie Williams has got "Angels" for weddings and we've got "Atmosphere" for funerals. Becky says that when I die she's going to play "Atmosphere" at my funeral—but by Russ Abbott. Thanks, love.

So no, "Atmosphere" isn't my favorite. If you were to ask me what was, it would have to be "Insight." I mean, it might change tomorrow, but it's "Insight" right now because it's just so simple but so powerful—and it doesn't have a chorus. That was one of the things I really liked about Joy Division, that the songs didn't have to have a chorus or a middle eight. I used to love it about New Order, too, until we started to get all formal about the writing, until by the end every song had a verse, chorus, and middle eight, which to me just made everything bland.

But "Insight" doesn't have all that. To me it's the sound of a group of young musicians working out the possibilities of what they can do, and working them out together. Changing the world. It reminds me of a time when writing music was easy but most of all fun.

The release of the "Transmission" seven-inch in October had proved to be a disappointment for Tony Wilson, who had hoped that its chorus of "Dance, dance, dance to the radio" would win it radio airplay. Plans to hire a radio plugger were shelved at the insistence of Rob Gretton and Martin Hannett, who felt that to promote the single went against the Factory ethos. As a result, and despite critical acclaim, just three thousand of the ten thousand copies ordered by Wilson were sold. Rob Gretton was to orchestrate the band's next act of commercial defiance, striking a deal with French label Sordide Sentimental. Set up in France in 1978 by Jean-Pierre Turmel and Yves Von Bontee, it had piqued his interest with a superbly packaged release of Throbbing Gristle's "We Hate You (Little Girls)," and a deal was made to release two Joy Division songs in similar fashion: "Atmosphere" and "Dead Souls," produced by Martin Hannett during sessions at Cargo in October. Finally released in March 1980, The Licht und Blindheit *EP was limited to just 1,578 copies, mail-order only, with most fans having to content themselves with taping it from the John Peel program.*

The tracks that Throbbing Gristle put out on Sordide Sentimental were never going anywhere else. I mean, they were harsh even by the standards of Throbbing Gristle. Whenever I put that EP on, my cat used to run out of the room. Us? We put two of our best songs on it. On a limited edition that we never even got any money for. The run was 1,578 copies; I found out years later that 1578 was also the last date the French beat the English in a war.

Having said that, it didn't bother us at the time—this came during a period when we were continually writing great songs, so it didn't seem like such a big deal, to be honest. And, looking at it in terms of the whole Joy Division story, well, it's just "us" isn't it? That special attitude championed by Rob and accepted by Tony that was either total naïveté, utter stupidity, incredible foresight, or a weird mix of all three. I honestly don't know. I mean, people said we were mad at the time—other bands and their managers, I mean. But Rob loved it. He loved being bloody-minded and contrary and he liked nothing better than winding up Tony.

"Atmosphere" was originally written in two halves. The bass and drums was one idea—me and Steve came up with it together. The vocals and the keyboards was another idea. We'd been working on them separately, just tinkering with them, really, then put them together and got the song that we called "Chance," featuring our Woolies organ borrowed from Barney's gran.

It would be a few years yet before we got overdrawn at the riff bank. This was the time, after all, that we also wrote "Love Will Tear Us Apart" and ended up recording it for the first time as part of a second John Peel session in November. It was a song we'd written during rehearsals at TJ's. I had the riff, Steve built the drum part, and Ian mumbled some words then said he was going to go home and write some lyrics for it, which he did, using the bass riff as the melody for the chorus. But Christ, if he'd written that song about me I'd have been heartbroken. I'm not sure who it was written about. I never asked. But whoever it was deserves all of his money just for that.

· *Chapter 24* ·

"He's possessed by the devil, that twat"

Still with the Buzzcocks tour, we were traveling farther afield in the UK and Ian began having more fits. He had a really bad one in Bournemouth. He was so tired by the time we got there. We all were, of course—absolutely knackered—but the rest of us weren't on heavy medication. We didn't have a wife and a baby, and our affairs of the heart weren't quite so complicated.

After a gig in Guildford the night before, Rob had shaved the band's hair with clippers. Ian, Bernard, and Steve got sheared; only I got away with it. We were staying at a B&B where Bernard had to go and sleep in the bathroom to get away from Rob's snoring—the start of a regular habit for him—there was a lot more booze involved and it was all a bit of a riot one way or another. The upshot being that by the time we reached Bournemouth we were shattered—especially Ian. Most of the seizures he had occurred toward the end of gigs but this one was near the beginning of the show, which we had to stop. It lasted about an hour and a half, with me and Rob taking turns holding him down in the dressing room; once again with me holding his tongue in his mouth to stop him from swallowing it. Christ, it was scary.

He came round and was looking at us, his eyes all glassy.

"Ian," I said to him, "Can you hear me, mate? We're going to have to get you to the hospital." He shook his head: he understood me all right but he didn't want to go to the hospital. Never did; didn't want to be a bother. That was him all over.

"Look, Ian, mate; it's not right; you've been fitting too long. We're taking you whether you like it or not."

He was still dead reluctant to go and in a funny sort of way he was right. You take a guy who's just had an epileptic fit to the ER and the nurse looks at you like you've just dropped in from Venus. And that's exactly what happened when we'd bundled Ian into the car, got him to the nearest hospital, and waited hours for our turn to be seen.

They did at least have the good grace to take him into a consulting room, while we hung about in the waiting room. After a while he came out. A bit pale, bit downcast. Otherwise okay.

"You all right, Ian?"

"Yeah, yeah, I'm okay. Don't worry about it."

He went back to the gig, where the Buzzcocks had only just come on, and there was no sign of Twinny anywhere. After searching for a while I found him in a cupboard, all curled up in a ball like he was hiding from something.

"What the fuck are you doing in here?" I said.

"He's possessed by the devil, that twat."

"Get up, you soft bastard," I said, dragging him out. "Stop fucking around. Go and see him. He's back to normal now."

Whatever "normal" was. For Ian "normal" was getting hardly any rest, eating shit food, getting pissed, traveling all the time, driving from city to city. The precise opposite of everything he should have been doing. I look back and keep seeing where we should have stopped. It's the part of doing this book that's the hardest. Writing it all down, I can pinpoint the moments where we should have said "enough is enough"—because now they seem so obvious. But at the time he just carried on and so did we. Selfishness, stupidity, willful ignorance, and a refusal to accept what was going on right in front of our noses—we were all guilty of it, even Ian. Because this was what we'd worked and waited for. All that freezing in TJ's and fighting with the Drones and feeling ignored and overlooked was paying off at last. I wish sometimes I could tell the younger me, "Slow down, mate, what's the big hurry? You've got another thirty or forty years of this," knowing that the twenty-two-year-old me would curl his lip and tell the old me to fuck off, because when you're twenty-two it feels like if you don't seize the moment then it'll be gone in a puff of smoke.

Even so, I find it mind-boggling that someone didn't slap Rob Gretton and the rest of us and drag Ian off home to bed. But nobody did. Things just got more and more manic. On the Buzzcocks tour the practical jokes continued. Unsuspecting victims would open doors and get wastepaper bins of rubbish or water dumped on their heads. Or they'd sit in chairs we'd balanced on Coke cans so they'd topple over.

Of course there were times it got right out of hand. One night, around about the time of fireworks night, the whole lot of us—me, Terry, Dave Pils, Rob, and Steve—burst in on Ian and Barney, who were with a couple of girls in a hotel room, Barney in one bed, Ian in the other. Dave lit a couple of bangers and threw them into the room, where one of them landed on Barney's shirt and set it on fire.

Barney went berserk—absolutely wild. After he'd put the shirt out, he was calling us all sorts and shouting at us to fuck off and waving his burnt shirt around. In return we were giving him the V's and telling him he could fuck off and that he deserved it (although I'm not sure he did, actually; it was probably jealousy on our part, but there you go). Ian thought it was hilarious and these two girls, both completely naked, were absolutely terrified, poor things, the room suddenly full of Northerners chucking fireworks around, setting clothes alight, and swearing at each other. Hardly the erotic feast they might have been hoping for.

We would have spent all night screaming at one another had the hotel porter not arrived and kicked off. As he was shouting at us, Barney stormed out of the room, giving it all, "Right, you fuckers, I'll show you," as a parting shot, and we were like, "Yeah, yeah, fuck off," as he went.

Everything calmed down. Most of us went to the bar for a drink, gave the girls a bit of privacy at last, and as we were sitting there Barney came in, still raging.

"Where've you been?" we said.

"You'll see,' he was saying. "You'll fucking see, you bunch of bastards."

We were like, "Fuck off, twatto," finishing our drinks. Only to discover the following morning that the stupid twat had let all four tires down on the car.

I was like, "What you do that for?"

"You burnt my fucking shirt."

"But you've japed yourself. You have to travel in that car as well, you stupid twat."

Of course, it took us hours to get the four tires pumped up. We had to buy a foot pump then take it in turns. We were all sweating like bastards, including Barney.

A lot of the japes took place between us and the Buzzcocks and their crew, and in the run-up to the last gig of the tour, which was at the Rainbow at Finsbury Park, their guys were telling us that they were going to spring something really big on us, really nasty, for our last night.

"Oh, we're going to get you. We're going to get you," they were saying. "When you're onstage, mate, mid-performance. We got something very special in mind for you."

But fuck 'em: they were messing with the kings and straightaway we formed a council of war to concoct our retaliation. What we came up with involved the purchase of twelve live mice—we wanted rats but we couldn't afford them—ten pounds of live maggots, ten cans of shaving foam, and five dozen eggs. That was all we could afford. A fortune was spent on this jape, but it was going to be worth it.

The plan was to get the Buzzcocks with the maggots during their performance. They'd think that was all we had to offer, but in the meantime we'd have put the live mice inside their tour bus and used the shaving foam on the doors and windows. They'd deal with the shaving foam, board the bus, see the mice, run screaming off the bus and we'd egg as they came out. Brilliant. We were as good as inventing japes as we were at writing songs.

So it got to the gig. Even though we knew we had something lined up we were still worried about what they'd do to us. Their crew was all sniggering. We'd been threatened with the jape to end them all. All week they'd been leading up to this. What would they have come up with? What horrors lay in store for us?

They put some talcum powder on the snare drum.

That was it. That was the full extent of their world-beating jape. A bit of talcum powder on the snare drum. I didn't even notice at the time. As we were coming off I said to Steve, "What's happened to the Buzzcocks' jape, then?" and Steve told me that they'd put a bit of talc on his snare drum and when he'd hit it a little cloud had come up. That was it.

What a bunch. Oh dear: our response was going to look a bit on the disproportionate side. Still, more fools them for doing such a lame joke, we thought, and seeing them chortling away, thinking they'd been dead funny with their talc-on-the-snare-drum trick, just made us even more determined to set about our reply as planned. We waited until they came on and launched phase one of the plan: the maggots.

Ten pounds of them, we had. That's a lot of maggots. That's five bags of sugar's worth of maggots. Toward the end of their set, as they started playing "Boredom," we livened things up by creeping up behind the crew with our bags: a couple of bags of maggots each, emptying them first onto the flight cases where the Buzzcocks' crew sat to watch the set, then onto the Buzzcocks' backdrop, which the maggots began crawling up, just as we'd hoped they would, and then onto the fold-back desk.

Barely holding it together we retreated to watch the mayhem from a safe distance, watching the maggots advance. The crew noticed something first. A tide of maggots had made its way from the flight cases up the backs of the crew, then into their hair. We watched as first one then another started to scratch and a horrible realization dawned on them. The next wave of maggots had by now worked their way up the backdrop and were falling on the Buzzcocks' drummer, John Maher. Now the guys on the fold-back desk were running around screaming. So was the rest of the crew. John Maher finished "Boredom" in a shower of maggots and the band came off, furious with us.

That was it, they thought. Jape over. How wrong they were. They had two buses outside, one for the band and their girlfriends and another one for the crew. We'd prized open the windows, dropped in the mice, coated all the door handles in shaving foam, then returned to the Rainbow for an end-of-tour party.

Sarge let us into the dressing room. At last. Allowed inside the sacred dressing room. And what a riot that turned into, everybody pissed. Their lot were laughing about the talc on the snare drum—ho-ho, what a funny jape—and we were laughing about the maggots, letting them think that was the end of it but secretly anticipating the carnage we'd prepared for when they got to their buses.

One food fight later and it was time to leave, so we scarpered out quick and piled into Steve's Cortina, parking up beneath an underpass or railway bridge or something, oblique to where the buses were and across the road, each bus primed with six live mice in it and the windows and door handles coated with shaving cream.

So we watched . . . And out came the Buzzcocks and their girlfriends and, in hysterics, we then watched them cursing us and wiping off the shaving cream. They saw us over the road and started screaming at us, but didn't even bother trying to get us—we'd have been out of there while they were still doing the Green Cross Code. We cradled our eggs as we watched them clean off the last bits of foam and board the bus, then we waited for them to come running out as soon as they saw the mice.

But they didn't. The bus drove off. We looked at one another. Shit. Still, at least we had the crew to come. Sure enough, a little bit later, out came the crew; they now saw their bus with shaving cream all over it, started wiping it off, spotted us, and were shouting insults while we sat there killing ourselves and holding on to our eggs, watching them clean up and board their bus.

This time it worked a treat. Seconds after the bus door had shut it opened again and out poured the road crew, falling down the steps, screaming, "Rats! Rats!"

Brilliant. We were already out of the car and legging it across the road, where we started pelting the lot of them with eggs. It was all over in seconds. We covered them in egg then scarpered back to the Cortina, busting a gut with laughter—only to find a couple of coppers standing there.

Behind us over the road was complete mayhem, with the crew only just recovering from the egg attack, their bus covered in egg and shaving foam, and shitting it about the rats inside. One of the coppers pointed over. "You do realize that's vandalism?"

Then, for some reason, Dave Pils went, "Is this 'cause I'm black?"

Which was funny, because he isn't black.

"But you're not black, Dave."

"It's 'cause my girlfriend's black."

Jasmine was black—he was right about that.

"Dave . . ."

"It is, isn't it, you racist bastard?"

"*Dave.*"

We managed to calm the police down but it took us about fifteen minutes, by which time the Buzzcocks' crew had got rid of the mice, got in their bus, and fucked off back to the hotel to meet up with the band.

"Fucking Joy Division put rats in our bus. Did they get you?"

"No," said the band, "they wouldn't fucking dare put rats in our bus."

But Sarge told us later that he'd been in the bus, and Steve Diggle was in there chatting to his girlfriend when Sarge had looked down and seen a mouse in her handbag.

"I thought I was tripping," he told us later. Looking around he saw a load of beer cans in the corner, and another mouse. Then another. And another. But he'd decided to keep it to himself, guessing that all hell was going to break out if anyone noticed. Instead he just waited till the band got to their hotel and ushered everyone off as quick as he could before dealing with the mice by stamping on them. We didn't like that—we were animal lovers—but I wasn't going to argue. The idea of the Buzzcocks unaware that their bus had been overrun with mice was somehow just as funny as them finding out.

I've got to say, that was a great end to what had been an eventful year to say the least. At the beginning of December we played at Eric's, which was quite a landmark gig, really, because it was the first time Gillian ever joined us onstage. There had been the usual horseplay, with us hanging around the venue in between the sound check and the doors opening and working our way through a crate of beer that Roger had given us. Barney and Rob had been play fighting, messing about with beer bottles, and one of them cut a finger open. Just our luck it was Barney, who couldn't play the gig because of it. I think it was Rob who suggested that Gillian join us on guitar, because she'd played guitar in the Inadequates—he was always a bit sweet on her, to be honest.

Fortunately Barney was okay for our next gig, at Les Bains Douche in Paris, where Steve told us that he'd be able to negotiate our way around because he had an O-Level in French.

"Oh," he said, "I used to love speaking French. Really good at it, I was."

He never spoke a word of French the whole trip. Not even in the petrol station, the bit he had been practicing: "Fill her up, mate" only came out in English.

Anyway, so we got on the ferry and, fuck, the waves were enormous. They were so big they were actually spinning the boat; the captain had to let it drift. Like a bunch of twats, me, Dave Pils, and Twinny went out on deck to have a look. We were the only passengers stupid enough—the wind was howling, there were huge waves slapping against the side of the ship and pouring rain.

We made it to the stern, hanging on to the rail, grinning maniacally. It started getting too rough even for us and we made our way back to the door, got there, and pulled ourselves in—just as the biggest wave I've ever seen in my life engulfed the whole of the stern where we'd been standing, taking everything that wasn't bolted down. We just stood there, shaking, knowing that another second and it would have been us.

Rob, meanwhile, was down in the casino, pissed and gambling, swearing that he wasn't gambling with the band's money; because, as he always said, "I keep the band money in this pocket, and me own money in this pocket."

But by the end of the night it looked to me as if both pockets were empty, pulled out like an elephant's ears. Things got even more interesting after that. When we arrived at the gig we discovered that an ex-girlfriend of Steve's had followed us over, trying to win him back from Gillian. The venue was an old Turkish bath, an early design by Philippe Starck, actually, quite weird: all the baths were still in place, and some still had water in them, so people could—I don't know—throw money in them, make a wish, or paddle or something.

So anyway, we were playing this gig, two numbers into the set, when suddenly the backstage door opened and Steve's ex, Stephanie, appeared. She stuck her head out and started calling him.

"Steve! Steve!"

Oh dear—he nearly died. He went bright red and kept his head down and then, as she carried on shouting at him—"Steve! Steve, I love you!"—started played faster and faster.

As if keeping up with Steve wasn't exhausting enough, afterward we had to make a dash for it in order to avoid her. Eventually we ended up looking for this street Rue Saint-Denis, which we'd heard was full of hookers. Not to partake, just to gawp. And this is one of my lasting impressions of Ian—an image I have in my head of him, like the image of him chasing the drum down the motorway or pissing in the ashtray. It's of Ian, who liked to read Burroughs and Kafka and discuss art with Annik, asking this French guy where all the girls were. "Girls," he was saying. "Where are all the girls?" Holding his arms to his chest and waving them up and down like a pair of jiggly boobs. "Where are all the girls?"

· *Chapter 25* ·

Unknown Pleasures Track by Track

I really recommend listening to the record while you read.

"DISORDER"

I've got the spirit, but lose the feeling . . .

Because we recorded *Unknown Pleasures* so quickly, there wasn't the time to rerecord much (with the exception of Steve's drums, obviously) so there are a few bum notes on the album, most of which are courtesy of yours truly. The ones that are most noticeable—and these are the only ones I'm going to point out—are on "Disorder," where it sounds like it could be Bernard's guitar but it's not, it's me. The funny thing is, though, they're now part of the song, even though they're bum notes. It's where I was playing the lower string and catching the A and D with my plectrum, which has given it that guitar sound. Playing it back, I can't imagine "Disorder" without those sounds. Some of the low notes are a bit wild too but, hey, we were young. Like Pete Saville's theory, now we'd stop and go, "Hold on, Hooky's played a wrong note. He's caught the strings, we'll have to fix that!" It's a mistake, but it ended up being a good mistake; to me it sounds really interesting.

"DAY OF THE LORDS"

This is the room, the start of it all . . .

We'd only ever played these songs live before, never demoed them. I think the only ones we'd demoed were "She's Lost Control" and "Insight."

"Day of the Lords" is a slow song, but it's a great song. The guitar's loud and swept along by the bass. Martin overdubbed the keyboards. At the time we were all like, "What? keyboards? If we want fucking keyboards we'll get a fucking keyboard player." So he overdubbed them when we weren't there. We didn't even hear it until he'd done the mix. He played us the mix and me and Barney were pulling faces behind his back because he was putting keyboards on things. He was right, though, Martin. The keyboards sweeten it and make it better. Bleeding keyboards, soon to be the bane of my life. Great snare sound.

"CANDIDATE"

I campaigned for nothing, I worked hard for this . . .

Martin needed two more songs so he said to me and Steve, "You've not got enough songs. You need to go in and write more songs."

We were like, "'Go in and write'? We can't 'go in and write'! What do you mean?" That just wasn't the way we came up with songs. We jammed them as a band; we didn't write them like that.

"Just go in there and write two more songs."

"Oh, for fuck's sake!"

So we took ourselves off and started "writing"—well, jamming. We got "Candidate" immediately—and also "From Safety to Where," which ended up not making it on to the album. If you listen closely to "Candidate," it has that feel of a song that's not quite finished—well, it does to me, anyway, because I know that it's a jam that Ian went and put a vocal on. A great song, yes; but, like I say, not completely worked out. Great for that reason, though.

So we had these two tracks and Martin said, "Right, Bernard, go and put some guitar on those songs; they're really good, these." So Bernard went and was sitting there with his guitar for ages, not playing on the tracks—well, hardly playing at all—because he didn't like them. This was the guitarist's equivalent of a huffy teenage strop. Like when you tell a kid to tidy their room and two minutes later they go. "*Happy now?*" That's what I mean when I talk about his "economical" playing. He's a brilliant guitarist but woe betide you if he didn't like the song; he'd either refuse point-blank to put guitar on it or do such half-arsed guitar you wish you hadn't bothered.

Martin decided to turn the twenty-four-track tape over and play the track backward, pushing him to play over it forward, which he seemed to quite like; he perked up a bit and we did actually get some good guitar. Martin then spun the tape back over so the guitar's backwards. It actually worked. "From Safety to Where" was Barney's economical guitar playing at its very best.

"INSIGHT"

Reflects a moment in time, a special moment in time . . .

"Insight" is one of my favorite songs and also one of my favorite bass riffs. I mean, the great thing about Joy Division was that we used the bass to write the songs. Most bass players are just used to back up a song, to fatten it up: to "follow the root notes," as they say. I don't do that. I remember, very early on in our career, Barney turning round to me and saying, "Can't you just follow the guitar?"

"No, I can't. You follow me. Ha!"

The lyrics are wonderful and there's no chorus. There's repetition in the lyrics, but no chorus. That sound at the beginning is the creaky old freight lift in Strawberry that Martin had miked up and recorded, adding fantastic atmosphere to the track. Steve's snare has such great presence. It's well known that Martin used a lot of echo plate and digital delays on *Unknown Pleasures*, which gives it a very unique sound. The very sound me and Barney hated for years—that was "his" sound. There was a rumor that he'd recorded the lead vocal down a telephone line to get the distortion just right, but I doubt that's true; in those days it would have been very difficult to achieve. I reckon he would have "pumped" the vocal. This was a technique he pioneered, where you used an external speaker in a very ambient room. Using a fader on the desk, you'd send the signal out into the room at a suitable volume and bring it back through a microphone into the control room to mix in with the original track. A great trick. Martin used it on the piano on "Transmission," putting a speaker underneath the strings and recording it back, then adding it into the track as ambience. We also used it to great effect on the bass drum on "Blue Monday" at Britannia Row.

"NEW DAWN FADES"

A change of speed, a change of style . . .

"New Dawn Fades" is the track that most people say is their favorite. This seems an odd choice to me, because it's very, very, simple and very economical, certainly from my point of view, because the bass is pretty much constant all the way through.

This riff reminds me of my old amp. I had a hundred-watt Marshall Lead Amp, wired for bass. I don't know what the difference is—something to do with the frequencies—but it had a fantastic rich, warm sound, especially when you played high. All the songs on *Unknown Pleasures* were written and played on it; it sounded great. It used to sing to me, that amp: such sweet distortion. It was wonderful. I had to sell it because I needed to pay the gas bill. Rob said we didn't have any money, so I advertised it in the *MEN* and this kid answered. I even took the amp round to his house in its flight case.

He said, "You in a band?"

"Yeah, we're called Joy Division."

"Never heard of you."

I went, "Yeah, well, you know, we're up and coming."

"I'm in a band," he said, gloating. "Six hundred quid a week, on the cruise ships, on the liners. Fucking great. It's full of old biddies; knuckle-deep in Lily of the Valley, me, mate. Hundred and sixty-five, yeah."

I was like, "Whatever." He took my amp off me, my *beloved* amp. Me and Iris were going to have our gas cut off otherwise.

So I went back to Rob. "Right, you'll have to buy me an amp now, out of the group's money, because I haven't got one. I've sold it."

"You stupid twat," he said. "I would have bought it off you. I would have given you the money."

"Well, I asked and you wouldn't give it to me."

"Oh, don't be so fucking soft, Hooky."

What the fuck was "soft" about that, I don't know and never will. But anyway. That was the story of the amp. It really did contribute to the sound of the album, without a shadow of a doubt. I wonder where it is now. While we're on the subject of amplifiers a mention must go to Barney's acquisition of the Vox UL730, a wonderful find. This amp has a fantastic sound and was his pride and joy, and again added a lot to the album. Even Martin loved it. It famously took over a whole PA at Liverpool Eric's once. We'd all been complaining about how loud it was, so Barney had bought an Altair power soak, which supposedly enabled you to have the same sound only quieter. I don't want to get too technical, but the idea was you used the Altair to quieten the amp then took a DI from it to the PA. This we did, but the UL730 obviously had ideas of its own and took over the whole sound system. You could hear nothing else. This amp was stolen with all the gear in America on the first New Order tour. Even I grieved.

"SHE'S LOST CONTROL"

She walked upon the edge of no escape . . .

They used an aerosol to create some of the drum effects—

another of Martin's many innovations. He liked to record different sounds that he'd work on to sound like drums but different. For one of the tracks he recorded us kicking a flight case in time. Also I suspect a ring modulator on the real damped snare. The other thing you hear on this track is Steve's Synare, which was a drum synthesizer with a white-noise generator that he used on both "She's Lost Control" and "Insight." He was one of the first drummers to use them, if I'm not mistaken. That was one of the great things about him—and Barney, actually. They're both very experimental, always wanting to try out new things, which I must admit I resisted because I was always like, "Let's just play. We play great together. Why do you want to add stuff for?" In Barney's case it was a bit of a two-edged sword because, while it was great that he was always on the lookout to do things differently, you did tend to feel that he wasn't entirely happy with you. He loved all this new technology, and always did the whole time I knew him, but the technology was reducing the need for players. They say that's why drum machines were invented, so the lead vocalist didn't have to talk to the drummer. Bass synths so that the singer doesn't have to talk to the bass player. You could just program them yourself and find yourself in your own little world while we're all hanging on for grim death. I never believed in any of that. I always believed that in a group the strength comes from the camaraderie, the chemistry, the people playing together. You should never exclude anybody; you should encourage rather than exclude. No song is worth alienating a group member.

Ian was apparently moved to write this lyric after an incident at work. It's about an epileptic young lady who was having problems finding and keeping a job, who eventually died while having a seizure. That must have been terrifying for him. The first I knew of that was when Bernard mentioned it on a Joy Division documentary. Again, I wasn't really paying that much attention to the lyrics. It's teamwork. You just see your teammate doing his bit; he looks and sounds up to speed, so, great, that leaves you to concentrate on your own side of things. There's no analysis going on. Nobody was going, "Let's have a look at your lyrics, Ian. Let's have a talk about them. Let's dissect the lyric." He probably would have just gone mad and told you to fuck off. He delivered his vocals with the perfect amount of passion and spirit, exactly what we wanted. Saying that, reading the lyrics now, his use of repetition and onomatopoeic delivery is startling.

Now, of course, Ian Curtis is recognized as one of music's greatest lyricists, a fact that wasn't established during his lifetime. In interviews all they seem to pounce on was the Nazi aspects. That just used to upset him. It's a funny thing with interviews. When you're a struggling band nobody wants to know, so you just live without the press. You don't even consider it to be important. All of a sudden you're popular and everybody wants to talk to you. Then it seems vital.

"SHADOWPLAY"

As the assassins all grouped in four lines dancing on the floor . . .

This was the song that Barney wanted to sound like "The Ocean" by Velvet Underground. Again, the lyric doesn't repeat until the end and it has no chorus, which is something that I think Ian was very, very good at—the way he played with the structure of the lyrics but without ever losing what it was about the song that makes it strong. You don't listen to it and think, *Ah, what an interesting lyrical structure.* But it's all in the song. His love of art was showing here. The way he wanted to slightly subvert the normal conventions of rock and pop.

"WILDERNESS"

I traveled far and wide to Stations of the Cross . . .

I'm blowing my own trumpet here, but this is a fantastic bass line. I watched John Frusciante of the Red Hot Chili Peppers play it acoustically at their gig at the MEN Arena. I think I can safely say that, of the 19,000 people there, 18,950 didn't know what it was—but I did, and it brought a tear to my eye, definitely. Monster bass line. A bass line that every bass player dreams of and I got it, so thank you.

It's Ian's sideswipe at religion, the futility of religion, the things that are done and perpetrated in its name. It's poetry. Once you unlock the meaning of the lyrics, or at least what you think are the meaning of the lyrics, you can lose yourself in them. Each one of his lyrics is like a wonderful little story in itself. Rob didn't like this track.

Great guitar, too. The two instruments interplay very well. I do think that Barney's guitar playing is underrated. He's a fantastic guitarist. One of the things that puzzled me when he started working with Johnny Marr is why he gave up the guitar. I prefer his playing. Maybe it's that thing about always wanting to move on to something else, whereas I've always been quite happy to capitalize on what I've got. This reminds me of when I got Donald Johnson of A Certain Ratio to teach me how to do slap bass. Everyone was doing it and I was feeling the pressure, shall we say. I tried once, one lesson; he just laughed, squeezed my arm and said, "Hooky, stick to what you're great at!" Lovely guy.

"INTERZONE"

Four twelve windows, ten in a row . . .

Me singing the main vocal while Ian does the low, backing vocal. Ian was very good like that; there seemed to be no ego with him. He was perfectly happy to let you sing, to let anyone sing. In fact he'd encourage you to do it. He was very, very generous in that respect. Strangely enough we were always trying to get Barney to sing but he was never interested.

This was the song that they tried to get us to do at RCA. The cover of "Keep On Keepin' On"—well, not the actual song itself but the inspiration for it—and you can hear the riff in it a little.

"I REMEMBER NOTHING"

Violent more violent his hand cracks the chair . . .

We had been playing this one for a while very loosely; it had no real order. So we jammed it in the studio and Martin added the shattering glass and other effects. This was also Barney's first foray into using the Transcendent 2000. He'd bought *Sound Engineer* magazine, or *Sound International* or something, and you got a free piece of an electronic kit every week—the idea being to build your own synthesizer, which is what he'd done; he soldered together the Transcendent 2000. Built it himself: quite an achievement. It's used a lot on the track. One of the interesting things about Joy Division is that people can never tell who's playing what; is it keyboard or bass or guitar? This is a great, atmospheric track and came together very quickly. In the New Order days, especially toward the end, we'd hammer our tracks to death. Budgeting a month per track to record. You'd try everything bar the kitchen sink and end up mainly coming back to exactly what you started with. Then it was blighted by the huge waste of time and money. Ending up with everyone in the group hating one another. We should have just looked at *Unknown Pleasures* and made every album that way. We'd probably never have split up. But people change. Ah well, last thing is the notable use of the Frank Sinatra lyric "Strangers."

TIMELINE FOUR

JANUARY 1979–DECEMBER 1979

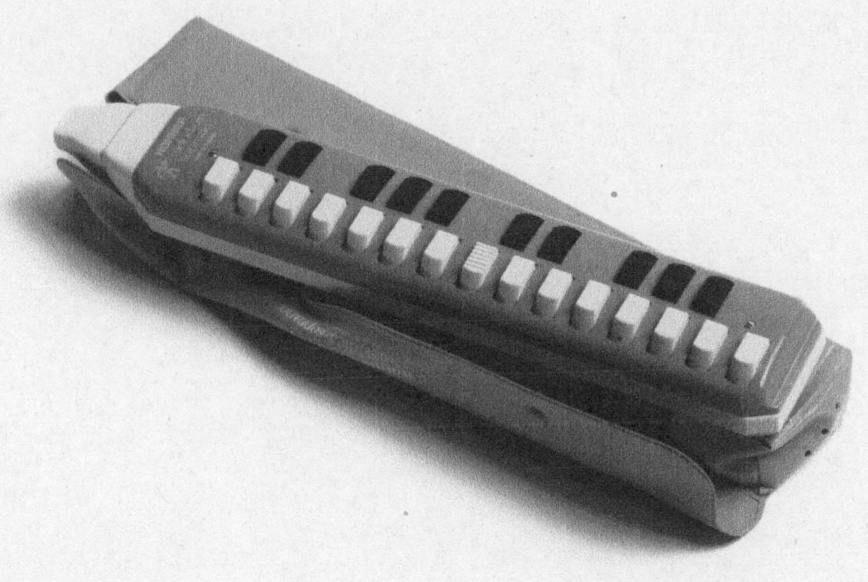

JANUARY 1979

The* A Factory Sample *EP (FAC 2) is released, priced at £1.50. Recorded at Cargo Studios, Rochdale. Produced by Martin Hannett. Track list (Side A [Aside]): Joy Division, "Digital"; Joy Division, "Glass." (Vinyl etching:* EVERYTHING.*) Track list (Side B [Beside]): the Durutti Column, "No Communication"; the Durutti Column, "Thin Ice (Detail)." (Vinyl etching:* IS REPAIRABLE.*) Track list (Side C [Seaside]): John Dowie, "Acne"; John Dowie, "Idiot"; John Dowie, "Hitler's Liver." (Vinyl etching:* EVERYTHING.*) Track list (Side D [Decide]): Cabaret Voltaire, "Baader Meinhof"; Cabaret Voltaire, "Sex in Secret." (Vinyl etching:* IS BROKEN.*)

JANUARY 6, 1979

Kevin Cummins takes his famous Princess Parkway shots of Joy Division.

I remember it was really cold and I borrowed that coat that I had on. I think I borrowed it off Steve, actually. They were done really quickly. Kevin freely admits he only took seven shots. He was lucky. He didn't have any money either—didn't have money for any more film. He had one roll and he had to do four or five groups on it. Quite punky, really. I mean, now, you sit there, they take fucking thousands of shots and wade through them to get one. But in the old days you had to get it finished and get it out. You know what I'm going to say, don't you? That's right. I liked it much better that way.

JANUARY 12, 1979

Joy Division plays Wythenshawe College, Manchester.

JANUARY 13, 1979

Ian Curtis appears on the cover of* NME; *the shot of him smoking was taken during the Kevin Cummins session on January 6.

JANUARY 23, 1979

Ian Curtis diagnosed with epilepsy.

JANUARY 26, 1979

Joy Division plays the* A Factory Sample *EP release party, the Factory, Russell Club, Manchester, with Cabaret Voltaire and John Dowie.

JANUARY 31, 1979

Joy Division's first John Peel session, produced by Bob Sargeant for the BBC. Tracks recorded: "Exercise One," "Insight," "Transmission," "She's Lost Control."

We weren't quite as green as we used to be in terms of being in the studio, so, instead of just sitting around watching other people get on with it, we were a bit more hands-on, happy that we were getting to use this great studio and were being treated well with a trip to the subsidized canteen. I loved that session. I love working for the BBC, actually.

FEBRUARY 2, 1979

Sid Vicious found dead of a drug overdose.

FEBRUARY 10, 1979

Joy Division plays the Institute of Technology, Bolton, supported by the Curbs.

Little Hulton's right next to Bolton, so I had to drive all the way to Salford to get the gear, pick everybody up, and then drive past my house to do the gig. At the end of the night, when we'd finished, I had to drive past my house, drop everybody off, go all the way to Salford and then back home. Fuck me. Who'd be the driver, eh?

FEBRUARY 16, 1979

Joy Division plays Eric's, Liverpool, supported by Cabaret Voltaire.

FEBRUARY 28, 1979

Joy Division plays Nottingham Playhouse as unbilled support for John Cooper Clarke.

Joy Division was late appearing, so John Cooper Clarke went on first, then introduced Joy Division (his distinctive accent leading at least one fan, Dominic, writing on joydiv.org, to expect "Geordie Vision"); John Cooper Clarke then played a second time.

We were using Sad Café's PA, which was operated by my cousin, Chas Banks—who was the first person to ever give me a guitar to hold, when I went round to his house in Stretford. I was fourteen. Fantastic guy, a real legend. We were waiting for the PA to turn up—you can't do anything until the PA turns up—and I remember being at the back door when Chas appeared, bruised and battered, and went, "Just crawled in from a motorway wreck; let's get on with it." We went out and the van was fucking hammered. It had been in a huge crash on the motorway. All the gear was trashed and everyone was frantically trying to put it back together. Proper rock 'n' roll. That was why John ended up going on twice: because we weren't ready.

MARCH 1, 1979

Joy Division plays the Hope & Anchor, London. Admission: 75p. "Cellar bar re-opening. Now with real ale!"

This was the gig where Dave Pils and his girlfriend, Jasmine, introduced themselves to us. They ran Walthamstow Youth Centre, which is why we ended up playing there. Dave would become a big part of our lives. He became our roadie and friend and stayed with us for years. Every time we played in London we crashed at their place, which saved us a lot of money. A pair of lovely people. I wonder where they are now. . . .

MARCH 4, 1979

The Genetic Records demo session, Eden Studios, London. Produced by Martin Rushent. Tracks recorded: "Glass," "Transmission," "Ice Age," "Insight," "Digital."

MARCH 4, 1979

Joy Division plays the Marquee, London, supporting the Cure. Set list: "Soundtrack" ("Exercise One"), "She's Lost Control," "Shadowplay," "Leaders of Men," "Insight," "Glass," "Digital," "Ice Age," "Transmission."

There's a set list from this still knocking around, written by Steve: it starts with a track called "Soundtrack," which became "Exercise One"; we thought it sounded soundtracky. . . . It was exciting being in the Marquee, for obvious reasons, and it was really crowded, but the night was ruined by the fact that we had to drive home afterward. The Cure never even acknowledged us. Everyone was rocking except us: we just played then got dragged off to drive home, which was a bit of a downer.

MARCH 13, 1979

Joy Division plays Band on the Wall, Manchester, supported by the Fireplace. A Manchester Musicians' Collective gig. Unconfirmed set list: "Walked in Line" (also known as "They Walked in Line"), "She's Lost Control," "Shadowplay," "New Dawn Fades," "Day of the Lords," "Insight," "Disorder," "The Only Mistake," "I Remember Nothing," and "Sister Ray."

A band with a name like the Fireplace could only be in a collective.

MARCH 14, 1979

Joy Division plays Bowdon Vale Youth Club, Altrincham, supported by Staff 9 (featuring Paul and Steve Hanley and Craig Scanlon, who later join the Fall). Set list: "Exercise One," "She's Lost Control," "Shadowplay," "Leaders of Men," "Insight," "Disorder," "Glass," "Digital," "Ice Age," "Warsaw," "Transmission," "I Remember Nothing," "No Love Lost."

Absolutely cracking. A fucking great set list, that one. I wouldn't put "Disorder" after "Glass," mind you; I'd change that bit round. But that's a great set list. Maybe it's a bit up and down, though, come to think of it . . . so maybe it's not that great a set list. Great songs, though.

"She's Lost Control," "Shadowplay," and "Leaders of Men" were filmed by Malcolm Whitehead for his Joy Division *short film, which was premiered at the Scala, London, on September 13 as part of* The Factory Flick *(FAC 9). The footage was also later released on the "Substance" video.*

That was very exciting, being filmed. Malcolm was a lovely geezer. His idea was to use us in a film he was doing, but in the end the film became more about us than anything else. There are photographs of that gig, too, taken by a very young Martin O'Neill, who started crawling round the stage while we were playing, right up into the drums. I kicked him up the arse and told him to piss off. Photographers they think they're it. If you want to annoy one just say "shared copyright"—that should see them off.

I met him years later and we laughed about it; he wanted an autograph, and I wrote, "I told you to fuck off."

"No," he said, "you told me to piss off."

MARCH 30, 1979

Joy Division plays the Walthamstow Youth Centre.

Dave Pils's girlfriend, Jasmine, was a youth worker looking after kids in Walthamstow, presumably trying to keep them on the straight and narrow or whatever, so it was a weird crowd. Very young kids there, running about, ignoring us, like a school hall–type gig. I do remember being horrified when we saw the poster, though. Dave had designed it: a bunch of Nazis on a tank. We were hoping to put all that stuff behind us! Dave was also the singer in SX, the support band.

MARCH 31, 1979

Joy Division starts recording* Unknown Pleasures, *Strawberry Studios, Stockport. Tracks recorded: "Disorder," "Day of the Lords," "Candidate," "Insight," "New Dawn Fades," "She's Lost Control," "Shadowplay," "Wilderness," "Interzone," "I Remember Nothing," "Autosuggestion," "From Safety to Where," "Exercise One," "The Kill," "Walked in Line."

APRIL 16, 1979

Natalie Curtis born, Macclesfield.

MAY 2, 1979

The Unknown Pleasures *recording session ends, Strawberry Studios, Stockport.*

MAY 3, 1979

Joy Division plays an Amnesty International Benefit, Eric's, Liverpool, with the Passage and Fireplace. Admission: 75p.

> When Joy Division left the stage I felt emotionally drained. They are, without any exaggeration, an Important Band.
>
> Ian Wood, *NME*

MAY 11, 1979

Joy Division plays a Factory Records night, the Factory, Russell Club, Manchester, with John Dowie, A Certain Ratio, and Orchestral Manoeuvres in the Dark. Admission: £1.20; tickets available from Discount Records and Pandemonium.

I liked OMD a lot as a group. I always thought they were really, really good; nice guys, too. Although it was those two who got me into cocaine, the bastards, at the premiere of *Pretty in Pink*. And come to think of it, wasn't one of them responsible for Atomic Kitten?

MAY 17, 1979

Joy Division plays* A Factory Sample *night, Acklam Hall, London, supported by John Dowie, A Certain Ratio, and Orchestral

Manoeuvres in the Dark. Admission: £1.50 at the door or £1.25 in advance from Small Wonder, Rough Trade, and Honky Tonk record shops.

This would have been the first gig for Final Solution, which was Colin Faver, who went on to become a big DJ—one of the house-music pioneers in the South of England—and Kevin Millins, who went on to run Heaven for Virgin and became a great friend of ours. It led to some great gigs, more for New Order than Joy Division. Acklam Hall became a club later on, and Davina McCall used to do the door. I have a wonderful memory of her bending over the table in my hotel room, with her silver hot-panted bottom stuck right up in the air. I always remind her of it whenever I see her.

OMD also had a guitar stolen and were very upset.

MAY 23, 1979

Joy Division plays Bowdon Vale Youth Club, Altrincham, supported by John Dowie and A Certain Ratio (OMD pulls out).

JUNE 4, 1979

Joy Division plays Piccadilly Radio session, Pennine Sound Studios, Oldham. Produced by Stuart James. Tracks recorded: "These Days," "Candidate," "The Only Mistake," "Chance" ("Atmosphere"), "Atrocity Exhibition."

Stuart James went on to become New Order's roadie. I saved his life once in Texas.

JUNE 7, 1979

Joy Division plays the F Club, aka the Fan Club, Leeds, with OMD.

JUNE 14, 1979

Unknown Pleasures *(Factory Records FACT 10) released. Produced by Martin Hannett. Engineered by Chris Nagle. Recorded at Straw-*

berry Studios, Stockport. Cover design by Joy Division, Peter Saville, Chris Mathan. Track list: "Disorder," "Day of the Lords," "Candidate," "Insight," "New Dawn Fades," "She's Lost Control," "Shadowplay," "Wilderness," "Interzone," "I Remember Nothing."

JUNE 16, 1979

Joy Division plays the Odeon, Canterbury, supporting the Cure, with Back to Zero. Set list: "Disorder," "She's Lost Control," "Shadowplay," "Wilderness," "New Dawn Fades," "Glass," "These Days," "Something Must Break," "Interzone," "Atrocity Exhibition."

I don't think the Cure liked us. I think they resented us in some way, because we'd managed to stay cool, credible, and independent and they'd, well, sort of sold out a bit. The problem was on their side; it wasn't on our side. But I think they thought, *Wish we were Joy Division.*

JUNE 17, 1979

Joy Division plays the Royalty Theatre, Kingsway, London, supporting John Cooper Clarke, with Fashion. Set list: "Atmosphere," "Disorder," "Digital," "I Remember Nothing," "Candidate," "New Dawn Fades," "These Days," "Interzone," "Transmission."

We did a series of three gigs with Fashion, both of us supporting John Cooper Clarke, and the idea was that we'd switch: Fashion would open one night then us the next. They were pretty big at the time but I hated their music. It was awful. They were supposed to open in London and us in Manchester. But we ended up being stiffed in London. They left us off the bill then insisted we go on first. It was bedlam backstage that night. Rob threatened everybody. The upshot was that we ended up going on before the doors had even opened. It was either that or don't play. We played "Atmosphere" and "Disorder" to a completely empty room. Three people came in during "Digital." The place was beginning to fill up when we finished our set.

JUNE 19, 1979

Joy Division plays the Nuffield Theatre, Lancaster University, Lancaster, supporting John Cooper Clarke, with Fashion.

Horrible gig. Fucking Fashion. I fucking hated 'em.

JUNE 22, 1979

Joy Division plays Good Mood, Halifax.

JUNE 25, 1979

Joy Division plays the Free Trade Hall, Manchester, supporting John Cooper Clarke, with Fashion.

They went on first. HA!

JULY 1, 1979

The first "Transmission" demo session, Central Sound Studios, Manchester. Produced by Martin Hannett. Tracks recorded: "Transmission," "Novelty," "Dead Souls," "Something Must Break."

Quite a pleasant session, this one. I remember Martin being very nice and helpful.

JULY 5, 1979

Joy Division plays Limit Club, West Street, Sheffield, supported by OMD.

This was the first time we ever went over the Snake Pass and the van was so knackered it was really struggling up the hills. Twinny was really annoyed and reckoned he could run faster. So we took him up on it and he jumped out of the van to race us. Of course, we beat him up the hill easy. By the time he joined us up at the top he was huffing and puffing, all red-faced, calling us bastards for not stopping. Me and Terry had eaten all his sweets while we waited. He didn't talk to us all night for that.

If I remember rightly Phil Oakey and the other lads from the Human League helped us load in. They were very nice. I met the drummer from Manicured Noise here. It was her twenty-first. Stephanie. Lovely girl. She had a pet rat.

JULY 11, 1979

Joy Division plays Roots Club (Cosmo Club), Chapeltown, Leeds. Set list: "Dead Souls", "Shadowplay," "She's Lost Control," "Candidate," "These Days," "Disorder," "Interzone," "Glass," "Transmission," "Atrocity Exhibition," "No Love Lost."

I'm pretty sure this was where Right Said Fred supported us.

JULY 13, 1979

***Joy Division plays the Factory, Russell Club, Manchester. Set list: "Dead Souls," "The Only Mistake," "Insight," "Candidate," "Wilderness," "She's Lost Control," "Shadowplay," "Disorder," "Interzone," "Atrocity Exhibition," "Novelty," "Transmission." The concert appears on CD2 of the September 2007 remastered edition of* Unknown Pleasures.**

JULY 20, 1979

Joy Division appears on* What's On *for Granada TV, playing "She's Lost Control."

JULY 27, 1979

Joy Division plays a Year of the Child benefit concert, the Imperial Hotel, Blackpool, with OMD, the Final Solution, Section 25, the Glass Torpedoes, and Zyklon B. Promoted by Section 25. Set list:

"Dead Souls," "Glass," "Disorder," "Autosuggestion," "Transmission," "She's Lost Control," "Shadowplay," "Atrocity Exhibition."

I remember looking out the dressing-room window and seeing a Ford Escort sat outside with the *Unknown Pleasures* logo on its bonnet. Cool, that was. This was also the gig where we met Section 25, who became great friends of ours. Ian and Rob took a shine to them and ended up producing their first single, which came out on Factory. That must have been a scream and I would have loved to have been there, because Rob and Ian were both hopeless at that sort of thing. Rob's only advice when you were recording was, "Make it go *Woomph*." That was it. "Make it go *Woomph*." And Ian, well, he had the ear but he was useless at anything technical.

You may or may not know, but Larry from Section 25 died recently, in 2010. Very sad. I'll tell you one story about him that made me laugh so much. I mean, he was a proper "character," and enjoyed fully the rock-'n'-roll lifestyle and some of its foibles, shall we say. His one true love was those flight simulators you get on the computer. What he used to like doing was staying up all night flying long-haul flights in real time. His brother Vinny was telling me that he'd done one where he'd been up all night, flying to New York from London, off his head, and crashed on landing. It had taken him eleven hours to get there! I tell you what, heaven's got to be a lot livelier with that lot there. Him, Ian, Tony, Rob, and Martin. What a crew.

But yes, the relationship between us and Section 25 was really very solid, much more so than with A Certain Ratio. They never had the acclaim we had and that was something that I think never bothered Section 25, whereas I think A Certain Ratio got annoyed because they felt in our shadow.

JULY 28, 1979

Joy Division plays the Mayflower Club, Manchester, a Stuff the Superstars Special, with the Fall, the Distractions, John the Postman, the Frantic Elevators, the Hamsters, Ludus, Armed Force, Foreign Press, and Elti Fits. Admission: £1.50.

> It's almost impossible to match a recording as good as theirs with an equally good performance. Joy Division pulled it off. THEY WERE BRILLIANT, I MEAN BRILLIANT!
>
> *City Fun* fanzine

There was always intense rivalry between us and the Fall. They started the same time as us and did a lot better than us more quickly than we did. So we were a bit jealous. There always is rivalry between groups. Never with DJs but always with groups.

JULY 28–AUGUST 4, 1979

The second "Transmission" demo sessions, Strawberry Studios, Stockport. Produced by Martin Hannett. Tracks recorded: "Transmission" (single version) and "Novelty" (single version).

AUGUST 2, 1979

Joy Division plays the YMCA, Prince of Wales Conference Centre, London, with Teardrop Explodes and Echo & the Bunnymen. This is the first show of a four-night alternative-rock festival at the Prince of Wales Conference Centre. Set list: "Dead Souls," "Disorder," "Wilderness," "Autosuggestion," "Transmission," "Day of the Lords," "She's Lost Control," "Shadowplay," "Atrocity Exhibition," "Insight."

> The truth is they were phenomenal—the most physical hard rock group I've seen since Gang of Four.
>
> Adrian Thrills, *NME*

It was a great gig, that one, and it's where the famous pictures of us come from—where we're drinking backstage, post-gig, out of cans, and where Ian's got the cig and we're sat on the step. They're all from backstage at the YMCA, very famous nice pictures. We all look very happy.

AUGUST 8, 1979

Joy Division plays the Romulus Club, Birmingham, supporting Dexys Midnight Runners.

Dexys were diabolically dressed, like something out of *Star Trek*. This was way before theirs became a big name, of course, but Kevin Rowland still swanned around like he was a god. They were playing jokes on a reel-to-reel tape recorder in between songs: very strange. This was the night I ripped my favorite blue shirt that Rob bought me, on my own bass cab. I was devastated. Stayed in a mad B&B afterward, complete with a saucy landlady.

AUGUST 11, 1979

Joy Division plays Eric's, Liverpool (matinee and evening shows), with Swell Maps. Admission: £1.10 for members. Set list (matinee): "Transmission," "Untitled," "Disorder," "New Dawn Fades," "Glass," "Shadowplay," "Colony," "Interzone," and "Ice Age." Set list (evening): "Insight," "Autosuggestion," "Digital," "She's Lost Control," "Day of the Lords," "Wilderness," "Atrocity Exhibition," "Transmission," "New Dawn Fades" (instrumental), "Interzone," "Dead Souls." Ian has a fit during "New Dawn Fades" and is carried from the stage. He returns during "Interzone."

AUGUST 13, 1979

Joy Division plays the Nashville Rooms, London, with OMD and A Certain Ratio. Set list: "Atmosphere," "She's Lost Control," "Exercise One," "Disorder," "Colony," "Candidate," "Autosuggestion," "Ice Age."

Annik Honoré saw the band for the first time and met us briefly. This was the night of the van crash, of course. But it was a great gig. Look at that set list, starting with "Atmosphere." It didn't have the connotations then that it does now that it's sort of Ian's death march. Back then it was a good song to start with—well, we thought so anyway because we were awkward bastards. We liked to come on and defy expectations by starting with something slow and reflective, before building up to the faster songs.

AUGUST 24, 1979

Joy Division plays the Walthamstow Youth Centre, London. Afterward Annik interviews the band at Dave Pils's and Jasmine's flat.

AUGUST 27, 1979

Joy Division plays Leigh Open Air Festival, Plank Lane, Leigh, with the Distractions, Echo & the Bunnymen, OMD, A Certain Ratio, Teardrop Explodes and Lori & the Chameleons. Billed as "Zoo Meets Factory Half Way," this is the last day of the festival. Admission: £2. Set list: "Disorder," "Leaders of Men," "Colony," "Insight," "Digital," "Dead Souls," "Shadowplay," "She's Lost Control," "Transmission," "Interzone."

I remember being really upset by Martin Moscrop of A Certain Ratio at that gig. We did "The Sound of Music" at the sound check and I had a bit on the song where I sang, "Hi, hi, hi, hi, higher." Martin turned round to me at the end and said, "You sounded like the fucking laughing policeman, mate, ha, ha, ha."

I've never been able to think of that song in the same way since. He ruined it for me in that one moment. "The Sound of Music" was one I played guitar on and Bernard played bass. But yeah, ruined for me from then on.

AUGUST 31, 1979

Joy Division plays the Electric Ballroom, London, with A Certain Ratio, Scritti Politti, and the Monochrome Set. Set list: "The Sound of Music," "Wilderness," "Colony," "Day of the Lords," "Shadowplay," "Transmission," "Interzone," "Disorder," "She's Lost Control," "Insight."

Great gig, this one. I was very impressed that the Monochrome Set's singer was an Indian prince.

SEPTEMBER 8, 1979

Joy Division plays the Queens Hall, Leeds, third on the bill, with A Certain Ratio, Cabaret Voltaire, and OMD, and with Public Image headlining. This is the opening day of the three-day Futurama Festival. Set list: "I Remember Nothing," "Wilderness," "Transmission," "Colony," "Disorder," "Insight," "Shadowplay," "She's Lost Control," "Atrocity Exhibition," "Dead Souls."

This was a great concert too. We went down an absolute storm. It was our first gig with John Keenan, who was a very interesting man to work with financially, and our first indoor festival.

SEPTEMBER 13, 1979

Premiere of* The Factory Flick *(Factory FAC 9, 1979), the Scala cinema, London. This 8mm film comprises: "No City Fun—Joy Division" (12 min), by student filmmaker Charles Salem, featuring three tracks by the band; "All Night Party—A Certain Ratio" (3 min); "Red Dress—Ludus" (3 min); and "Joy Division" (17 min),

by Malcolm Whitehead, featuring footage of "Shadowplay" and "She's Lost Control" shot by Malcolm Whitehead at Bowdon Vale Youth Club.

SEPTEMBER 15, 1979

Joy Division appears on* Something Else*, playing "She's Lost Control" and "Transmission."

SEPTEMBER 22, 1979

Joy Division plays the Nashville Rooms, London, supported by the Distractions. Admission: £1.25. Set list: "Atmosphere," "Wilderness," "Shadowplay," "Leaders of Men," "Insight," "Colony," "Transmission," "Disorder," "She's Lost Control," "Atrocity Exhibition," "Glass," "Exercise One."

Terry couldn't make it, so Twinny said to me, "Can I bring my mate as a roadie?" and I was like, "Yeah, 'course," thinking that was nice. Then his mate turned up and he was on crutches. I took Twinny to one side. "Look, he's on crutches. How's he going to help if he can't walk?"

Twinny was like, "Oh come on, Hooky, he's a nice guy. He needs a night out." I was just shaking my head. I mean, what a liability: some kid on crutches along for the ride. Anyway, at the end of the night we couldn't find him—he kept us waiting for ages—and when we eventually did he was snogging the face off some girl. So not only had he turned up on crutches, done fuck-all, and drunk all our rider, but he'd ended up copping off as well, the lucky bastard.

SEPTEMBER 28, 1979

Joy Division plays the Factory, Russell Club, Manchester, with Teardrop Explodes and Foreign Press (formerly Emergency). Set list: "Atmosphere," "Wilderness," "Shadowplay," "Insight," "Colony,"

"Twenty Four Hours," "Interzone," "She's Lost Control," "Transmission" (encore; fight occurs), "Atrocity Exhibition" (encore, minus bass).

The big fight. I was ashamed.

SEPTEMBER 29, 1979

Joy Division plays the Mayflower, Manchester, with Foreign Press.

OCTOBER 1979

The* Earcom 2 *compilation (Fast Products FAST 9b) released. It features two Joy Division tracks, recorded by Martin Hannett as part of the* Unknown Pleasures *session: "Autosuggestion" and "From Safety to Where."

OCTOBER 1979

The "Transmission"/"Novelty" seven-inch single (Factory Records FAC 13) released. Produced by Martin Hannett. Sleeve design by Peter Saville. Later rereleased as a twelve-inch with new cover (FAC 13.12).

OCTOBER–NOVEMBER 1979

The Sordide Sentimental session, Cargo Studios, Rochdale. Produced by Martin Hannett. Tracks recorded: "Atmosphere," "Dead Souls," "Ice Age."

OCTOBER 2, 1979

Joy Division plays Mountford Hall, Liverpool University, as part of the Buzzcocks tour. Set list: "Wilderness," "Ice Age," "Candidate," "Shadowplay," "Insight," "She's Lost Control," "Twenty Four Hours," "Disorder," "Transmission," "Warsaw."

OCTOBER 3, 1979

Joy Division plays Leeds University as part of the Buzzcocks tour.

The anguished singer had achieved total physical self-expression by the climax of "She's Lost Control" and, evidently having lost control, he was helped offstage at the conclusion of a set which, for practical reasons, could not be extended.

Des Moines, *Sounds*

OCTOBER 4, 1979

Joy Division plays City Hall, Newcastle, as part of the Buzzcocks tour. Set list: "Disorder," "Shadowplay," "Colony," "Day of the Lords," "Glass," "Transmission," "She's Lost Control," "Atrocity Exhibition."

OCTOBER 5, 1979

Joy Division plays Apollo, Glasgow, as part of the Buzzcocks tour.

I remember freaking out at the height of the stage: it was one of thc highest I've ever played on.

OCTOBER 6, 1979

Joy Division plays the Odeon, Edinburgh, as part of the Buzzcocks tour. Set list: "Leaders of Men," "Digital," "Day of the Lords," "Transmission," "Shadowplay," "She's Lost Control," "New Dawn Fades," "Disorder," "Transmission."

OCTOBER 7, 1979

Joy Division plays Capitol, Aberdeen, as part of the Buzzcocks tour.

Sarge threw a kid out of the backstage area for having a Scottish accent. He was trying to say he had an interview with Pete Shelley for a fanzine. "I can't understand a word you're saying, dickhead, OUT!"

OCTOBER 8, 1979

Joy Division plays Caird Hall, Dundee, as part of the Buzzcocks tour. Set list: "Atmosphere," "Wilderness," "Interzone," "Colony," "These Days," "New Dawn Fades," "Transmission," "Shadowplay," "She's Lost Control." Ian collapses.

OCTOBER 10, 1979

Joy Division gig at Ulster Hall, Belfast, canceled. Part of the Buzzcocks tour.

OCTOBER 11, 1979

Joy Division gig at Kelly's, Portrush, canceled. Part of the Buzzcocks tour.

OCTOBER 13, 1979

Joy Division gig at City Hall, Cork, canceled. Part of the Buzzcocks tour.

OCTOBER 16, 1979

Joy Division plays Plan K, Brussels. Set list: "Love Will Tear Us Apart," "Wilderness," "Disorder," "Colony," "Insight," "Twenty Four Hours," "New Dawn Fades," "Transmission," "Shadowplay," "She's Lost Control," "Atrocity Exhibition," "Interzone."

OCTOBER 18, 1979

Joy Division plays Bangor University, as part of the Buzzcocks tour.

OCTOBER 20, 1979

Joy Division plays Loughborough University, as part of the Buzzcocks tour.

OCTOBER 21, 1979

Joy Division plays Top Rank, Arundel Gate, Sheffield, as part of the Buzzcocks tour.

OCTOBER 22, 1979

Joy Division plays the Assembly Rooms, Derby, as part of the Buzzcocks tour.

OCTOBER 23, 1979

Joy Division plays King George's Hall, Blackburn, as part of the Buzzcocks tour.

The Blackburn lot ended up being great supporters of both New Order and the Haçienda. Mad football fans.

OCTOBER 24, 1979

Joy Division plays the Odeon Theatre, Birmingham, as part of the Buzzcocks tour.

OCTOBER 25, 1979

Joy Division plays St. George's Hall, Bradford, as part of the Buzzcocks tour.

OCTOBER 26, 1979

Joy Division plays the Electric Ballroom, London, supported by the Distractions and A Certain Ratio, during a break from the Buzzcocks tour. Set list: "I Remember Nothing," "Love Will Tear Us Apart," "Wilderness," "Colony," "Insight," "Day of the Lords," "Shadowplay," "She's Lost Control," "Transmission," "Disorder," "Atrocity Exhibition," "Interzone."

Something I remember about the Buzzcocks tour is that they played the same set every night, whereas we always varied ours.

We did it to keep ourselves interested, so that all the songs got an airing, to try to find that ultimate moment and sometimes, again, just to be bloody awkward. If the audience was really wild, we'd start with "I Remember Nothing," just to wind them up. One thing that punk taught you was to be challenging—always try to break the rules, to forge your own way. Being on Factory reinforced those ideals. It was like, whatever the game was we weren't going to play it. Whatever was expected of us we did the opposite. I was really inspired by Throbbing Gristle back then. Genesis P-Orridge, what a man. I loved how awkward they were—how they used to try to drive their audience away every night. I wouldn't have minded us being a bit more like Throbbing Gristle, actually.

OCTOBER 27, 1979

Joy Division plays the Apollo Theatre, Manchester, as part of the Buzzcocks tour. Set list: "Dead Souls," "Wilderness," "Colony," "Autosuggestion," "Love Will Tear Us Apart," "Shadowplay," "She's Lost Control," "Transmission."

OCTOBER 28, 1979

Joy Division plays the Apollo Theatre, Manchester, as part of the Buzzcocks tour. Set list: "The Sound of Music," "Shadowplay," "Colony," "Day of the Lords," "Twenty Four Hours," "Disorder," "Walked in Line," "I Remember Nothing," "Transmission."

OCTOBER 29, 1979

Joy Division plays De Montfort Hall, Leicester, as part of the Buzzcocks tour.

OCTOBER 30, 1979

Joy Division plays the New Theatre, Oxford, as part of the Buzzcocks tour. Set list: "Walked in Line," "The Only Mistake," "Leaders of Men," "Insight," "Ice Age," "Love Will Tear Us Apart," "I Remember Nothing."

NOVEMBER 1979

A photographic session with Anton Corbijn results in yet more iconic images of the band and sees the start of a relationship that will eventually culminate in the multi award–winning film* Control, *Corbijn's biopic of Ian Curtis.

What I loved about Anton was that he did the pictures really quickly, with no fuss, no fucking about: bang, bang, bang, and it was over. At the time, I thought, *Now, that's how a photo shoot should be.* Those shots he took of us in the tube station: absolutely brilliant. The way that he works, he almost does it like a throwaway gesture. When he did New Order in America, he was with us for four days, pissed as a fart, having a great time; when we were all sat on the grass outside the gig on the afternoon of his last day he went, "Oh, I'm sure there's something I've forgotten. What have I forgotten?" Then the color drained out of his face and he went, "Oh my God, I've forgotten to take any pictures."

All his gear had gone to the airport so he rushed to a garage across the way, bought a couple of instamatic cameras, and took us into a fairground opposite the venue, where he got Steve to wear these daft glasses and did the photo shoot. He'd been there for four days and did the shoot as the car was waiting to take him to the airport. Class. And this is the thing—they were brilliant. The guy is either a fucking genius or somebody up there likes him, without a shadow of a doubt. He's a nice guy as well, really easy to be with. He's sweet and patient—one of those people that you feel so comfortable with and happy to be with—which is a gift for a photographer. He did a great job of *Control* and I knew he would. He is a perfectionist, though, and in that respect working with him wasn't easy. Doing the soundtrack was the last nail in the coffin for New Order. I realized after that me and Barney were poles apart, too far apart, and no one seemed able to bring us back together. I thought our management was useless and Steve seemed lost. It was awful. The music was great, though. Typical: you're always better when you're full of anger. One thing I was happy about was that Natalie Curtis was included in the publishing for the songs. The credits are "Curtis-Hook-Morris-Sumner."

NOVEMBER 1, 1979

Joy Division plays the Civic Hall, Guildford, as part of the Buzzcocks tour. Set list: "No Love Lost," "These Days," "Disorder," "Candidate," "Shadowplay," "Autosuggestion," "Warsaw," "Transmission," "The Sound of Music."

This was the night that Pete Shelley slipped Twinny (£3.50) to get the key to his room so he could play a practical joke on Dave Pils. Dave was awoken by a drunken Buzzcock tickling his feet under the covers. Dave ran away screaming.

NOVEMBER 2, 1979

Joy Division plays the Winter Gardens, Bournemouth, as part of the Buzzcocks tour. Set list: "I Remember Nothing," "Love Will Tear Us Apart," "Interzone," "Colony," "Insight," "These Days," "Digital," "Transmission," "Atrocity Exhibition." The set is cut short because Ian has a fit and is taken to the hospital.

NOVEMBER 3, 1979

Joy Division gig at Sophia Gardens, Cardiff, canceled. Part of the Buzzcocks tour.

NOVEMBER 4, 1979

Joy Division plays Colston Hall, Bristol, as part of the Buzzcocks tour.

NOVEMBER 5, 1979

Joy Division plays the Pavilion, Hemel Hempstead, as part of the Buzzcocks tour. Set list (possibly incomplete): "Dead Souls," "Wilderness," "Twenty Four Hours," "New Dawn Fades," "Digital," "Disorder," "Interzone."

The practical jokes went up a gear here. The Buzzcocks' road crew told Terry that swallowing a huge lump of dope would give him a mild buzz. He was incapacitated. We arrived to find him leaning against a wall outside the venue, whimpering. We put him tenderly in Steve's car to recover and sleep it off, then Twinny, me, and Barney took it in turns to shove lit bangers up the car exhaust and repeatedly scared him to death. Rob did the sound for the gig.

NOVEMBER 7, 1979

Joy Division plays the Pavilion, West Runton, as part of the Buzzcocks tour. Set list: "Colony," "These Days," "Autosuggestion," "Twenty Four Hours," "Love Will Tear Us Apart," "The Sound of Music," "Atrocity Exhibition."

NOVEMBER 9, 1979

Joy Division plays the Rainbow Theatre, London, as part of the Buzzcocks tour. Set list: "The Sound of Music," "Shadowplay,"

"New Dawn Fades," "Colony," "Insight," "Love Will Tear Us Apart," "She's Lost Control," "Transmission."

NOVEMBER 10, 1979

Joy Division plays the Rainbow Theatre, London. The last date of the Buzzcocks tour. Set list: "Dead Souls," "Wilderness," "Twenty Four Hours," "Day of the Lords," "These Days," "Interzone," "Disorder," "Atrocity Exhibition."

NOVEMBER 26, 1979

Joy Division records their second John Peel session, BBC Studios, Maida Vale, London. Produced by Tony Wilson (not the same one). Tracks recorded: "The Sound of Music," "Twenty Four Hours," "Colony," "Love Will Tear Us Apart."

DECEMBER 8, 1979

Joy Division play Eric's, Liverpool (matinee and evening shows), with Section 25.

DECEMBER 18, 1979

Joy Division plays Les Bains Douches, Paris. Set list: "Passover," "Wilderness," "Disorder," "Love Will Tear Us Apart," "Insight," "Shadowplay," "Transmission," "Day of the Lords," "Twenty Four Hours," "Colony," "These Days," "A Means to an End," "She's Lost Control," "Atrocity Exhibition," "Interzone," "Warsaw."

DECEMBER 31, 1979

Factory office party at Oldham Street, Manchester.

Rob bought about two hundred cans of beer for 25p each—the idea being to sell them for 50p and make back the money that we paid for the PA and the lights, so we'd break even. It was a nice idea; quite forward-thinking, actually. Rob said, "Right, I'll sell the fucking beer. I can't trust you bastards. I'll do it." But what he didn't do was get a float, so when the first kid came up with a pound note to buy a 50p drink, Rob had no change. So he said, "Fucking have two cans."

The kid said, "I don't want two cans. I want one."

"Look, we've got no change."

"Well, give me the beer then."

"Come back later and get your fifty p."

"No, no, I'll come back later and give you fifty p."

Rob was like, "Oh, fucking hell!" and gave him the beer.

Anyway, so the next kid came up: same story. Rob had to keep giving the beers away and in the end he got so fucking fed up he just went, "Fuck off, the lot of you; you can have it." And he just walked away and left the bar open.

That was when we discovered that it was easier to give drink away than it was to get people to pay for it—an important lesson, that, and one we made great use of during the Haçienda years.

PART FIVE

"CEREMONY"

Failures of the Modern Man

Dont speak of the safe Messiah
Failure of the Modern Man
To the centre of all lifes desires
As a whole not an also ran

Love in a hollow field
break the image of your fathers son
drawn to an inner feel
he was thought of as the only one

He no longer denies
all the failures of the Modern Man
He no longer despies
No now he cant pick sides
sees the failures of the modern man

Wise words and sympathy
tell the story of our history
New strength gives a real touch
Sense and reason make it all too much

With a strange fatality
breaks the spirits of a lesser man
some other could see
in his way he was the only one

now that its right to decide
in his time he was the total man
taken from Ceasars side
kept in silence just to prove us wrong.

I. Curtis(November, 1977).

· *Chapter 26* ·

"A right mother hen"

Joy Division began the new decade with a ten-date, eleven-day tour of Europe, where Ian was joined by Annik.

As I've said, I liked Annik. She really, really cared for Ian and she looked out for and after him. Being Belgian she seemed impossibly exotic. She was strong, independent, very into her music, intelligent, and pretty into the bargain.

But none of that could make up for the fact that she was a royal pain in the arse on that tour. She didn't like us being at all laddish and was always pulling us up on our manners. God help you if you farted in the minibus or something. She disapproved of us chatting up girls and generally being dirty bastards, and didn't like our bad language. She was a right mother hen, in other words, clucking round us all the time.

Ian seemed to love it, of course, but that's because he changed when he was with her—that chameleon aspect of him coming out again. Was he more himself when he was with Annik, or more himself when he was pissing about with us? There's the eternal question. All I can remember is that with her he became a bit . . . Well, Barney probably put it best when he said "poncey." With us: chasing groupies and pissing in ashtrays and looking at turds in toilets. With her: talking about Burroughs and Dostoyevsky. The perfect friend or partner for Ian would have combined all those things, but if that person exists they were nowhere near our social scene, so he had to be the chameleon, moving from one to another. You have to say he was bloody good at it. In her book Debbie says he would have made a good actor, and I think she's spot-on there.

So the tour was hard. Not just because of Annik, though she hardly helped, of course. But because we had no money, we were hungry, it was cold and miserable, we were driving around in a minibus, and we really got on each other's tits, and the gigs were small too.

Worst of all, there was never any privacy. Nowhere could you go to be by yourself for a bit. I'd not been abroad for any length of time, had a bit of my mother in me when it came to food, and wouldn't touch anything that wasn't "English." So at the end of a gig when the promoter brought us Chinese, I went hungry. Never had rice, you see. I was in my early twenties and had never had rice. Well, maybe rice pudding. So I just used to sit there, tummy rumbling, watching that lot eating and going hungry. If it wasn't Chinese then it would be lentils—most of the promoters were hippies—and just the sight of lentils used to turn my stomach. So again I ate nothing.

Added to the hunger was the cold. The van was freezing. You'd spend the whole journey twisting and turning, hugging yourself trying to keep warm, with everyone bitching and moaning around you . . . Jesus.

I just wanted to go home. To warmth, and the cat, and proper food. When we got to Antwerp it was like heaven because we had a hotel lined up and we were looking forward to getting a proper wash and a decent bed for the night, rather than kipping on a promoter's floor.

But on our arrival at the hotel any thoughts of luxury were well and truly dashed when the promoter announced that we weren't allowed to check in until after one a.m. Huh? What kind of hotel can't you check into until one o'clock in the morning? Annik was grumbling off about that, quite rightly on this occasion, because Ian was ill and she'd made it her job to ensure he was as comfortable as possible—which must have been especially hard for her, considering his policy of behaving like nothing was wrong. She was on damage control, I suppose you'd have to say.

Either way, we went off, did the gig, then returned to the hotel just after midnight. Perhaps they'd take pity and let us in before one.

But of course they didn't. So we had to wait in the freezing cold, moaning about the van and watching people coming and going from the hotel. There were some right choice fuckers coming out of there, I'm telling you. Tarty women and fat geezers.

Then all of a sudden Annik sat bolt upright and went, "I know what ziss is—eet's a brothel."

Me and Barney were like, "*Really?*" looking forward to getting in there even more. But she started having this flaming row with Rob.

"You peeg," she was saying. "You peeg. You are deesgusting to bring us to ziss brothel," which the rest of were cracking up about—right up until she announced that there was no way we could stay there, no way.

Then we stopped laughing. Because let me tell you we'd been really looking forward to a bed for the night. It didn't matter to us that it was a brothel. It was the wash and bed we were desperate for. But she was really kicking off about it, shouting at Rob and calling him immoral or something, which was the wrong thing to say because Rob squared up to her, pushed his glasses up his nose, and said, "I'm immoral? *I'm* immoral? I'm not the one fucking a married man with a kid."

Which wasn't strictly speaking true, of course. Ian's medication meant that fucking anybody was out of the question; and, like I say, it's public knowledge that he and Annik never—what's a nice way of saying it?—*consummated* their relationship. Even so, what Rob said was close enough to the bone to shut Annik up and she agreed that we could go in, which we did, only to discover that it was indeed a brothel. Everything was neon and there were neon strips everywhere—under the tables, which looked really good. (Come to think of it, I'll have it to suggest that to Becky for our house.) And in every room there was a speaker under the bed, so that when music was playing it vibrated (but I won't suggest that).

Oh, and there was hot water and a mattress. The fourth date of the tour and it was the first time I'd had a proper mattress. Fucking luxury.

Annik still didn't like it, though. She and Ian ended up with the promoter at his house and when we all met up the next morning there was, shall we say, an "Atmosphere" in the van.

Things took a weird turn the next night, after the gig in Cologne, when this guy gave one of our entourage—all right, you've twisted my arm, it was Steve—a tab of acid. A "red star," this guy called it. I think he'd got the idea from an interview that Steve was into hallucinogens—which obviously wasn't that far from the truth, because Steve said, "Thank you very much," and swallowed it.

At which point the Dutch guy's eyes widened and he went, "Oh my God, you Mancunians are *wild*."

"What do you mean?" said Steve. "Why?"

"You've just taken *five* hits of acid in one go. You're supposed to break a corner off to take it." And the guy walked off shaking his head at how wild we Mancunians were, while Steve sort of looked around at us, the color draining from his face.

To paraphrase Hunter S. Thompson, we were at the promoter's house when the drugs began to take hold.

It had a mezzanine section, this house, where we were all sleeping. You got to it by climbing up a ladder, and Steve was getting more and more fucked by the second. Barney could see the writing was on the wall, grabbed his sleeping bag, and escaped down the ladder. Which left me, Twinny, and Steve, who by now was a proper space cadet and was starting to talk about how he was going to get an ax and chop me and Twinny into little bits.

Twinny, you'll recall, is easily spooked at the best of times, so the next thing you know he'd fucked off as well—except that because he was so freaked out by all the talk of Steve chopping us up with an ax he moved the ladder so Steve couldn't get down into the main bit of the house. But then again, neither could I.

It was the beginning of a very long night. Stuck alone with Steve, who had reached a kind of zoned-out, off-in-another-world stage of this trip, I'd nod off and every time I woke up he'd be staring intently at me and I'd go, "Fuck off, Steve. Stop staring."

He was still spaced out the next morning. Much to our relief he was okay to play, but he didn't speak—not a word for three days—which was quite weird. We'd be in the bus and you'd look and Steve would be staring at you.

Then the next time you looked he'd be staring at Barney and

it would be Barney's turn to feel uncomfortable. Thank God there was no ax available, that's all I can say.

Still I wasn't eating. By the time we reached Rotterdam I could have eaten the hind legs off a rotten donkey, I was that hungry, and it was bloody Chinese again. They'd taken us to a Chinese restaurant, where I sat feeling sorry for myself until this waitress who spoke really good English came over to ask why I wasn't eating.

I was a right little kid, going, "I can't eat it. I don't like it. Me mam says it's dirty."

Evidently she was taking pity on me and said, "What *can* you eat?"

"English food."

"Ah," she said. "That's a shame because we only have Dutch food—steak and chips, egg and chips, sausage and chips."

Oh God, it was like I'd died and gone to heaven. My deep affinity with the Dutch began that night as I ate like a lord—two steaks, two full dinners. It was brilliant. It was all my mother's fault, of course. That's how deep the indoctrination went. Even though all the rest would be tucking greedily into their Chinese and somehow managing not to fall down dead, and despite the fact that I was fucking *starving*, I still couldn't accept the evidence of my own eyes and eat some special fried rice or whatever. When I did—I must have been at death's door to do it, but I eventually did—it tasted incredible. I loved it. I was like, "*Mother!* . . ."

The same thing happened years later with New Order, when we went for a meal with Cabaret Voltaire. There I was, heart sinking as we pushed open the door to a Sheffield curry house, knowing I was going to have to order whatever was the one dish they had for unadventurous bastards like me: Maryland Chicken, which tasted like they hated making it. One of the Cabs had this amazing-smelling curry.

"Can I have a taste?" I said.

"Yeah, 'course . . ."

It was delicious. Fabulous.

"*Mother!* . . ."

But that moment in Holland ended up being among the best of the tour. It was funny, though, because then more than ever—because of the discomfort, probably—we played some of our best gigs. We always loved playing so much and during that tour in particular it felt like the only refuge—from the cold, the hunger, Annik's clucking, the band bickering—was being onstage. We'd play and be brilliant and really click as musicians, then come offstage and immediately resume our former positions at one another's throats.

What was at the root of it all, I'm not sure. Definitely we felt a bit frustrated that, with our album doing so well (it had featured in a load of best-of-year lists from 1979), and us being such a hot band, we could still be so cold, freezing in a minibus, and on people's floors. I'll tell you this for nothing: I've never been so happy to return to Manchester as I was when we got back.

· *Chapter 27* ·

"We carried on"

We played a lot with Killing Joke around that time. They were a tough bunch to work with but we became friends, and years later they were the only group ever to ask me to join them. Primal Scream almost did, just changing their minds right at the end: they were worried they'd sound too much like New Order. Anyway, Killing Joke got back together after a long time apart to make an album, *Pandemonium*, but their bassist, Youth, was getting into production and didn't want to tour, so I got the call: did I want to play bass on tour with Killing Joke?

Because New Order had split up, and I'd finished doing Revenge, I was at a bit of a loose end; so I decided that at the very least I could listen to the album they wanted me to play. Plus the wages they were offering were very good: a grand per gig. *Per gig.*

We were actually working together on a German concept album, *Freispiel*, in Cologne's Stadgarten Studio; it was a collaboration of rock and avant-garde musicians. We worked with Rüdiger Elze (guitar) and Rüdiger Braune (drums) both from the group Kowalski. Afterward I ended up back at the lads' hotel. I was drinking then, and doing whatever else was going round—and there was plenty of it going round that night.

In the room were me, Geordie and Jaz, and two girls. We all sat down to listen to their new album and when it was over they stopped, looked at me, and said, "Well? What do you think?" Now, because I was completely off my tits, I said, "I can't play that shit."

But I didn't mean, like, "shit," like the music was shit. I meant shit, as in "that shit," meaning the bass, which was the normal, low-end, chord-following rumble, which is just not what I do; I don't play bass like that. I can't play bass like that. Not that the album was shit. Far from it. Just that I don't play "that shit."

Being off my face, though, I couldn't get this point across. But Geordie and Jaz were just as wasted as I was, and they weren't getting it either. They thought I was talking about the album. I wasn't.

The more I tried to dig myself out of it, the worse it went, until the atmosphere had become really heated and we were getting to our feet. If it wasn't for the girls breaking it up, we'd have ended up fighting there and then—and they would have kicked the shit out of me. Meaning "the shit."

Anyway, the situation was defused thanks to the feminine intervention and a couple of weeks later I was surprised to find that the offer still stood. By this time I was thinking that a grand a gig was simply too good an offer to pass up. Fuck it, I'll follow chords for a grand a gig. So I decided to swallow my pride and play that shit. I got my head round it too, and was starting to look forward to being on the road with Killing Joke. Then I spoke to either Jaz or Geordie and they said that Youth had changed his mind: couldn't bear to have someone else playing his bass lines, apparently. Yeah, me, I know. . . .

Anyway, as a result of all that me, Jaz, and Geordie decided to do a bit of work as a side-project, and we put six or eight tracks together. We even had meetings with their management, E.G., about setting up a band together. Never got as far as a name, but we were thinking about who we were going to have drumming for us, and I'd even persuaded Jaz that he should do more singing, rather than his normal, more shouty, style, when suddenly it all went quiet. Never heard from them, never got a postcard, a phone call, whatever—complete media blackout. Until one day I started getting PRS royalties on a weird song that I'd never heard of and didn't remember playing on and it was a Killing Joke song. They'd used me on one of their albums, the cheeky buggers. Saying that, I do hold Jaz and Geordie in the absolute highest regard; not being in a band with them is one of my only regrets in music.

So that was that. They always were a right bunch, though, to be honest, and they'd be jockeying for position on the bill all the time. They were very ambitious and driven; ruthless. I mean, that night at the ULU, they were trying to fuck things up for us. They were trying the old Fast Breeder trick of being the support but going on late so it looked like they were the headliners. Meanwhile, we were having trouble with another support group, from Manchester, called the Smirks, who were aptly named because they were a right bunch of arrogant smirkers. That almost ended in fisticuffs too.

Plus my bass amp blew up while we were sound checking. Of course in those days you didn't have somebody who would come and fix your gear. You didn't have a "guitar roadie." And you didn't carry spares. What you did was get your manager to ask the support group if you could borrow their amp. Oh, but our support was Killing fucking Joke and the Smirks, and Killing Joke was doing their level best to fuck us right up with all their time-keeping shenanigans, and I'd almost had a fight with the Smurfs, so of course they both refused to help.

It was quite funny, really: because I'd done so badly at school I knew nothing about electronics when I joined the band, and when I had to fix the gear I did wish I'd paid more attention in physics. But there I was—I had to take the whole cab apart, hundreds of screws, then check the wiring, which was okay. Shit, one of the speakers had blown.

As I was doing that, Killing Joke came on. I was stuffed in the back of the cab, with the Joke sound checking more loudly than usual, it seemed, me holding a soldering iron and trying to see with a cigarette lighter. I ended up rewiring the cab and managed to get through the gig. Fuck me, that was traumatic.

Not quite as traumatic as what happened next, though, because it was around this time that Ian started cutting himself up.

After getting back from the European tour he'd apparently downed a bottle of Pernod and slashed himself with a knife—a fucking kitchen knife. We talked to him about it in practice afterward.

"What the fuck did you do that for, Ian, you daft bastard?"

"Oh, it was just one of those things," he said, shrugging. "I got pissed and got carried away. You know . . ."

"Yeah, yeah . . ."

But, actually, *no.* I didn't know.

Of course—you know what I'm going to say. We brushed off the fact that he'd added self-harming to the list. We avoided the subject. We carried on like everything was all right and pretended that Ian wasn't ill, wasn't struggling with the responsibility of the band, and didn't have some heavy, heavy affairs-of-the-heart stuff to contend with. We carried on. With Ian's blessing we carried on; Ian, who out of all of us most wanted us to taste the fruits of success and didn't want his illness to get in the way; Ian, who always buoyed us up after a bad review or a shit show. Who, even though he was the front man and the focal point, always insisted that we were a group, who used to say, "All I do is the words and sing. The others do the music."

Because that's the thing, and I can't say it enough: nobody wanted the group—*the whole group*—to do well more than Ian did. So he lied. Either to us, or to himself, or both. He lied when he said that it was no big deal to get pissed and start carving away at yourself with a knife.

He was having fits more frequently, too. He'd have a fit at gigs. There was one when he just froze, mid-strum on his guitar. Another one when he fell into the drum kit and was thrashing around; Steve played on as Ian kicked his drums out from beneath him and Twinny and Terry rushed on to haul him off the stage. Another where he kicked the flight case the synthesizer was on and sent it spinning off the stage. More than anything Ian hated having a fit onstage and I can see why. Being at your most vulnerable, just flipping out like that, with some of the audience laughing, some scared, some cheering, some thinking you're a freak. It must have been horrible. But we'd stop him from swallowing his tongue and he'd get up, tell us he was fine, and, well, you know the rest.

It got so that recording our next album was almost a break. Almost.

· Chapter 28 ·

"He thought we were pricks—and how right he was"

By now plans were being made to tour America, and Joy Division was due to record their second album at Britannia Row studios in London. Things were going less smoothly for Ian Curtis, however. During a confrontation in which Debbie smashed his copy of Bowie's Low, *he admitted his affair with Annik. Despite assuring Debbie that he would break it off, he didn't, and continued writing to Annik, his letters to her reflecting his inner turmoil. He told her about the obligations and responsibilities that weighed heavily upon him; that his epilepsy seemed to be worsening, the attacks growing more frequent and more intense; and that his dog, Candy, was to be sent away. Finding it increasingly difficult to cope with Candy during Ian's absence, not to mention the cost, and with Ian unwilling to either contribute or discuss the issue, Debbie felt she had no choice and had made arrangements for the dog to live on a farm in Rochdale. Ian, meanwhile, was taking barbiturates for his epilepsy, which have a numbing, deadening effect.*

Next, the band decamped to London for the recording sessions, leaving Terry Mason and Twinny at home and using Dave Pils as a roadie. He stayed at home in Walthamstow, Martin Hannett in a hotel, while Rob

Gretton and the band rented two flats in York Street. The cost of this, however, meant that the band members had very little to live on.

We had enough to get some food and maybe a pint, the usual. Both Sue and Iris worked, so at least me and Barney didn't have to worry about providing, but Ian had a wife and kid back home, so, just like everything else in this story, it was harder for him.

It's funny really, when you look at it like that, because nowadays if we'd released an album like *Unknown Pleasures*, we'd have been nominated for the Mercury, be swanning around Glastonbury fighting off mates of Kate Moss, and sitting on sofas with Fearne Cotton. Back then things moved much more slowly. Independent music stayed underground. Ian on the cover of *NME* was as big as it got. We never felt like we were stars at all, and we never acted like it.

For a start, we didn't have any money, hadn't really earned any yet. We let Rob take care of all of that and he did it very well, keeping it all close to his chest. One of Tony's favorite sayings was: "Always keep your bands poor. That way they make great music." He may well have been right. There's nothing like sudden fame and wealth to turn a band's heads.

But just every now and then it would have been nice to have tested his theory instead of being forced to prove it.

It made us a better band, though. I mean, Rob, you'd have to say, was very good at keeping you grounded, making sure your feet stayed firmly on the ground. His thing was: just get on with it, play live and record. That was how we went in to record *Closer*. We were keen to do an album as good as *Unknown Pleasures*, but it wasn't like there was huge pressure—not from Rob and not from Factory. All the pressure we felt came from within and we were brimming with confidence back then. Ian's illness was the only black spot on the horizon. Otherwise we were rocking.

By that time we'd already recorded "Love Will Tear Us Apart" at Pennine but weren't happy with it so had another crack in Strawberry. Martin was up to his old tricks. He'd stay up till two in the morning then phone Rob and go, "Right, I'm going in the studio now with Chris to mix 'Love Will Tear us Apart,' and Rob would phone me up and go, "You're nearest: fucking get down to Strawberry now, Hooky; they're mixing," and I'd go, "Fucking hell, it's two in the morning."

He'd just say, "Fucking get down there." Because he didn't have a car, you see. So I'd drive to the studio at half two in the morning, buzzing the buzzer for hours before they'd let me in, and Martin would say, "Oh, you turned up, did you?"

"Yes, why are you doing it now?"

"Oh, it's the only time we could get." But it wasn't—it was just so you weren't there, so you didn't turn up. Because one of the most famous things about Martin was that he hated having the musicians around during the mix, so he'd make it really difficult. The night he did "Love Will Tear Us Apart" the air-conditioning was cranked up as usual. I was freezing while Martin and Chris sniggered. He may well have been a genius, Martin, but that didn't stop him from being a right twat sometimes.

All of which didn't bode well because we were due to record our second album with him, a prospect we might well have been dreading but for the fact that we were going to London to record it, in Britannia Row studios, owned by Pink Floyd, just like proper rock stars.

Our families didn't like it, of course. We got a lot of grief: "Why can't you just record at Strawberry?"

I think Rob liked the idea of getting Ian away for a bit and of course Ian loved it because he got to shack up with Annik. Martin wanted to use Britannia Row because it was state-of-the-art at that time and he did like his toys. Chris Nagle got the elbow, though. Martin wanted to use this other guy he'd met, John Caffery, who wasn't wildly imaginative but was a nice bloke, while the tape operator was Mike Johnson, who later became New Order's engineer on everything we ever did. We liked him and really got on with him; he was very imaginative and willing to try anything.

So we decamped to London, where Rob had hired two flats above a shop, which were opposite each other across a corridor, both two-bedroom. They were probably quite small but they seemed huge to us at the time, with open-plan kitchens and everything. Ian and Bernard had one side—with Annik in with Ian when she stayed over—while me Steve and Rob had the other side. Our flat wasn't as cozy—it was a bit bigger, colder, and more sparsely furnished—but was still okay.

Martin was in a hotel because he wanted to be as far away from us as possible because he thought we were pricks—and how right he was.

Then there was Britannia Row itself. The studios we'd used in Manchester were a bit old-fashioned. All wood-paneling and heavy drapes and cork tiles on the walls. Britannia Row was like something out of *Star Wars* in comparison. It was a bit more austere and clinical than anywhere we'd been at home. It had an enclosed spaceship atmosphere, with the control room in particular really packed full of stuff. There wasn't much room for anybody else; we had a bench seat against the wall. Me and Bernard would position ourselves on either side of Martin, looking over his shoulder.

He was in his element there, Martin was. He loved the airless quality of Britannia Row. He loved how it felt sealed off from the outside world and started working at night to take advantage of it at its most silent and dead. Listen to the finished product and you can hear all of that in the album.

There were offices, too, so loads of staff hanging around—Pink Floyd's staff, I think—and there was a PA company based there, plus they had a recreation room with a pool table in it. Islington was a very interesting area. There was a famous taxidermy shop called Get Stuffed full of very exotic animals and a military shop on the corner where I used to stand staring in at the window, looking at these really expensive World War II flying jackets, lusting after them.

Every day we'd clamber into Steve's car and drive the few miles from York Street to Islington, Martin arriving in his old beat-up Volvo. He'd ripped the speakers out and replaced them with two Auratone monitor speakers, studio speakers that are very flat but faithful. Martin said if we could make the mix sound good on the Auratones then it would sound good on anything. Nobody in their right mind would listen to Auratones for pleasure because they sound rotten; they soak up all the reflections and echo and wetness on a track, make everything sound dead dry and boring. But that was Martin's scheme: make the record sound good on them and it'll lop your head off on a set of decent speakers. Listening to a mix with him meant getting in his car and having him drive you around while you checked out how it sounded. He hadn't bothered screwing them down, these speakers, so they just used to roll around the floor of the Volvo, and because Martin was such a terrible driver they did a lot of rolling around.

But of course we weren't using him for his skill as a driver. As a producer he was getting the best out of us, and at the same time we were learning from him. It was him who encouraged us to use the piano; they had a grand piano at Britannia Row. He put it on "The Eternal," trying it on nearly every track. He showed Bernard how to use keyboards properly, how to layer them to give the sound a real richness and depth. Christ, he used to get pissed off with us, especially me and Barney: we were about as welcome as a dog at a bowling alley.

"Oh, Martin, what do you reckon about making the hi-hat a bit brighter?" one of us would say, strictly taking turns.

He'd scream at us. "Fucking shut up, you pair of twats."

I've since discovered that Martin was on heroin then, and that one night he drove to Manchester and back to score, he was that desperate for it. But to be honest, there was no evidence of that in the studio. He was smoking a lot of dope, as he always did, but otherwise really efficient and really creative. He introduced us to the ARP synthesizers and sequencers, which he and Bernard used a lot, and to audio gates, used so that the drums would trigger synthesizer sounds and sound really crisp and powerful.

Martin's big thing was still clarity. He always said that for a recording to have lasting effect and impact it had to have clarity and separation. Now, remember: me and Barney still didn't like the sound of *Unknown Pleasures*. I mean, I suppose that by then we'd grudgingly accepted that it was a great album, and knew that part of that was due to the work Martin had done, but it still wasn't how we heard Joy Division. We wanted a harder, harsher, more metallic sound, like a group playing in a garage with metal walls, like the Stooges or the Velvet Underground. He wanted us to sound like—how did he describe it?—adult gothic music or something.

Well, he was right and we were wrong. Sorry, Martin, if you're up there. But it didn't stop us bitching at the time because he'd make us play the song then take it apart.

"Right, let's concentrate on this bit," he'd say, and would do a lot of work adding effects and synth parts. He spent many a happy hour messing about with the synths and the sequencers, too—much to the studio manager's delight, because it was an expensive studio, Britannia Row, around £40 an hour; considering I was only earning £12 a week, this was an absolute fortune.

So workwise it was great. As far as socializing went, this was when a division appeared in the band. The first, I suppose you'd have to say. It was caused by Ian finding his arty feet and us not handling that all too well.

By finding his arty feet I mean behaving a little bit pretentiously. There were other influences in his life now and he was soaking them up. One of these was Genesis P-Orridge from Throbbing Gristle. Now, I like Genesis, and I fucking love Throbbing Gristle, but I can't get on with the whole none-more-arty attitude that goes with that scene. Genesis wrote the book on all that.

Then of course there was Annik. Although she had her flat in Parsons Green, she and Ian had set up house in his room in the flat across the way and were acting like a right pair of arty Bohemian types. Every five minutes they'd be announcing that they were off to some art exhibition or some gallery, with their noses in the air, making it perfectly clear that whatever they were doing wasn't for the likes of us.

The fact that in return we gave it loads and called him all sorts of pretentious tossers wasn't very nice of us, of course. If I'm honest, we were pretty horrible to him about it. So what if he wanted to go to an art gallery with his new girl? It was really none of our business.

But you know what it's like. Young lads, their mate suddenly going off with his new girlfriend, taking on airs and graces: they rip the piss. I've no doubt that the likes of Genesis and Annik thought they knew the "real" Ian, and that he was most at home in "their" world. But we thought *we* knew the real Ian. Probably Debbie did too. What I've realized in the years since is that the truth was a lot more complex and in-between than any of us really knew at the time. Thinking about it, I bet even Ian didn't know who the "real" Ian was.

About halfway through the recording, Rob announced that we should get our other halves down, and sent them money for train tickets. Debbie didn't come, much to Ian's relief. She used the money to pay a bill. I can't remember the sequence of events, but that's because it was a day best forgotten. For a start, we left them waiting around at the station for a couple of hours. Then they had to hang around while we finished in the studio, which didn't exactly improve the mood. Later I accidentally blabbed to Iris about Annik being with Ian all of the time. Me and my big mouth. She kicked off, which added to the general air of gloom. She then told Rob's wife, Lesley.

In short, the day was a complete debacle, because it was really expensive and everybody was as miserable as sin and I don't even know why that day was chosen, because we were in the studio anyway, which didn't help matters. So you had Sue, Lesley, Gillian, and Iris all twiddling their thumbs, dead fucking pissed off at being dragged to London only to have to sit around, and fuming that they were apparently banned from the whole process while Annik was hanging around.

We breathed a big sigh of relief when it was all was over, I can tell you, and Rob celebrated by putting cornflakes in everybody's bed. However, in order to escape suspicion, he put them in his own bed as well and was walking around scratching his head, going, "Well, if we've all got cornflakes in our beds, then who's fucking done it, then?"

A few days later the truth emerged and we were like, "You barmy bastard. What's the point in japing yourself?"

Another night we overheard Ian and Annik getting ready go out, and Annik saying, "Ian, Ian, hurry and do the i-ron-ing." Just like that. "I-ron-ing." And there stood Ian, all done up ready to go out, doing Annik's ironing with a cigarette hanging out of his mouth.

We were like, "I-ron-ing. I-an, have you done the i-ron-ing?" which really pissed him off and he got really angry. Me and Barney noticed that they had a teddy bear in the eiderdown in their room and laid into him about that, too.

He was like, "Fuck off, you pair of twats. Just fuck off and leave us alone, would you?"

I feel terrible about it now, of course. Now I'm older and wiser, and now I've looked at his lyrics and worked out what a tortured soul he was. We should have left him alone to have his love affair but we didn't because he wasn't tragic Ian Curtis the genius then. He was just our mate and that's what you did with your mates up North: you ripped the piss out of them.

One particular evening we got back before Ian and Annik, who were still out somewhere, probably at a gallery or an exhibition or something, and Barney said, "Come on, let's jape their room."

So we went in and the first thing we did—what a bunch of bastards—we took out the bed. No mean feat. Then we unfolded the i-ron-ing board, made the bed over the i-ron-ing board, and tucked the teddy in the top. We hid in Barney's room, looking through the keyhole waiting for them to come back. Didn't have long to wait. A few minutes later the front door opened and Ian and Annik came into the flat and then went into the bedroom.

Next thing you know, she screamed. "Ian, Ian, what have

zey done to our room?" We pissed ourselves laughing. Then Ian kicked off. Really kicked off. Shit. He heard us laughing from the other side of Barney's door and launched himself at the door, screaming, "You fucking cunts, you fucking bunch of twats," kicking hell out of the door.

We weren't laughing anymore. We were scared, because let me tell you, he was going mental. Absolutely mental. What if he had a fit? What if he smashed the door in?

He calmed down enough for us to make our escape. But of course we still had their bed, which was in bits in the other flat. As we scarpered across there we had Annik on our tails and she launched herself at the door.

"You peegs," she was screaming. "You fooking English peegs." Kicking the glass window in the door.

Of course we were in hysterics again, which just made it worse. God knows how we got the bed back together.

Part of the problem was that we were jealous of Ian, I think. Annik was fit and exotic, and Ian was living with her in the flat while we were all slumming it. Or that's how it felt, anyway.

Plus he was Martin's favorite. As far back as *Unknown Pleasures*, Ian had developed a special relationship with Martin—the two of them seemed to feed off each other creatively—and I think we sort of resented that, too, like Ian was the teacher's pet or something. Especially since Martin treated the rest of us like shit.

Ian would say to Martin, "Do you need me for a while, Martin?"

Martin would say, "No, mate, you're all right; come back at eight."

So Ian and Annik would happily go off together, whereas me and Barney were always "that pair of bastards." We'd play the tracks with Steve, and Ian would do a guide vocal but then he'd return to record the proper vocals at night, when it was quieter in the studio. Which is fair enough—it's a normal thing to do—but it did create a bit of a them-and-us situation.

It went both ways, of course. It's a well-known fact that we totally pissed him off during the making of *Closer* because he wrote a letter to someone—Rob, I think—saying that he wasn't happy with the album, partly because of us lot, "sneaky, japing tossers," he called us. But in his letters to Annik he says he was very happy with the album: strange.

You've got to say he had a point. I remember being in the flat one night and A Certain Ratio were around having a smoke with Rob. Me and Barney didn't bother with all that so Barney was going, "What shall we do to them? Come on, we got to do something. . . ."

So they're all sitting there, squinting at us through clouds of dope smoke, going, "What are you up to, lads?" as we set about our plan. First we smeared their minibus handles and windscreen in jam and marmalade, and tied toilet rolls to their exhaust; then we prepared eggs and pots and pans full of water.

When ACR finally made their way out we were waving good-bye to them from the flat windows, watching as they got to the bus and found the jammy traps. Next thing we were pelting them with water and eggs and killing ourselves as we watched them trying and failing to wrench open the doors and get out of the line of fire. Finally they managed it and tore away, with two long trails of pink bog paper hanging off the back off the bus.

So Ian had a point. We *were* sneaky, japing tossers. Not long before he would have been a part of it too. So if we resented him for being Martin's favorite and having a fit foreign girlfriend, well, maybe we also thought, *We're losing our mate here.*

His illness hung over us, though. One night we were in the

studio. He was working on his vocals and he seemed a bit rattled about something and went off by himself. We were waiting for him to do a vocal and after a while Martin was going, "Where is Ian? Where the fuck is Ian? Hooky, go and find out where Ian is and drag him back here."

So off I trotted and found him in the toilet, where he was sparkled on the floor, big gash in his head. He'd gone to the toilet, had a fit, fallen forward, and banged his head on the sink, which had knocked him out.

Guess what? We brought him round, he said he was all right, and we carried on. I should call the book that, shouldn't I? *He Said He Was All Right So We Carried On.*

The other thing I remember is recording one afternoon and a bloke calling in to reception to see Martin. There was a group with him, a young group. They wanted to talk about Martin producing their first single.

So Martin went off to talk and of course, being nosy, I poked my head around the door to get a look at these kids, who it turned out were called U2. I don't know if it had been raining outside but they looked like something the cat had dragged in, and they were sitting in reception staring at Martin with complete awe. Very funny.

They were huge fans of Joy Division, it turned out, and wanted Martin to produce their first single, "11 O'Clock Tick Tock," which he did.

Years later I got the shock of my life when Tony told me one story about Bono. It seems that after Ian had died Tony met Bono somewhere, and Bono was telling Tony not to worry because he would take over from where Ian left off.

Very strange. But nice . . . Well, he did in a way, didn't he? We may have been laughing at them in reception that day, the star-struck young pretenders, but just look at how our two careers went. Seven years later we'd been stung with a tax bill for nearly a million quid and losing all our money on a nightclub, while they'd gone off and made *The Joshua Tree*, become the biggest band in the world, and hadn't opened a nightclub. And we all know how they feel about tax. They did everything right, in other words.

For the cover of Closer, *as well as the twelve-inch of "Love Will Tear Us Apart," Peter Saville showed the band a series of photographs taken by Bernard Pierre Wolff of crypts in Genoa's Staglieno Cemetery. Of course, these images would later take on an extra, tragic significance.*

"I guess it worked for Ian," said Saville. "Perhaps if I'd been sent a draft of the lyrics, and had any kind of sensitivity, I might have thought, I'm not going to indulge that route. Let's have some trees. . . ."

The "Love Will Tear Us Apart" single cover was done before *Closer.* We went to Peter's studio on Portobello Road. He'd just seen an article about a photographer who'd taken some photographs of a cemetery on the outskirts of Genoa that was used by rich Italian merchants. These rich families had gotten into a macabre competition with the tombs, each building more and more elaborate monuments.

I loved the images and I loved Peter's cover. I was always fascinated by the way the apostrophes both go the same way. They don't frame the word *Closer* as you expect them to. I did ask him recently what that was all about, and it turns out that what I thought were apostrophes are actually full stops from the second century BC, and the reason they go that way is to do with the angle the original stonemason leaned when he was tapping out the words and punctuation marks. So there you go.

It's a beautiful cover. We all loved the pictures, especially Ian. I wonder: when he chose them did he realize how symbolic they would be? I don't know; nobody does, I suppose. In my gut I think not but I do think that he saw them and saw how they fit perfectly with the music on the album—which itself was a kind of soundtrack to his suffering, I guess. Quite shocking really. By the time we chose those pictures, he had less than two months to live.

· Chapter 29 ·

"His mum got the blood out by washing it in a bath of saltwater"

With the American tour due to begin on May 21 at Hurrah nightclub in New York, Joy Division next embarked on a busy schedule of UK dates partly aimed at raising funds, including a Factory mini-residency at the Moonlight Club in Hampstead, as well as a prestigious support slot for the Stranglers at the Rainbow Theatre in Finsbury Park.

Prior to this gig, however, the Stranglers' front man Hugh Cornwell was sent to Pentonville Prison for possession of heroin, cocaine, and cannabis, and the show was instead reconfigured as "The Stranglers & Friends" with other well-known artists (Toyah, Hazel O'Connor, Robert Smith, and Richard Jobson among them) filling in for Cornwell.

The night would also prove eventful for Joy Division, which was scheduled to perform there before returning to the Moonlight in Hampstead for the last night of the Factory residency. Onstage at the Rainbow, Ian had a fit triggered by strobe lights and collapsed into the drum kit but recovered enough to play the Moonlight just over an hour later. He then had another fit during that set—though the performance was still rated a triumph by NME*'s Neil Norman, who wrote: "Unlike the Fall, who make me want to go out and kick a cat, Joy Division convince me I could spit in the face of God."*

Though the pressure was evidently becoming intolerable, and Ian spoke of opening a bookshop with Annik and even, according to Genesis P-Orridge, hatched plans with him to form a breakaway group, Ian nevertheless insisted to his bandmates that they continue with the schedule.

It got chaotic now. Really, really busy. First off we had this label residency at the Moonlight Club in Hampstead, loads of Factory bands playing over three nights: Section 25, Crawling Chaos, John Dowie, A Certain Ratio, Kevin Hewick, Blurt, the Durutti Column, X-O-Dus, and the Royal Family.

And us. Being the biggest, it fell to us to attract the punters. Factory was apparently nervous that the other bands wouldn't be enough of a draw but I found that hard to believe, because the venue was tiny.

Anyway, we'd stayed down in London after recording *Closer*, and went on to do the first two nights of the Hampstead gig, the second and third of April, which went well—as in we turned up, played, did good gigs. One of the nights was attended by this A&R guy from Polydor called the Captain, who's a bit of a legend in the industry. He's a very tall, broad guy with a military bearing, hence the name, but a nice bloke. I've since met him many times over the years. He looks after U2 now, and was a big help in their career, but before all that came to see us, which Ian was dead excited about.

"Oh God, Hooky," he was going, "there's an A&R man from

Polydor here. He's called the Captain. He's great. Come and meet him—we might get some free drinks."

Great. Free drinks. Well up for that. So after the set the band and Rob went to meet the Captain and discovered, firstly, that he was dead posh—"Hello. How are you, Peter?"—like that; and secondly that he was going to get a round of drinks in: "Now, what can I get everybody?"

We were like, "Fucking great," and really took the piss, ordering triple vodkas and orange and two beers—each. But he just looked amused, said, "Fine, fine," went to the bar, ordered the drinks, and handed them out.

"Tuck in, everybody, tuck in. It's all you chaps deserve after such an excellent gig."

Then he turned to the barmaid. "How much is that, my good woman?"

"Eight pound fifty, darling," she said.

The Captain reached into his jacket and pulled out a checkbook. At which point the barmaid looked absolutely incredulous, as though he was offering to pay with a huge purple marrow, and said to him, "We don't take checks, darling."

So the Captain turned to us, looking suitably embarrassed and said, "I'm terribly sorry about this, but can anybody lend me eight pounds fifty to pay for the drinks?"

I think it was Ian who lent him the money to get the round in and the guy made a check out to him for the round of drinks, then slunk off as soon as he could.

Then came the gig at the Rainbow, where the Stranglers' crew behaved like complete bastards. Before the doors opened I was onstage ogling Jean-Jacques Burnel's setup, which was split into high/mid/bass, like a proper PA. Oh, it was great. He had a really huge rig and I had a really small, cheap setup in comparison. I was jealous. The problem was their crew wouldn't let us move any of it so we could sound check. That day the Stranglers' crew was swanning about as if they owned the place because there were all these "pop stars" hanging around, like Toyah and what have you. It was as though it had suddenly become this huge event or something. They were recording it to release as an album, too, which didn't help.

All day the crew was just rude, to be honest. Because Jean-Jacques Burnel was one of my heroes I'd been really, really looking forward to that Rainbow gig, so for them to treat us so badly was gutting and I held a grudge about it for a long time. Same with Rob.

It was at that gig, in fact, that we swore to ourselves that we'd make sure we never treated a support band the way the Stranglers had treated us, and thus a policy was born—one that arguably got out of hand in the Haçienda years, when visiting bands were treated like royalty. I used to moan and whinge about it at the time, but Rob would always remind me of that Stranglers gig.

He'd say, "Treat your bands how you want to be treated." And he was absolutely right.

The crew problem went right across the board, including the lighting guys. At most gigs Rob would position himself in the lighting booth so that if the technician went to the strobes he was there to sort it out straightaway. We'd always know about it onstage because the lights would kick in then stop almost immediately, and you could just imagine Rob pushing his glasses up his nose and telling the technician to kill them or else. But that night we didn't even get a sound check, so there was no way Rob was going to get in the lighting booth. Sure enough, during "Atrocity Exhibition" the guy went to the strobes.

They were blasting away and not stopping like normal, and I

thought, *Uh-oh,* and no doubt so did Barney and Steve, and the next thing you know Ian's dancing had fallen out of time and suddenly he'd lost it; his legs went, he stumbled back and into the kit and the lighting guy realized something was wrong and brought the lights down just as Twinny and Terry dashed on and me and Barney took off our guitars and went to help Ian, who was having a fit in the drums.

We carried him off, got him to a room backstage and stayed with him for a while until he'd recovered. He was going, "Thanks, lads. Sorry lads. I'm all right now. Let's get over to the Moonlight, eh?"

We were telling him, "No, mate, no you're not fucking going on again tonight. They can manage without us."

Tony was down to see us that night but bollocks to that—even Rob was adamant that Ian needed to rest. But Ian insisted. You know why? Because he was a man of his word, simple as that. He wasn't a wimp. You put Ian on a battlefield and he'd be the guy still fighting with his arms hanging off. He said, "Don't worry, I'll be fine. A couple of aspirin, no problem. Let's go."

Definitely his own worst enemy. So we went to perform at the Moonlight, and of course things didn't get any better. We were as good as our word. We played. But Ian collapsed again. He was really, really tired by this point, almost weary. But instead of resting, which of course he should have done, we went to Malvern the very next night, did a storming gig with Section 25, drove home that night, and dropped Ian off. The next day, I got a phone call from Rob to tell me that Ian had tried to kill himself.

It was on Easter Sunday that Ian took an overdose of phenobarbital at home in Macclesfield. It's been suggested that after taking the pills he had second thoughts, fearing the possibility of brain or liver damage rather than death, or that his attempt was a cry for help. Whatever his reasons, he alerted Deborah and was immediately taken to the hospital in Macclesfield and had his stomach pumped.

The following day, Easter Monday, Tony Wilson, Alan Erasmus, and Rob Gretton took Debbie to visit Ian in the hospital. There it was suggested that Ian stay with Tony and his wife, Lindsay Reade, at their cottage in Charlesworth in order to ease Ian's marital pressure. It was agreed that the stay would begin the following day, Tuesday, April 8.

Meanwhile, Rob Gretton had decided that the next day's gig, at Derby Hall, Bury, was to go ahead as planned, only without Ian. Alan Hempsall of Crispy Ambulance, a big Joy Division fan, was asked to stand in and duly began learning lyrics. When he turned up on the night, however, he was surprised to find Ian Curtis at the venue. Gretton had apparently visited Ian in the hospital and persuaded him to perform—for at least one or two songs. . . .

We should have canceled of course. I mean, looking back now, you start to see the gigs we should have got rid of. That Stranglers support at the Rainbow, for one, and that one at Derby Hall, Bury, for another. But we decided to go ahead with it for whatever reason. Whether we needed the money for the American tour or would have been penalized financially for pulling out, I don't know, but we went ahead with them.

I hate to say this, but in an awful sort of way it was quite exciting, really, to consider being able to play a gig without worrying about Ian for once. Because, after the initial shock of him trying to top himself, you felt like, *Right, okay, that's a fucking scary thing, but at least he* didn't *go through with it. He pulled back in time. He changed his mind. He chose not to die. He wants to live.*

So you felt that he'd turned a corner somehow. He'd had a go at the suicide thing, decided he didn't like it, and that would be that. Plus, to sound very, very callous for a moment, it was nice to think of playing a gig without the fear of one of the band members collapsing onstage. We could actually enjoy the music for once. Yeah, that does sound callous. Maybe I should take that out.

It was a lovely venue, actually, Bury. There was a large, ornate chandelier that hung above the stage, and a covered grand piano that had been pushed up to the stage. Of course they're kidney-shaped, aren't they, those pianos, so muggins here stepped onto it, thinking it was part of the stage, and shot straight through to the floor and nearly killed myself, which was my only brush with death for the day—or so I thought at the time.

So anyway, Minny Pops played their set, then Section 25 came on, did most of their set, and finished with "Girls Don't Count," which was the song that Ian and Rob had produced and was supposed to be released as a single but hadn't yet come out—delayed because of the sleeve, I think. So they were playing that, and me, Barney, and Steve went onstage to join them, along with Alan from Crispy Ambulance and Simon Topping from A Certain Ratio, who would be singing the Joy Division songs.

Maybe the idea was to try to dazzle the crowd with the amazing array of Factory talent onstage so they'd be so bowled over they wouldn't notice that Ian wasn't there—I don't know. What I do know is that the crowd was getting more and more rowdy.

Now, the venue was sold out and was at capacity: four hundred. But earlier, after the sound check, the bands and Rob had gone for a bite to eat and returned to find a bunch of kids hanging around outside the venue. They'd caught sight of Rob and started hassling him to get in, and for some strange reason he took pity on them and put them all on the guest list.

Little did he know that these kids were a right bunch of troublemakers, and immediately on entering the gig had gone to the fire escapes to let in all their mates—loads of them—which swelled the numbers inside to around six hundred. The mood, as they say, started getting ugly.

What didn't help matters was Ian coming on to sing "Decades" and "The Eternal," but with nothing like his normal spark, which sort of brought the evening down, to be honest. It eludes me, actually, the point of him coming on, because it definitely made matters worse. I mean, up until then it was going all right. I dare say there were plenty in who didn't even realize Ian wasn't onstage. Of course the true fans knew, but then they weren't the ones most likely to cause trouble. When Ian went off again the crowd became even more restless and we played "Sister Ray" then left, just as it started to get rowdy.

Really rowdy. Most of the bands were backstage when it all kicked off. I found out later that Larry from Section 25 had got caught out there and had to hide behind the curtains. But the rest of us were in a dressing room at the side of the stage, kept separate from the main venue by a huge drape that ran down one side. So we didn't see one of the idiots throw a pint pot that shattered in the chandelier above the stage, showering the stage with broken glass. We didn't see Rob dive into the crowd to try to lamp the idiot who'd thrown the pint pot. Didn't see Twinny dive in after him and get set upon by a bunch of thugs who started kicking the hell out of him. Or Terry grab a microphone stand and jump offstage to help them.

Twinny went down, his head smashed open and bleeding badly, and they would have kicked the shit out of him if Terry hadn't smacked a couple of them with the mike stand, which at least gave Twinny the chance to pull himself to his feet and fight back, still bleeding badly.

The thing was: he had my shirt on, the fucker. That afternoon he'd asked if he could borrow it and, even though it was my favorite (after the blue one, of course), I'd let him have it because he promised me he was going to be dead careful with it, and absolutely not get a battering from a load of thugs and bleed all over it.

Later on his mum got the blood out by washing it in a bath of saltwater. The salt lifts the blood out, she told me later, and she was absolutely right because the shirt was fine. Little tip for you there.

So anyway, it was all kicking off out in the venue, a proper riot. These guys weren't messing about. Twinny was badly hurt and they were coming back for second helpings, Terry swinging his mike stand around his head trying to keep the crowd off him. He was so scared he actually pissed himself, but luckily he hadn't borrowed my trousers.

Backstage the first we knew of it was when Tony Wilson came bursting into the dressing room, screaming like a girl: "Oh fuck, it's all gone off. Everyone's getting beaten up."

Hysterical, he was. Imagine the suave intellectual Tony Wilson you've seen on telly. Now imagine the opposite and that was how he was.

Next thing, the door opened again. With it open all we could hear was the sound of shouting and glasses smashing from out in the venue: the sound of it all really going off. Then Rob was standing there, out of breath, in complete disarray, saying one word: "*Fuck.*"

I was straight out of my seat, "What the fuck's going on?"

"It's a fucking riot, mate," he said. "They're going fucking ape shit out there. Terry, Twinny, and Dave are out there. We've got to help them, mate, come on. . . ."

He opened the door, we poked our heads out, and straightaway there was a hail of bottles. I'm not kidding, it was like a fucking mortar attack—all these bottles shattering around us. Rob darted out and I grabbed two empty bottles of beer off the dressing-room table, shoved one at Alan Hempsall, and shouted, "Come on, let's get out there."

Alan Hempsall stood there like I was trying to hand him a dog turd. Wouldn't take the bottle. I looked from him to the rest of them.

"Come on, then."

They all stared at me. The rest of Joy Division, Tony, Lindsay, Iris, all of Minny Pops, A Certain Ratio, and Section 25, all of them at the back of the dressing room and staring at me, wide-eyed and shitless.

Well, fuck 'em, I thought, and turned to follow Rob when all of a sudden I was being grabbed from behind, held back, arms going around my waist, someone else grabbing on to my arm.

Tony was holding me, Lindsay was holding me, Iris was holding me; Paul from Section 25, too. One of them had long nails and really hurt me but that was my fault for struggling, I suppose, because I was going mental and the bastards wouldn't let me out; they ended up pinning me down and sitting on me in the dressing room. I was shouting that we could have them if we all stuck together, how we should be out there helping our mates and all that. Calling them all the names under the sun.

They were right, though. I'd have been toast if I'd got out there. A member of the band? The bastards would have kicked seven shades of shit out of me. So I can say that now: they basically saved my life. But at the time all the thanks they got was me struggling and swearing at them and calling them rotten. But save my bacon they did. They held on to me until at last the trouble had ended. Then, like survivors emerging from a nuclear shelter, we ventured outside.

The place was trashed. Twinny had a massive gash in his head, blood all over him. Terry was in a terrible state; they all were.

Ian had disappeared, though, and I found him in a stairwell with his head in his hands, and one of our lot (she shall remain nameless) screaming at him: "This is all your fault. This is all your fault."

I was going, "Will you get the fuck out?" I gave this bitch a shove out of the way and said, "Are you all right, Ian?"

He was just like, "Yeah, I'm all right, Hooky, I'm all right. Just leave me for a minute; I'll be okay."

Ian wasn't much of a fighter, especially when he was sober. He was obviously really shocked and shook up. Tony came to have a word and I left them to it, went out to see the others who were in the process of calling an ambulance for Twinny. Lindsay ended up taking him to the hospital, telling him on the way that she had stockings and suspenders on, even showing him them at the traffic lights. He just said, "Under the circumstances, Lindsay, I'm not really interested!" When they got to the emergency room who else should be there, getting stitched up, but the two lads Terry had battered with the mike stand. Nice one, Terry.

After the Bury gig Ian went to stay with Tony and Lindsay, where he spent a few days listening to records and smoking dope. Debbie attended the next Joy Division concert at the Factory II on April 11, but during the course of the evening learned more about Ian's relationship with Annik—specifically their living arrangements during the Closer *sessions. After the concert the couple argued and Ian returned to Charlesworth. However, he left at some point during the weekend and stayed either with Bernard or his parents, missing Natalie's birthday on April 16. He returned home briefly then departed for Derby, where Joy Division was playing at the Ajanta Theatre on Saturday April 19.*

This was to be the band's penultimate gig. There Ian met up with Annik, and that night the pair stayed at a hotel in Rusholme. The following day they visited Rob Gretton, who by coincidence Debbie phoned during their visit. On Monday, Annik returned to London and Ian home to Macclesfield, but at this point both Ian's and Debbie's parents became involved and on Tuesday, April 22, there was apparently a showdown involving all concerned—as well as Rob and Lesley Gretton—at the Curtis home in Macclesfield. The same day, Debbie phoned Annik at the Belgian embassy and by her own admission "screamed" at her that she planned to divorce Ian and would be naming Annik as co-respondent. Though advised to hang on by her parents in order to win a larger divorce settlement when Joy Division was a bigger band, Debbie chose not to. "It was difficult initiating the divorce," she writes in Touching from a Distance, *"but once I had made the decision it felt wonderful. It seemed as though a huge weight had been lifted from my shoulders."*

For her part, Annik has said that the call forced her to confront the fact that Ian was married—something she had downplayed. "I realized I was hurting somebody," she said.

Meanwhile Ian went to stay with Rob and Lesley Gretton, then with Bernard, while the band—despite taking a break from playing live—busied themselves with rehearsals and preparations for the upcoming US tour. Now at new rehearsal rooms, Pinky's in Broughton, they wrote two new songs, the first since the Closer *sessions: "Ceremony" and "In a Lonely Place."*

• Chapter 30 •

"We were so excited about going to America"

Ian saw Annik for the final time on Friday, April 25, at a Factory night held at the Scala cinema in London's King's Cross—where Joy Division had been due to play but pulled out. The following day, Annik was scheduled to leave the UK for an Egyptian holiday; by the time she returned Ian should have been leaving for America with Joy Division.

They left the venue in the early hours and returned to her flat so she could finish packing. Then in the morning they went to catch their respective trains, bidding farewell at the station. She never saw him again.

Meanwhile the band pressed ahead with plans to film a video to accompany the single release of "Love Will Tear Us Apart."

We'd worked him nearly to death in March. Then we'd done quite a bit of working him to death in early April.

Ian had responded by trying to kill himself.

We'd paid him back with a debilitating riot and then at last—at long bloody last—we pulled some gigs. Every gig, in fact, that we could pull. We did it because of Ian, because he needed a rest.

But sometimes I wonder if it wasn't the gigging break that did him in in the end. At least when we were playing we were away, our minds were distracted. With the gigs canceled and us staying close to home, Ian also ended up staying so much closer to the source of all his domestic problems.

Not that we were aware of all these troubles, the depths of his problems, at the time, mind you. It's only recently, since the explosion of interest in Joy Division, you might say, and while I've been researching the book, that I've really started to get a clear picture of the kind of shit Ian was going through and the very short timescale involved.

At the time he kept it mainly to himself. As far as we were concerned he was dead excited about going to America, really looking forward to it. Yet you read about him telling people that he didn't want to go. According to Genesis P-Orridge, Ian said he'd "rather die" than go on tour—and maybe he did say that, but not to us he didn't: no way. With us, Ian was bang into the idea and maybe if he'd been spending more time with us, and less at home, and less talking to the likes of Genesis, then he'd have been buoyed up by it all. I think he'd have gone to America, where, looking at it, the schedule wouldn't have been exhausting, and I think he would have loved it.

I'm not saying his problems would have gone away, of course. Just that they wouldn't have been crowding in on him quite so much. I really think that if he'd made it to America he'd have lived.

Or maybe I'm just talking out my arse again. Barney always said that it was his medication that made him suicidal, and that could have happened anywhere—Macclesfield or New York.

Anyway, what else could we do but stop? Ian was exhausted, his illness getting worse. He *had* to rest. Even though, in a funny kind of way, he did the exact opposite: he was drifting between staying at his mum and dad's and with Barney; he had Debbie and everyone on his case; he went to London to say good-bye to Annik, so was probably upset about all that. Then, a couple of days later, we were recording the "Love Will Tear Us Apart" video, and that seemed to take forever.

We'd arranged to film it in TJ Davidson's, even though we weren't really using it anymore. Looking for more basic comforts we'd ended up in Pinky's near Broughton Baths (quite near North Salford Youth Club, actually, the second youth club I ever went to, with Barney; I got chased away from the first, South Salford) but it wasn't big enough to make the video.

Now, it probably won't surprise you to learn that we hated the whole idea of a video where you mimed or acted to the track. In fact we were never into it, all through New Order. God, you feel like such an idiot miming. So what we decided to do was hire a PA and a mixing desk, play "Love Will Tear Us Apart," and record while we filmed, so the video would be a live performance of the song.

We set up for the filming with a long runway so the cameras could come in and out on a track, like a mini-railway. Then off we went and did a few run-throughs, trying to get the sound right. But we couldn't, because there wasn't a separate room in which to mix the sound. It was confused with the racket that we were getting off the instruments and through the amps. It didn't really work, and the tape we ended up with, the soundtrack to the video, sounded pretty rushed and bad, to be honest. Nor could we overdub any backing vocals—or anything else, for that matter.

Even so, we were very happy with it as it happened. It was

raw, dirty, and arty. We liked that: it was us all over, of course. As usual it never really occurred to us that anybody else might have a problem with it. If they did, well, that was their problem. Trouble was, hardly anybody we sent it to would play it. It got shown a little, but not nearly as much as we'd hoped, so it had seemed a bit of a waste of time.

Ah, but then we heard that it had gone down well in Australia, and of course we thought, *Good on the Aussies. They've got good taste, they have. They know art when they hear it.* And thus began an affection for our like-minded brethren down under.

It wasn't until years and years later that we visited Australia—as New Order, of course—and discovered the truth. Somebody at the Australian record company had simply laid the actual record over the film, and it wasn't even properly synchronized. It looked well dodgy, actually—well, we thought so. But this became the version that ended up being the "official" (for want of a better word) version. Now, of course, it's perfect, capturing us at our youngest and freshest with a great soundtrack.

I suppose you could say it was yet another of those slightly questionable self-defeating decisions, to do the video that way: like insisting on performing "Blue Monday" live on *Top of the Pops* (which they're not set up for) and seeing it go ten places down the charts as a result. But we didn't care, not really. Our ultimate aim was just to be ourselves, to do things the way we wanted them done, and we'd insist out of sheer bloody-mindedness. Rob was always in our corner. Tony was always in our corner. You might call them mistakes but at least they were mistakes made on our own terms. Mistakes that then became legends.

A few days later we played Birmingham. We didn't know it then, of course, but it would be our last-ever gig as Joy Division.

It was a good one too. We later released it on the album *Still*.

Ian had a bit of a wobble during "Decades" but was fine for "Digital." Even so, it was one of those gigs—like all of them were around then—where you were looking at Ian wondering if, or *when*, it was going to happen, and that was because it was now happening at every show. With hindsight you can look back and say he probably wasn't going to be right at any gig, whether in America or outer space. Even so, the idea of canceling or rescheduling America never came up.

We were so excited about going, so wound up about it and desperate to do it. Ian, the fan of the Doors and Lou Reed and Iggy Pop and Burroughs, especially. I don't care what Genesis P-Orridge says, he was looking forward to going. I mean, we had so much going for us then. The word was getting out that we were a great group to see live. We had "Love Will Tear Us Apart" up our sleeve. We were on the way up.

That's what always gets me about what he did. Sometimes you can see just why he did it, and it makes a kind of sense.

Other times, it just makes no fucking sense at all.

· *Chapter 31* ·

"I never said good-bye"

Ian killed himself in the early hours of Sunday morning. The last time I saw him was on the Friday night, when I gave him a lift back to his mum and dad's in Moston, just past where my house on Minton Street was. You drove to the top of the road and his mum and dad lived in Failsworth, literally a quarter of a mile from my house. So, yes, I drove him home that Friday night and he was cock-a-hoop, full of it. We'd had a great practice and I was dropping him off. We were laughing and joking and every now and then one of us would go, "I can't believe we're fucking going to America!" We were screaming in the car, jumping up and down on the seats, properly shouting, whooping, hollering: "Yeah! America!"

No "rather die" about it.

This was on the Friday night. We were due to leave after the weekend. If the silly bugger hadn't killed himself, we would have been on a plane to America on Monday. If he'd known all along that he planned to kill himself, as some say he did, was he just putting it on, all that excitement? Was he *that* good an actor?

Barney spoke to him on Saturday. There was a phone at his

mum and dad's, whereas he didn't have a phone at home, so you were able to phone him there but not in Macclesfield. Barney rang to see if he wanted to come out but Ian said no, because he was going to go to Debbie's, and of course that's what he did. He went up to Debbie's. They had an argument and she went to work.

And he went and hanged himself.

Before he was supposed to leave for America, Ian had been staying with his parents and seemed well, according to his mother, Doreen. On Saturday morning he received a letter regarding his divorce and told his mother he wanted to go to Macclesfield to see Natalie, to say good-bye. Doreen and Kevin, Ian's father, gave him a lift to Piccadilly Station, and the last they saw of him he was waving to them from the station approach. Natalie was staying with Debbie's mother, but Debbie saw Ian at the house on Barton Street on Saturday afternoon before she went to work behind the bar at a wedding reception, promising to return after work to see him. She did, finding that he'd been drinking spirits and coffee, having watched the Werner Herzog film Stroszek, *and they continued discussions about the future of their relationship. Ian told her that he had spoken to Annik earlier; he also asked Debbie to drop the divorce. As he became more and more worked up, Debbie began to worry that he might have a seizure and offered to spend the night. She then drove back to her parents' to tell them she intended to stay. However, when she returned to Barton Street, Ian seemed to have calmed down.*

He asked her to leave and to give him her assurance that she wouldn't return to the house before ten the next morning, when he was due to leave for Manchester. After she left, he listened to The Idiot *by Iggy Pop on repeat, drank more coffee and spirits, then wrote a long letter to Debbie, in which he said that he wished he was dead but made no mention of any intention to kill himself.*

At about eleven thirty the next morning Debbie returned to the house to find Ian dead, kneeling on the kitchen floor with a rope around his neck, the other end tied to the kitchen clothes rack attached to the ceiling. A neighbor had cut him down.

I was having Sunday lunch with Iris when I heard. I got up from the table to answer the phone. It was the police, Detective Sergeant Somebody, who said, "We're sorry to have to inform you that Ian Curtis took his own life last night. We're trying to get in touch with Rob Gretton. If you speak to him, could you ask him to ring us, please?"

I said, "Right," and went numb. (I stayed numb for days, actually, as though my brain were frozen.)

In that state I went and sat back down at the dinner table, picked up my knife and fork, and carried on eating. I didn't say anything to Iris. Just sat back down and continued eating my food, except not really tasting it now, feeling all of a sudden like I was no longer in my own body. As though I were looking down on myself.

After a while Iris said, "Who was that on the phone, by the way?"

"Oh, that," I said. "That was the police ringing to tell me about Ian."

"What about him?"

"He's killed himself."

I don't remember anything then. I don't remember anything for a long time after that. I mean, I remember that we spent a lot of time together sitting in a pub: me, Barney, Terry, and Twinny, just sitting having a drink, playing darts, spending time together, going to see Rob, talking to him, sitting round, trying to make sense of it all. There was no shouting or crying, just a perpetual stunned silence that being together seemed to make bearable. Steve was in Macclesfield, but the rest of us, we kind of huddled together for warmth. Just stayed together because we were all going through exactly the same thing. Gradually the details of Ian's death began to seep through: the divorce, hanging himself, the whiskey, Iggy Pop. All the stuff that we discovered in dribs and drabs and absorbed with that same sense of numbness.

He was lying in state at the chapel of rest, but I didn't go to see him. Steve and Rob and Tony and all that lot went, but me and Barney were like, "No, we don't want to see his body. We're going to the pub."

I really regret that now and always will. We acted like kids in a way, but it seemed okay. It was sort of allowed because it was like the grown-ups were sorting it all out, Tony and Rob and everyone else.

I rented a car for the funeral.

There were loads of people there for the funeral. But the funny thing is I don't remember much about it. Just that there were loads there, all the bands, the guys from Factory Benelux, but not Annik, obviously, because of Debbie and the family. I remember sitting at the back at the funeral and Ian's sister screaming really loudly when the curtain closed behind his coffin. But it all seemed surreal; I felt strangely detached. Afterward we went to the pub down the road: me, Steve, Gillian, Barney, Rob, and Terry. Twinny couldn't face it, so he didn't go. We sat and had something to eat, had a couple of pints. That was when Rob said, "Don't worry. Joy Division will be really big in ten years' time." He was right, of course. Ten, fifteen—twenty, too. Not that any of us gave a shit at that precise moment in time. We finished the afternoon off watching the Sex Pistols film at Factory's office, a kind of wake. A truly dismal affair.

Afterward we made arrangements to go back into the practice room on Monday. I remember writing the intro and verse to "Dreams Never End" on my six-string bass in the back bedroom of Minton Street over the weekend. The beginning of our new life as New Order. It was as though a film of Factory records had paused for a moment while Ian was scrubbed out of the picture. Then the film started again and continued as though nothing else was different. In the end it would be years before we would start talking about Joy Division, and Ian, and start to face up to it, to ask ourselves what went wrong. What we could have done differently. How we might have saved him.

Oh, and I remember going to the inquest later, with Rob, and maybe Steve, which was even more surreal because there was bad feeling toward us—toward the band. Like his mum and dad thought we were responsible. I can vividly recall Debbie's dad giving evidence about Ian, saying, "He was on another plane." I was thinking, *Fuck, I wish it had been that plane to America.* They were talking about him as if he were a stranger and the inquest found that he'd taken his own life under the influence of alcohol.

Me, I felt guilty. Guilty that I never went to see him when he was lying in state. Guilty that I never said good-bye. Guilty that, like everybody else, I went along with Ian when he said he was all right; that I was so wrapped in my own bit of me, of the band, that I never took the time to listen to his lyrics or him and think, *He really needs help.*

So, yes, I felt all of that, and still do. I'm sure I'm not the only one. In a way we're all of us to blame, but none of us are. Years later I remember Dave Pils telling me that when we'd last stayed with them in Walthamstow Ian had left his raincoat behind, the famous mac he always wore. Dave had grabbed the mac and gone running after the car when we left, but it was too late, we were gone. That was the last time Dave saw Ian.

"What did you do with the mac?" I asked.

"Took it down the charity shop, Hooky,"

I thought, *You silly sod. The charity shop? Who would do something like that?*

But then even later I was talking to one of our roadies, Corky (Mike Caulfield). He was reminiscing about our old practice place in Cheetham Hill and how it used to have Ian's scarf hanging on the back of the door. A proper old man's woolly scarf, it was, brown and gray and black. We'd brought it from the rehearsal room at Pinky's when we moved.

Corky said, "What happened to it, Hooky, that scarf?"

I thought, *Oh fuck*—because with a sudden jolt I realized I'd taken it to the charity shop. I'd forgotten it was Ian's scarf and donated it. *What an idiot*, I thought. *Who would do something like that?*

Well, I had. I suppose in the end it's almost too easy to look back and say what you should have done, how you might have changed things. How you might have done things differently and ultimately stopped Ian from doing what he did. What's harder—what's much, much harder—is to accept what you actually did do. Accept what you did and live with it. At that point I thought that the worst thing that had happened was me losing a friend, the band losing a member. It took me a long time to realize that a child had lost a father, a mother and father had lost a son, a sister had lost a brother, a wife had lost a husband, a mistress had lost a lover. All a lot more important than me and the band; we pale in significance. You're selfish when you're young and I suppose in many ways that's self-preservation. Now I'm embarrassed to have put us first. Even after writing and researching this book I'm no clearer as to why he decided to end it on that night. About what made that night different. The only odd thing I see is the dog story: Candy going to the farm. It seems like such a cliché. Did they have the dog put down, I wonder? Was that what was too much for him to bear on top of everything else? I will never know.

EPILOGUE

We packed everything in a little box once he'd gone, and put it away. Now, of course, Ian's with me all the time, and even this book is as much about him as it is about me. But back then—then it was like the group disowned the group. I mean, Joy Division's popularity skyrocketed: "Love Will Tear Us Apart" came out and was a great success, then *Closer*, but we didn't promote them, didn't play them, didn't read reviews of them, didn't want to know about sales, nothing. Didn't care about them.

The only thing we took from Joy Division—the only two things, actually—were the songs Ian had left us: "Ceremony" and "In a Lonely Place." To one another we said, "See you on Monday," and that was it. Me, Barney, and Steve got together on the Monday to work on the songs. I took the riff for "Dreams Never End" into rehearsal. It was weird because I was looking for Ian to tell me if it was any good or not. Realizing that we'd lost our spotter, our mentor. Realizing that suddenly we had to find a new way of working that didn't rely on him. We had to learn to record everything, play it back, and pick out the good bits ourselves.

We never considered carrying on as Joy Division, though. We

had made a pact years before that if one of us didn't want to do it anymore, or if anything happened to any one of us, then Joy Division would be over. The group was finished. I mean, the desire to carry on was uppermost, but as for trying to carry on as Joy Division with one of us lot singing, or even getting in a new lead singer, it never even came up. We just knew that Joy Division was over. But we wanted to continue as a band, to carry on making and playing music. From a purely practical point of view, we did have the core of a band so it seemed right to carry on. There was, of course, the problem of who was going to sing the songs. That wouldn't be resolved for a while. In fact, right up until we played our first gig as a three-piece, all three of us were singing two or three songs each, but we got there in the end.

Then there was the business of finding a new name. We sat down one day to try to come up with one, thinking that we were going to learn our lesson this time, and that whatever name we came up with wouldn't be anything even vaguely Nazi-sounding.

No way, we thought. No fucking way were we going to make that mistake again.

· *Chapter 32* ·

Closer Track by Track

JOY DIVISION

May		
19th	Fly In	
20th	Day Off	
21st	New York	Hurrahs
22nd	New York	Hurrahs
23rd	New York	Hurrahs
24th	Day Off	
25th	Toronto	The Edge
26th	Day Off	
27th	Chicago	Tuts
28th	Madison	Merlins
29th	Minneapolis	Duffies
30th	Day Off	
31st	Day Off	
June		
1st	New York	Pop Front
2nd	Fly to San Fransisco	
3rd	Day Off	
4th	Day Off	
5th	Day Off	
6th 7th	San Fransisco	American Indian Hall
8th	Los Angeles	Flippers?
9th	Day Off	
10th	Fly Home	

I really recommend listening to the record while you read.

"ATROCITY EXHIBITION"

This is the way, step inside . . .

Me and Barney were bored writing on our own instruments so we just thought, *Let's swap*. Barney plays bass and I play guitar on "Atrocity Exhibition." I was nowhere near as proficient a guitarist as him, mind you, but I like the way it sounds. Great riff. Great bass, too.

During the recording Iris had insisted I go home for a christening or a wedding or something, and Martin mixed the first two tracks while I was gone: "Heart and Soul" and "Atrocity Exhibition." I remember coming back and being dead excited to hear them because I played the guitar really heavily on "Atrocity Exhibition" and I loved it. So there we were, sitting in Martin's Volvo. Barney put the cassette on so I could listen to the mixes and the bass was really low on "Heart and Soul," very dead and quiet, and I was, like, head in hands, *Oh fucking hell, it's happening again*. Unknown Pleasures *number two*.

As if that wasn't bad enough, he then put on "Atrocity Exhibition" and Martin had fucking melted the guitar with his Marshall Time Waster. Made it sound like someone strangling a cat and, to my mind, absolutely killed the song. I was so annoyed with him and went in and gave him a piece of my mind but he just turned round and told me to fuck off.

Rob said, "Fucking hell, Hooky, if you're going to fuck off home you've got to be prepared to take what happens in your absence."

"ISOLATION"

Mother, I tried please believe me . . .

This is an interesting track because it has no guitar on it. If we wrote "Isolation" now, Barney would not only have played the synth but would have done a guitar part too. We would have done a low part, a medium part, a high part; we'd have done a part you can't hear, a part on the left, part on the right; we'd have killed it. So it was the inexperience involved in us writing "Isolation" that just kept it dead simple, straightforward and very, very effective. What Martin did was take the original drum track, flange it and effect it through his synth, then get Steve to overdub the drums so they were separate; then he could have them really up front in the mix, not buried in a drum mix. Plus he used the drums to trigger his synth, which was, again, ahead of his time. Barney overdubbed the ARP over the Transcendent, playing the same part, and it sounds current even now. Nice vocal effect. I mean, Martin was a fucking genius, without a shadow of a doubt. The way the acoustic kit comes in halfway through the song is fantastic.

Martin had finished it with a dead stop and the echo going off. But there was a click on it and he wanted to edit it out. But John Caffery got in a right mess—too nervous, I think—and couldn't get the edit to work. And the more he tried to fix it, the more of the take he was losing—and this was the only copy of it. Don't forget that editing was done with a razor blade, physically cutting out the part you didn't want then sticking with tape the bits you did. He was working on the master, so the tape was getting shorter and shorter. In the end Mike Johnson, the tape op/tea boy, had to come in and rescue him, to rescue the edit. That was what impressed us so much about him and why, when we came back in to record as New Order, we got him in as our engineer. That's why "Isolation" sounds a bit weird at the end. It's a great song, though. If we'd believed in releasing singles off albums then we would have released it, but we always knew "Love Will Tear Us Apart" was going to be the next single and we were far too bloody-minded to put the singles on the albums.

"PASSOVER"

This is the crisis I knew had to come . . .

I'm playing six-string bass on this, the first time I used it I think. I got it on Barney's recommendation, actually. He'd seen it in Mamelok Music Shop on Deansgate and very graciously suggested I go and have a look at it. "You should get it, you should get it; it's fucking great. You could really use it, because the way you play is guitar-like." Which was very nice of him.

So I went and tried it out and, lo and behold, something about it got me playing it like a guitar. I suppose, in a way, I've always been a frustrated guitar player who plays bass, but what I've done is stuck with bass and made it a guitar. So getting the six-string bass actually felt quite natural. Around the same time we tried out some effects pedals, again on his recommendation, I got the Electro-Harmonix Clone Theory, because of the fragility of the six-string sound, and that really helped it, fattened it up. Everyone thinks it's a guitar but it's not; it's the six-string bass. It was quite a departure for me. Coupling the chorus with a short eighty-millisecond delay gave me the sound for the next phase of my career. This track has great crescendos and dropdowns and is one of my favorites. Ian's lyrics are insanely good with hardly any repetition.

"COLONY"

A worried parent's glance, a kiss, a last good-bye . . .

Great lyrics. "Colony" is on the four-string bass. These songs are the product of a great group, without a shadow of a doubt: music chemistry at its best. Steve's drum riffs, the bass riffs, and the guitar riffs are all excellent. The whole lot of them on every song are excellent. I shouldn't say it really, because I was in the band, but I love this album. There's not one dodgy track on it.

It's very atmospheric, very powerful. If you listen to *Unknown Pleasures*, there's a bit of reticence on some songs, but not on this LP. Every song is confident—which is strange, given the fact that most of the music is very melancholic, very fragile but intense.

"MEANS TO AN END"

Two the same, set free too, I always looked to you . . .

This is the pop song on the album. It's a fucked-up disco song. We had it worked out a little but finished it in the studio. Martin always liked it when we did that—it meant he could put his stamp on it. Weird: the verse has four ascending notes all next to each other, with no thought to sharps or flats. It's very unusual. I liked that.

"HEART AND SOUL"

Existence, well, what does it matter? . . .

This is so seductive, a very sexy song that has many layers. I wrote the low bass and we transferred it to the synthesizer. Martin showed Barney how to layer and structure the keyboards, the strings especially, and that's what he's doing here—playing the low bass, while nice and low in the mix you've got my six-string bass. This was another occasion when Martin really took the heat out of it during the mix, downplayed it, but it really adds to the atmosphere. I was upset when I first heard it but he was right and I was wrong.

Barney was moving from guitar to keyboards. Live, this had no guitar, but of course in the studio we would overdub some at Martin's request. I have a feeling Ian may have played the chord guitar. We continued with this way of writing, which felt quite natural. Barney would say, "Oh, why don't we put that low bass on the synth, and you can play over with it with your six string and add high strings for the breaks." This was what we did and we used it a lot in New Order too. I'd write a bass line then he'd put it on the synth to make it dancey and I'd play over it with the melody. Barney used to call me Mr. Melody, in his lighter moments.

"TWENTY FOUR HOURS"

Now that I've realized, how it's all gone wrong . . .

Ian had difficulty singing some of the songs he wrote because he didn't have the range in his key, but I've always felt very, very strongly that a great vocalist can write great music and doesn't have to sing it perfectly as long as the emotion's there. The emotion comes from the heart, the soul, the passion, which together make a perfect delivery. When Barney used to strain in his vocals it sounded a hell of a lot better to me than when he started writing them all in the right key. I thought then it became too perfect; I preferred the emotion and the vulnerability of it before. Ian had that too. I mean, I know I keep saying it, but what you want in life is strength and belief, and if someone has that, it doesn't have to be technically perfect.

People turn round to you and say, "God, you'd been hearing these lyrics for weeks—why didn't you realize he was so bad?" You hadn't. He wasn't slumped in the corner with a lone fiddle in the background; he was fucking going for it. I suppose that's the contradiction: on the one hand, he was ill and vulnerable; on the other, he was a screaming rock god. That's what was confusing.

"THE ETERNAL"

Cry like a child though these years make me older . . .

This is a great song. My favorite lyric. So dreamlike. Any band would die to have this under their belt, in their arsenal. It's instrumentally and musically powerful as well as vocally powerful. It's the six-string bass with the clone pedal, which gives you a slight double-track. It just makes it wobble and sound fatter. Barney's playing the keyboards and then at the end using the Transcendent as a white-noise generator. Steve's drum riff is amazing, so simple and strong. And there's a great use of echo plate on the snare by Martin. Listening to it now you can hear how well we played together; the solidity between me, Ian, Steve, and Bernard was very, very powerful. I don't think any of us will ever have it again. Classic.

"DECADES"

We knocked on the door of hell's darker chambers . . .

This is an interesting track. It begins with me playing low bass and, unusually, playing in sync with the bass drum; then there's overdubbing of another bass part, on the six-string, very rhythmic so it sounds like guitar. There's a great Syndrum sound, loads of echo plate in use. There's Barney on the keyboards, again layered wonderfully, and overdubbed guitar melodies. It's one of the most beautiful songs we ever did. I think it's more beautiful than "Atmosphere."

I find *Closer* much easier to listen to than *Unknown Pleasures*. I like it as a musical offering and find myself listening to *Closer* simply for pleasure, which I can't really do with anything else that I've done. Definitely not the New Order stuff, sadly. This is actually one of my favorite albums. My five favorites would be *Chelsea Girls* by Nico, *New Boots & Panties* by Ian Dury & the Blockheads, *Raw Power* by Iggy Pop, *Berlin* by Lou Reed, and *Closer* by Joy Division. Oh, I forgot John Cale, *Paris 1919*, and the Sex Pistols, of course . . . Oops, that's seven.

TIMELINE FIVE

JANUARY 1980–OCTOBER 1981

JANUARY 7–8, 1980

The first "Love Will Tear Us Apart" session, Pennine Sound Studios, Oldham. Produced by Martin Hannett. Tracks recorded: "These Days," " The Sound of Music," "Love Will Tear Us Apart" (version one).

JANUARY 11, 1980

Joy Division plays Paradiso, Amsterdam, Netherlands. The start of the European tour. The support band doesn't play, so Joy Division does both slots, performing two different sets for the price of one. Set list ("support" set): "Passover," "Wilderness," "Digital," "Day of the Lords," "Insight," "New Dawn Fades," "Disorder," "Transmission." Set list (main set): "Love Will Tear Us Apart," "These Days," "A Means to an End," "Twenty Four Hours," "Shadowplay," "She's Lost Control," "Atrocity Exhibition," "Atmosphere," "Interzone."

JANUARY 12, 1980

Joy Division plays Paard Van Troje (the Trojan Horse), The Hague, Netherlands, supported by Minny Pops.

JANUARY 13, 1980

Joy Division plays Doornroosje, Nijmegen, Netherlands.

JANUARY 14, 1980

Joy Division plays King Kong, Antwerp, Belgium.

> When finally the Joy Division company arrives the next day, we immediately bring them to the Boemerang . . . in a very friendly and polite way the manager tells us the place is "too scruffy" and request another place to stay . . . hell!
>
> In a hurry we manage to find some rooms in the Appelmans hotel near the central station, and this time the crew and band seem to be satisfied and get in.
>
> All goes well until Annik Honoré, the young girlfriend of Ian Curtis, pops her head in; she sees the red lights, the "special" furniture and erotic paintings on the wall and screams: "No way! You're not going to put us in this whorehouse! Don't you know Joy Division is an important band?"
>
> Curtis looks at her and laughs—he doesn't mind sleeping here with the others—but she bursts into tears.
>
> Excerpt from *The Night Ian Curtis Came to Sleep* by Marc Schoetens, from joydiv.org

JANUARY 15, 1980

Joy Division plays the Basement, Cologne, Germany. Set list: "Atmosphere," "Love Will Tear Us Apart," "These Days," "Insight,"

"Twenty Four Hours," "A Means to an End," "She's Lost Control," "The Sound of Music," "Glass," "Day of the Lords," "Shadowplay," "Interzone," "Disorder," "Transmission," "Atrocity Exhibition."

They were good gigs but fucking hell, Europe was cold. Thinking about it, what can't have helped was the fact that I'd gone skinhead. The rest of them were growing theirs back but I'd decided to shave all mine off. Ever since the time they'd japed me into dyeing it blond I'd been different with my hair—so if they cut theirs, I'd be growing mine; if they grew theirs, I'd get mine cut. That was the same all through New Order, too.

JANUARY 16, 1980

Joy Division plays Lantaren, Rotterdam, Netherlands.

JANUARY 17, 1980

Joy Division plays Plan K, Belgium. Set list: "Dead Souls," "Wilderness," "Insight," "Colony," "Twenty Four Hours," "A Means to an End," "Transmission," "Atmosphere," "Love Will Tear Us Apart," "Digital," "Warsaw," "Shadowplay," "Atrocity Exhibition," "Sister Ray," "The Eternal."

JANUARY 18, 1980

Joy Division plays Effenaar, Eindhoven, Netherlands, supported by Minny Pops. Set list: "Love Will Tear Us Apart," "Digital," "New Dawn Fades," "Colony," "These Days," "Ice Age," "Dead Souls," "Disorder," "Day of the Lords," "Autosuggestion," "Shadowplay," "She's Lost Control," "Transmission," "Interzone," "Atmosphere," "Warsaw." The band has some trouble with a bunch of young rockabillies. Some songs are shot on Super-8 ("Digital," "New Dawn Fades," "Colony," "Autosuggestion") and later appear on the **Here Are the Young Men** ***film.***

JANUARY 19, 1980

Joy Division plays Club Vera, Groningen, Netherlands.

JANUARY 21, 1980

Joy Division plays Kant Kino, Berlin, Germany. Set list: "Dead Souls," "Wilderness," "Colony," "Insight," "Twenty Four Hours," "A Means to an End," "Transmission," "The Eternal."

According to Ian's letters to Annik, he and Barney were very depressed after this gig because of the sound. I don't remember that. They had a few posters up advertising forthcoming films and I nicked a few, which we put on the wall in the practice place for inspiration. That's where we got loads of our New Order titles from: they're all old films. Very cheeky.

FEBRUARY 7, 1980

Joy Division plays a Factory benefit (in aid of the **City Fun** ***fanzine), the Factory II, New Osborne Club, Manchester, supported by A Certain Ratio and Section 25.***

I remember that when we came off Ian was dying for a piss so we couldn't go back on and do another encore. He was hopping about trying to find a toilet but there wasn't one backstage, so in the end we were going, "Oh, just piss in the corner," and he was going, "No, no, I can't! I can't piss in the corner! I can't do it, I can't do it."

Rob was going, "Fucking hell, Ian, you know, you're supposed to be going back on," and Ian was running round like a fucking madman, holding himself.

So in the end Rob went and got a pint pot and ordered him to go into a corner and piss into it so we could go back on.

After an age Ian came back, saying, "Aw, thanks for that, Rob—I was desperate." But the pot had only a quarter of an inch of piss in it—something to do with his meds, I suppose.

It was too late to go back on by then, so we didn't. But I do remember that it was nice to be back in Manchester, just to be home. I was the only one whose car wasn't broken into that night. I lived in Moston and knew the area, so I parked right outside the window of the pub opposite. I warned them all. But when everyone—audience included—came to leave they discovered that every single car round the club had been broken into.

FEBRUARY 8, 1980

Joy Division plays University of London Union, supported by Section 25, A Certain Ratio, and Killing Joke. Set list: "Dead Souls," "Glass," "A Means to an End," "Twenty Four Hours," "Passover," "Insight," "Colony," "These Days," "Love Will Tear Us Apart," "Isolation," "The Eternal," "Digital." This concert appears on CD2 of the September 2007 remastered edition of **Closer.**

MID-FEBRUARY 1980

Debbie confronts Ian about Annik.

FEBRUARY 20, 1980

Joy Division plays High Wycombe Town Hall, supported by Killing Joke and A Certain Ratio. Set list: " The Sound of Music," "A Means to an End," "Colony," "Twenty Four Hours," "Isolation," "Love Will Tear Us Apart," "Disorder," "Atrocity Exhibition." Both concert and sound check appear on CD2 of the September 2007 reissue of **Still.**

The reason that a lot of these gigs were so widely bootlegged was there were these two young lads—quite nice lads, actually—called John and Lawrie, who used to come and tape all the gigs then provide us with a cassette. We'd let them into the sound checks so they'd do them, too, which was quite nice of them—

because really they were bootlegging you with your consent, weren't they?

It was during this period that Ian's self-harming episode occurred.

FEBRUARY 21, 1980

Joy Division cancels their gig at Manchester Polytechnic.

FEBRUARY 28, 1980

Joy Division plays the Warehouse, Preston, supported by Section 25. Set list: "Incubation," "Wilderness," "Twenty Four Hours," "The Eternal," "Heart and Soul," "Shadowplay," "Transmission," "Disorder," "Warsaw," "Colony," "Interzone," "She's Lost Control."

We turned up on the day and everything that could go wrong went wrong. The PA was dreadful, our equipment was all over the place . . . Everything, actually, just went completely to shit. But for some reason we embraced it with humor, which didn't always happen, and it ended up becoming quite funny. You know the way it goes sometimes: when the more something goes wrong, the funnier it gets? Well, it was like that.

Years later Tony Wilson put out a bootleg of this gig because he loved it so much because you can hear everything going wrong. It was the beer pump—it kept cutting out the amps. Barney's guitar amp went. Then my amp went. Barney came over and tried to plug into my amp and I was going, "You're wasting your fucking time 'cause my amp's gone as well." Then the keyboards went off.

Rob was in the background screaming, "Play, you fuckers, play!" It's on the bootleg, him screaming at us. Occasionally one of us would go to the mike and say, "Oh, sorry about this; this has all gone wrong." It just completely fell apart but the audience didn't seem to mind, particularly. There weren't that many of them there.

There was a wonderful, glorious moment when some girl got up onstage while we were all busy trying to fix our equipment; we were all looking at her thinking, *What's she doing?* She just went up to the mike, grabbed hold of it and said, "The coach for Blackburn is leaving in five minutes." That's on the bootleg as well.

We just couldn't get it back then; we'd just lost it, you know, lost the whole gig. Complete disaster. So anyway, afterward in the dressing room there was a great atmosphere, with everyone laughing and joking, but the promoter came back and was fuming. He said we hadn't played and we could fuck off if we thought he was going to pay us. Then he stalked out of the dressing room.

We weren't having that. The dressing room doubled up as a food store and there was a freezer in there, so I kicked the lock off the freezer. Inside were about thirty frozen chickens that we took as wages. I remember Ian nabbed all these chickens to take home to Debbie—so I think he must still have been living at home with her then. He probably took them back as a peace offering: *Sorry I've got another girl on the go, love. Here are some defrosting chickens.*

FEBRUARY 29, 1980

Joy Division plays the Lyceum, London, co-headlining with Killing Joke, supported by Section 25 and A Certain Ratio. Set list: "Incubation," "Wilderness," "Twenty Four Hours," "The Eternal," "Heart and Soul," "Love Will Tear Us Apart," "Isolation," "Komakino," "She's Lost Control," "These Days," "Atrocity Exhibition." This concert features on the* Heart and Soul *box set.

MARCH 1980

Licht und Blindheit *seven-inch single (Sordide Sentimental SS33022) released: "Atmosphere"/"Dead Souls." Produced by Martin Hannett. Limited to 1,578 numbered copies.*

MARCH 5, 1980

Joy Division plays Trinity Hall, Bristol, supported by the Passage.

Around this time Ian himself started to get very worried about the frequency of his fits, worrying that they would take over his life and that he would not be able to carry on working.

MARCH 13, 1980

The second "Love Will Tear Us Apart" session, Strawberry Studios, Stockport. Produced by Martin Hannett (working sporadically over a period of three weeks beginning April 24). Tracks recorded: "Love Will Tear Us Apart" (single version), "She's Lost Control" (twelve-inch version).

Tony had visited us at Strawberry and again brought Ian a Frank Sinatra album. Tony tried to encourage Ian to emulate it here: I think he thought the combination of the timbre of his voice and this song would be perfect. I don't think it ended up like Frank Sinatra, though; just sounds like Ian to me.

At the time we all thought he was doing it to wind us up. But I know that in one of his letters to Annik Ian mentions how much he liked Frank Sinatra's voice, so obviously not. But Christ, the recording of "Love Will Tear Us Apart" was a marathon. We were in the studio overnight on these sessions, everybody was exhausted, and it still wasn't done—we ended up finishing it in Britannia Row during the recording of *Closer.* There were loads of different mixes of it too. Martin kept remixing it and must have done it ten to fifteen times; then Tony pulled the plug on him because it was costing so much money. Martin was never happy with it and kept searching, constantly, for the great mix. He tried different engineers but could never get the definitive mix. Funnily enough, I now don't like the mix he eventually chose for the single. I like the one that's got a dead-loud guitar overdub on it, a radio mix.

MARCH 18–30, 1980

Joy Division records* Closer*, Britannia Row, London. The band stays in two flats: the "party" flat, and the "intellectual" flat, living the rock-'n'-roll high life on £1.50 a day. Tracks recorded: "Atrocity Exhibition," "Isolation," "Passover," "Colony," "A Means to an End," "Heart and Soul," "Twenty Four Hours," "The Eternal," "Decades," "Komakino," "Incubation," "As You Said."

APRIL 2, 1980

Joy Division plays the Moonlight Club, West Hampstead, London, supported by Section 25, Crawling Chaos, and John Dowie. Set list: "The Sound of Music," "Wilderness," "Colony," "Love Will Tear Us Apart," "A Means to an End," "Transmission," "Dead Souls," "Sister Ray."

"Sister Ray" features on *Still*, but is wrongly credited to the Moonlight Club.

APRIL 3, 1980

Joy Division plays the Moonlight Club, West Hampstead, London, supported by A Certain Ratio, Kevin Hewick, and Blurt. Set list: "Love Will Tear Us Apart," "Glass," "Digital," "Heart and Soul," "Isolation," "Disorder," "Atrocity Exhibition," "Atmosphere."

APRIL 4, 1980

Joy Division plays the Rainbow Theatre, London, supporting a unique Stranglers lineup along with Section 25, Fashion, and the Soul Boys. Set list: "Dead Souls," "Wilderness," "Shadowplay," "Heart and Soul," "Decades," "She's Lost Control," "Atrocity Exhibition."

APRIL 4, 1980

Joy Divisions play the Moonlight Club, London, supported by the Durutti Column, X-O-Dus, and the Royal Family and the Poor. Set

list: "Transmission," "A Means to an End," "Twenty Four Hours," "Day of the Lords," "Insight," "Interzone."

APRIL 2–4, 1980

After an exhausting run of concerts Ian has a fit onstage. This comes shortly after an incident in which he wounded himself with a kitchen knife.

APRIL 5, 1980

Joy Division plays the Malvern Winter Gardens, Malvern. Set list: "Disorder," "Wilderness," "Twenty Four Hours," "Heart and Soul," "Atmosphere," "Love Will Tear Us Apart," "Isolation," "Interzone," "She's Lost Control," "Girls Don't Count," jam with Section 25.

> I met the band backstage. They were all very polite and friendly, apart from Hooky, who was being an arse. Ian was sat on his own. He seemed in good spirits, though looked tired and had a painful-looking shaving rash under his chin. He talked enthusiastically about the 'new songs' and actually thanked me (but I don't know what for!). He spoke in a soft, high-pitched voice, which surprised me. Fond memories indeed!
>
> Phil (fan), on joydiv.org

APRIL 6, 1980

Ian takes an overdose.

APRIL 8, 1980

Joy Division plays Derby Hall, Bury. Set list: "Girls Don't Count," "Love Will Tear Us Apart," "Digital" (all without Ian), "The Eter-

nal," "Decades" (or "Passover"; both with Ian on vocals), "Sister Ray" (without Ian). The gig ends in a riot.

APRIL 9, 1980

Following the Bury gig, Ian begins his stay with Tony and Lindsay.

APRIL 11, 1980

Joy Division plays the Factory, Russell Club, Manchester, supported by Minny Pops.

APRIL 12, 1980

Joy Division cancels their gig in Bradford (venue unknown).

APRIL 12–13, 1980

Ian leaves Charlesworth and spends most of the week away from home, either with Bernard Sumner or with his parents.

APRIL 16, 1980

Natalie Curtis's first birthday. Ian is absent, though briefly returns home before leaving for Derby on Saturday.

APRIL 18, 1980

"Love Will Tear Us Apart" seven-inch single (Factory Records FAC 23) released. Produced by Martin Hannett. Sleeve designed by Peter Saville. Rereleased on twelve-inch with a new cover (FAC 23.12 27.6.80). Track list: "Love Will Tear Us Apart," "These Days," "Love Will Tear Us Apart" (Pennine version).

APRIL 19, 1980

Joy Division plays the Ajanta Theatre, Derby, supported by Section 25 and XL5. Set list: "Dead Souls," "Wilderness," "Digital," "In-

sight," "Passover," "Heart and Soul," "Isolation," "These Days," "Transmission," "She's Lost Control," "Colony," "Girls Don't Count," jam with Section 25.

I remember that there was a bit of a weird atmosphere to this gig. Also we had a lot of equipment problems. The synthesizer in particular kept going out of tune—and I think if you listen to "Isolation" on the live tape, the whole thing's out of tune—and it was really off-putting. The sound was bad too, and you felt that Ian was unwell. So I really did get a feeling that something was wrong. With hindsight everything was falling apart.

APRIL 19–20, 1980

Ian and Annik spend the weekend at a hotel in Rusholme, going their separate ways on Monday: Annik back to London, Ian home to Macclesfield.

APRIL 22, 1980

Debbie calls Annik at the Belgian embassy, warning her of her intention to divorce Ian and name Annik as co-respondent. Debbie and Ian's parents become involved, and Ian's parents now learn about his suicide attempt for the first time. Debbie begins divorce proceedings.

APRIL 25, 1980

Joy Division cancels their appearance at the Scala cinema, London, because of Ian's poor health. A Certain Ratio, the Durutti Column, and Section 25 play.

We'd canceled but Ian still turned up at the Scala. He arrived about one thirty a.m. and sat at a table on his own, writing furiously in a notebook while watching Kevin Hewick play. Three songs later he was gone. He hadn't spoken to anyone. Kevin told me that Tony debuted *Closer* that night, playing a tape of the LP in between the live acts.

APRIL 26, 1980

Joy Division cancels their gig at the Rock Garden, Middlesbrough.

APRIL 26, 1980

Annik leaves the UK for Belgium, then on to Egypt for a holiday.

LATE APRIL 1980

"Ceremony" (though as yet unnamed) and "In a Lonely Place" demo session, Pinky's, Broughton. "In a Lonely Place" later released in the* Heart and Soul *box set as "In a Lonely Place (detail)."

People say that the recordings of these tracks were from TJ's, but they weren't. The only time we went into TJ's during this period was to record the "Love Will Tear Us Apart" video. Besides, we'd started taping everything by then, so there might be hundreds of those tapes—it's just that bootleggers get hold of them and make out it's the only one of its kind, which is what happened here. This is what happened: Rob lent a tape out to a fan and it got leaked, and then years later these songs are cropping up on bootlegs and now they're on YouTube and whatever. Exactly where the recordings are from—whether it's Pinky's or Graveyard in Prestwich—is difficult to say, but I do know this: they're definitely not from TJ's.

APRIL 28, 1980

The "Love Will Tear Us Apart" promo video is filmed at TJ Davidson's, Manchester. Directed by Stuart Orme. The video would be first shown on Granada's Saturday-morning children's show,* Fun Factory, *on June 26, 1980, introduced by Manchester DJ Ray Teret, who said: "Joy Division isn't a female vocalist; it's a band."

That's Rob Gretton's hand you see pushing the door, and the "Ian C" you see scratched onto the door originally said either

"Ian C is a bastard" or "Ian Curtis is a bastard" and was scratched there by a girl who Ian had, shall we say, "spurned" a while back, when we first started rehearsing there.

MAY 2, 1980

Joy Division play High Hall, Birmingham University, supported by A Certain Ratio. Set list: "Ceremony," "Shadowplay," "A Means to an End," "Passover," "New Dawn Fades," "Twenty Four Hours," "Transmission," "Disorder," "Isolation," "Decades," "Digital."

This was Joy Division's last-ever gig (it was recorded and later released on *Still*), and when we debuted "Ceremony," Ian wrote very positively about the gig—"It was our biggest crowd ever"—while berating himself for forgetting the last verse of "Transmission." He also said that the best number of the night was the new one, "Ceremony."

MAY 3, 1980

Joy Division cancels their gig at Eric's, Liverpool.

MAY 4, 1980

Ian is hypnotized by Bernard while staying at his flat in Worsley. The process regresses Ian to his childhood and then several lives before and leaves a marked impression on him.

MAY 5, 1980

Ian moves back to his parents' house.

MAY 8, 1980

Joy Division cancels their gig at the Astoria, Edinburgh.

MAY 9, 1980

Joy Division cancels their gig at the Albert Hall, Stirling.

MAY 13, 1980

Ian goes home to see Debbie and Natalie. He has his picture taken with Natalie: this is the last photograph taken of him.

MAY 14, 1980

Joy Division recording session, Graveyard Studios, Prestwich. Tracks recorded: "Ceremony," "In a Lonely Place." "Ceremony" is later released on the* Heart and Soul *box set.

I remember doing the session because it was downstairs in Stewart Pickering's house in Prestwich, which was next to a graveyard. (Hence Graveyard Studios.) But Martin was in a weird mood and it was very rushed, the whole thing, and a bit of an unsatisfactory session, which is why it was never used for anything—nothing official, anyway. But the plan, had everything turned out all right, was for these recordings to become the next single: the next record was going to be "In a Lonely Place" and "Ceremony." But, of course, this never came to fruition.

I know a lot fans think the "Ceremony" on the *Heart and Soul* box set comes from the same session as "In a Lonely Place," but it doesn't; it's from this session. "In a Lonely Place" is from a rehearsal tape and this isn't and I'll tell you how I know. Those drums are dead loud; it's not ducking the vocal. So I'd say that's a recorded version of a live rehearsal, because the drum sounds as fat as fuck but it's not making the cassette-player compressor duck and that's what had happened. That's the one we did at Graveyard, I swear it, and I can do that in court.

MAY 18, 1980

The day before the band is scheduled to leave for America, Ian commits suicide. The "joint" North American tour with Cabaret Voltaire would have opened at Hurrahs in New York on May 21, taking in Toronto, Detroit, Chicago, Minneapolis, San Francisco, and Los Angeles after that. Martin Hannett was committed to mix the live sound on this tour.

MAY 23, 1980

Ian Curtis is cremated. Factory holds its own wake at Palatine Road and screens the Sex Pistols film The Great Rock 'n' Roll Swindle.

JUNE 13, 1980

The inquest into Ian's death is held, Macclesfield.

JUNE 27, 1980

"Love Will Tear Us Apart" twelve-inch (FAC 23.12) released.

JULY 18, 1980

Closer *(Factory Records FACT 25) released. Produced by Martin Hannett at Britannia Row, London. Engineered by Martin Hannett and John Caffery, assisted by Michael Johnson. Photograph by Bernard Pierre Wolff. Designed by Peter Saville, Martyn Atkins, Chris Mathan. Track list: "Atrocity Exhibition," "Isolation," "Passover," "Colony," "A Means to an End," "Heart and Soul," "Twenty Four Hours," "The Eternal," "Decades."*

JULY 18, 1980

Free giveaway flexidisc (Factory Records FAC 28) released. Produced by Martin Hannett. Initial pressing: 10,000 copies. Track list: "Komakino," "Incubation," "As You Said."

For a while there had been talk of making *Closer* a double album, but we dropped that plan because we all hated the idea of a double. This did mean that we couldn't put the other three tracks on the album, so we came up with what we thought was a compromise: releasing a flexidisc with the album. You'd buy the album and get the flexidisc free. But the record stores didn't like that and decided to sell the flexidiscs—they didn't get the giveaway idea. So when you bought the album they'd say, "Yeah, you can buy the flexidisc as well to go with it: fifty p," or whatever, the rotten devils. Our intention was to give them all away.

SEPTEMBER 2, 1980

"Atmosphere"/"She's Lost Control" (Factory Records FACUS2/UK) twelve-inch single released. Produced by Martin Hannett. Sleeve photography by Charles Meecham. Typography by Peter Saville.

OCTOBER 8, 1981

Still ***(Factory Records FACT 40) double twelve-inch LP released. The final Joy Division album, a double LP comprising songs by the band never readily available and some formally unreleased; it also includes a live recording of their final concert. Produced by Martin Hannett. Engineered by Chris Nagle. Sleeve design by Peter Saville. First 5,000 with collectors' hessian cloth cover. Track list: "Exercise One" (*****Unknown Pleasures*** *session), "Ice Age" (October/November 1979, Cargo Studios), "The Sound of Music" ("Love Will Tear Us Apart" Session 1), "Glass" (Factory sample), "The Only Mistake" (*****Unknown Pleasures*** *session), "Walked in Line" (*****Unknown Pleasures*** *session), "The Kill" (*****Unknown Pleasures*** *session), "Something Must Break" ("Transmission" session), "Dead Souls" (from*** **Licht und Blindheit/*****Sordide Sentimental session),***

"Sister Ray," "Ceremony," "Shadowplay," "Means to an End," "Passover," "New Dawn Fades," "Transmission," "Disorder," "Isolation," "Decades," "Digital." Track 10 recorded live at the Moonlight Club, London, April 2, 1980. Tracks 11–20 recorded live at Birmingham University, May 2, 1980.

I bought this Joy Division bootleg the other day, and the strange thing was, the first track on it was recorded at TJM practice studios, "Shadowplay." I know for a fact we didn't even own a tape recorder, so I don't know how anybody else can have recorded it. When I listened, it wasn't from there, so I took it back and the bloke knocked me a fiver off it because the track list was wrong.

PETER HOOK INTERVIEW WITH JON SAVAGE, APRIL 1994

· ACKNOWLEDGMENTS ·

Much love and thanks to my beautiful wife, Rebecca, and my beautiful children, Heather, Jack, and Jess. I could not have done it without your love, patience, and understanding.

In memoriam, rest in peace . . . Jean Jackson, Derrick Jackson, Dave Dee, Rex Sargeant, Larry Cassidy, Mia Hook, Martin Rushent, and New Order.

Special thanks to . . . Andrew Holmes and David Sultan. Their hard work in making this book the very best it could be was fantastic. I am in your debt, boys . . . forever.

Thanks, in no particular order, to . . . Twinny, Terry Mason, Claude Flowers, Lesley Thorne, and all at Aitken, Alexander & Co., Phil Murphy, James Masters (the Fountain of Knowledge), Kelvin Briggs, Mike Jones, Emily Husain, all at Simon & Schuster, and Mike and Carol Georgieff-Jones. The people of Manchester and Salford, Aaron Mellor, and all at the Factory, Anthony Addis and all at OJK & Co., Stephen Lea, Mike Hall at IPS Law. THE LIGHT . . . Jack Bates, Nathan Wason, Andy Poole, and Paul (the Bear) Kehoe. Stephen Jones. Pete and Peasy @ Oxygen Management, Steve Strange at X-Ray Agency. The Mighty Sarge. Debbie and Natalie Curtis. The Buzzcocks. Alan Erasmus, Alison Bell, Amanda Dunlop. Dr. Hew Jones. Kate King at JMC Office Services. Joanne and all at the Alderley Edge Hotel. Spellcheck, joydiv.org. Chris and Tom Hewitt. John Brierley. My brothers, Chris and Paul Hook, and their families. Dianne Bourne and the *Manchester Evening News.* OZ PA. Dave Pils and Jasmine. All at Factory Records. Phil Saxe. Matt Greenhalgh and Anton Corbijn. Electro-Harmonix, Shergold Guitars, Crown Amps, Alembic, AMS Digital Delay. Michael Winterbottom and all the 24 Hour Party People. Kevin Hewick. Peter Saville and Alice Cowling. Paul Fletcher at One Love Music. Warner Bros. Music. Universal Publishing. The Sex Pistols. Roger Eagle. Jean-Jacques Burnel for the sound. Paul Simonon for the strap length. Cockney Rebel for turning me on to music. David Essex and Ringo Starr. The list is endless. . . .

JOY
DIVISION

INDEX